PEARSON CUSTOM

STUDENT SUCCESS & CAREER DEVELOPMENT

College and Career Professionalism
Owens Community College
BUS 102

D1307860

Pearson Custom Publishing

New York   Boston   San Francisco
London   Toronto   Sydney   Tokyo   Singapore   Madrid
Mexico City   Munich   Paris   Cape Town   Hong Kong   Montreal

Senior Vice President, Editorial and Marketing: Patrick F. Boles
Operations Manager: Eric M. Kenney
Marketing Manager: Kathleen Kourian
Production Manager: Jennifer Berry
Database Project Specialist: Sean Pantellere
Cover Designer: Kristen Kiley

**Pearson
Custom Publishing**
is a division of

www.pearsonhighered.com

ISBN 10: 0558182054
ISBN 13: 9780558182052

Package ISBN 10: N/A
Package ISBN 13: N/A

Contents

Understanding Your College

1

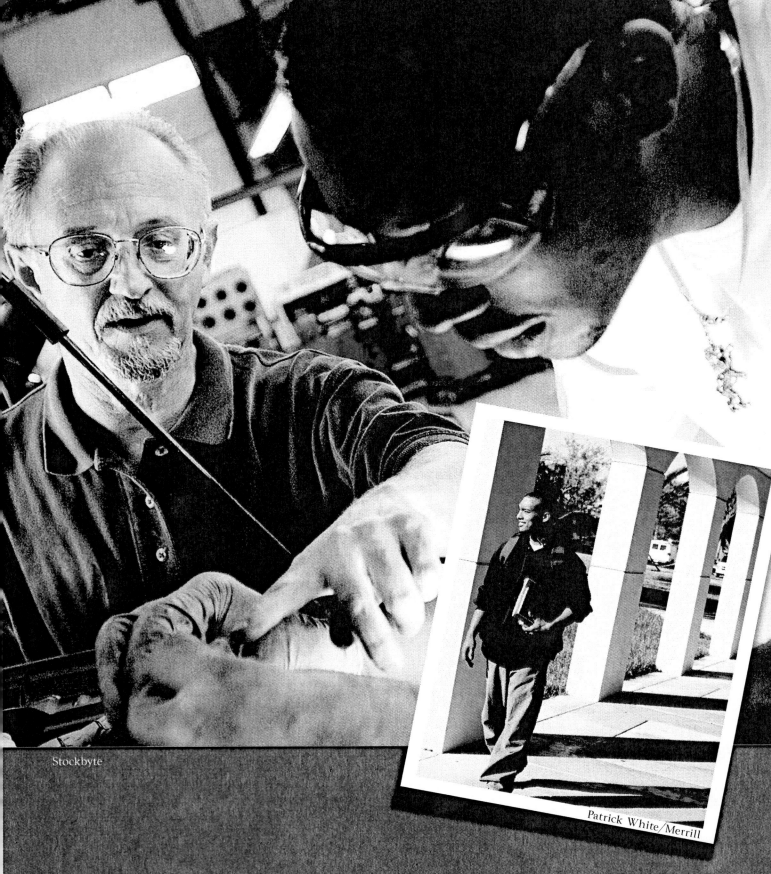

Stockbyte

Patrick White/Merrill

Understanding Your College

Rachel has learned that there is a different set of expectations in college than there was in high school. As she related, some "rules" do not apply anymore—there are new responsibilities and methods of communication. College students like Rachel realize that understanding college culture and becoming familiar with the campus are two important parts of starting college. In addition to the other information, Rachel told you that her VARK learning style is both aural and kinesthetic. It may be helpful to know that she learns best by hearing and participating in physical activities. Whether you learn best by hearing, seeing, participating, or reading, this chapter discusses the following topics, which will move you closer to being comfortable in college:

* What will college be like? What can I expect?

* What do professors expect from me? How can I meet their expectations?

* Should I worry about my grades? Are they important?

* How will I find my way around campus?

* How can I find the help I need when I need it?

1. **What was the biggest adjustment you had to make when moving from high school to college?**

   The biggest adjustment was realizing that because I can set my own schedule, I need to be responsible.

2. **Describe your college's culture. What is expected of you and others who are enrolled in college?**

   It is really relaxed and friendly. There is time to get to know each other. In college, we are expected to come to class because we are paying to be here. We also have to be responsible for our own work. You have to rely on yourself—there's no one to tell you that you are not doing well.

3. **What types of communication materials were you familiar with in high school? Which ones are new?**

   The communication materials are the same as they were in high school. We had a student newspaper, literary magazine, and website. However, few of my high-school teachers handed out a syllabus, so that is a new way to communicate.

4. **What is your VARK?**

   Aural and kinesthetic.

What Is College Culture?

QUICK AND EASY?

LOSE WEIGHT OVERNIGHT WITHOUT DIET AND EXERCISE!

LUNCH IN TEN MINUTES OR IT'S FREE!

BUY GIFTS ON THE INTERNET—NO WAITING IN LINES, NO LOOKING FOR PARKING

A COMPLETE GOURMET MEAL FOR YOUR FAMILY—IN 5 MINUTES

As these common slogans show, we are bombarded by offers to get something without effort and without sacrificing our precious time. We have come to value anything that is quick and easy. Unfortunately, the desire for "quick and easy" has spread from fast food and convenience items to higher education as well. Students who are strapped for time, but who also believe a degree will give them the financial stability and career success they want, often enroll in a community college because the programs are typically shorter than those at a four-year university—the "quick" students are looking for. Other students enroll in a community college because they believe that the courses are not as challenging as they are at other schools—the "easy" students are looking for.

Although the community colleges' degree programs are sometimes shorter, usually one or two years long, the reality is that more time may be necessary to complete a degree program if you enroll as a part-time student. You also may need developmental or remedial classes before you can start the required curriculum, which will delay the program's completion. Perhaps the biggest misconception about community colleges, however, is that the classes are less demanding.

Because of technical and industrial standards and licensing, many courses and programs are, in fact, very challenging. Instructors who teach in the technical, industrial, and business fields are expected to graduate students who can pass the licensing exams, which means the standards in the class must be high. If the courses are "easy," the graduates are unemployable. Likewise, students intending to transfer to four-year universities after completing their general education requirements will not be successful if the community college courses are not challenging. Community colleges want well-prepared and successful graduates; thus, the colleges must provide courses that require the best work from the students.

This chapter's objectives, then, are to introduce you to the culture of college, to reveal the truths about going to college and debunk the myths—the "quick and easy" myth, for one—and to prepare you to meet the challenges you will inevitably face. The first step, though, is to change your thinking from "quick and easy" to the belief that your college education is worth taking time to complete, and should be challenging and rewarding.

Reflection

EXERCISE 1

What are your early impressions of your community college? How do you feel about taking on such an exciting and important journey?

Companion Website

Higher Education and the Role of the Community College

Part of understanding college culture is to understand what higher education is and what it does. According to the American Association of Community Colleges' website, more than 1,000 community colleges exist today. The first community colleges provided a liberal arts education; that emphasis changed to job training during the 1930s to deal with unemployment during the Great Depression. Today, the AACC claims, over half of all undergraduates attend a community college. What sets community colleges apart from traditional four-year universities is their versatility and accessibility. Many community college mission statements demonstrate a commitment to offering higher education and continuing education to those who may not be ready or feel they are ready to pursue a four-year degree. At a community college, you can complete the first two years of general education credits toward a four-year degree, or you can work toward a degree or certificate in a highly specialized field. If you need help transitioning into higher education because of such issues as remediation and cost, a community college can be the perfect match for you.

Regardless of why you enrolled at a community college, be assured you made a wise choice. Community colleges are constantly adapting to the changing needs of their community, business and industry, and students. They pride themselves on being student-focused teaching and learning institutions that are uniquely capable of responding to changes in the workforce so the students receive the highest quality education. Community colleges also lead the way in innovative scheduling and accommodations because the students demand it. It speaks volumes when a community college reacts to students' special work and family needs by offering night, weekend, online, and special session classes. Because of their commitment to you, community colleges will continue to be a great way for people to start or continue their education or upgrade their skills.

What Does Your Community College Value?

As you will learn, determining your values is an integral part of understanding yourself better. The same is true for what your college values; understanding its values enables you to better appreciate the college's mission and services. To determine your community college's values, as well as its goals, look at its mission statement, its extracurricular activities, the types of degrees it awards, and its faculty and staff. All colleges and universities value students' success. Because schools value producing educated, dynamic members of the community, they focus their goals on helping their students achieve success. They may do this by offering tutoring and counseling services or by providing developmental courses for students who lack the preparation needed to be successful in college-level courses.

Colleges and universities also value diversity, although they may define the term differently, because without diversity, there is little need for college. Diversity—in people's backgrounds, in their opinions, and in their interests and activities—creates an environment in which ideas and values can be developed and shaped. Your school may celebrate ethnic diversity by sponsoring multicultural groups, promoting cultural celebrations, or working to include all types of people in decision making. Your school may value a diverse faculty, attracting and hiring professors from all parts of the world, with different world views.

Although you will find similarities between what you and people in the academic world value, you may occasionally find that your college's values do not mesh with yours. At the very least, you will meet one person (most likely dozens) who openly or implicitly challenges what you believe.

Making the Transition: What Is Expected

For some students, the move from high school to college seems fairly simple—both require reading, writing, testing, and attending class. Students taking the step from work to school may also see some similarities between their jobs and their classroom work—both require working hard, staying motivated, and following the rules. Despite the similarities between the cultures, some students have trouble adjusting to the "climate" of college because they are not sure what is expected of them. In order to be successful, students must know what is expected of them beyond the questions on the next test; they need to know how college works and how to navigate through not only their courses, but also the common challenges they will face as they work toward a degree or certificate.

Exhibit 1 illustrates some of the differences and similarities between high school, a full-time job, and college. Notice that the greatest differences occur between high school and college; although there are some similarities between a full-time job and college, there are also distinct differences.

With your transition into college in mind, consider the following information about what you can expect in college. Even though the expectations are different, you are in control of your success.

Attendance

Movie director, actor, and writer Woody Allen said, "Eighty percent of success is showing up." Definitely, in college classes, you can't be successful unless you attend regularly. That means you must go to class every time it meets whether or not you feel like it and whether or not there is something "important" going on. Unlike high school, college professors may not take attendance or make an issue of students who do not attend; however, do not be fooled by an instructor's laid-back attitude about your attendance. If you do not attend regularly, you will miss valuable information about assignments, tests, and grading—information the instructor is not obligated to review with you. Especially in courses that build on concepts (such as math and English), your lack of attendance can keep you from being successful later in the semester. Also, think of regular attendance as your leverage for negotiating. If you have an emergency that prevents you from taking a test on time, your regular attendance and your status as a good student can help get an extension.

Students who have held jobs better understand the importance of attendance. They know that they do not get paid if they do not show up, or they

EXHIBIT 1 *Comparisons and contrasts.*

HIGH SCHOOL	FULL-TIME WORK	COLLEGE
Attendance is mandatory to meet requirements	Attendance is mandatory to stay employed	Attendance may not be mandatory
At least six continuous hours spent in class each day	At least eight continuous hours spent at work each day	Different amounts of time spent in class and between classes each day
Very little choice in what classes you take and when you take them	May have little choice in work assignments and when the work is to be completed	More flexibility in which classes you take, in when you work on assignments, and in how soon you complete them before the due date
Moderate to no outside work necessary to be successful	Moderate to no overtime work necessary to complete job duties	Substantial amount of outside work to complete assignments and to be successful
Teachers check homework and keep you up to date on progress; they will inform you if you are not completing assignments and progressing well	Supervisors check completion and quality of work at regular intervals; they will inform you if you are not meeting the standards for the position	Professors may not check all homework or provide feedback on progress at regular intervals; they may not inform you if you are not meeting the standards of the course
Teachers go over material and expect you to remember facts and information	Employers provide basic information and expect you to use it to complete the job effectively	Professors provide concepts and theories and expect you to evaluate the ideas, synthesize the ideas with other concepts you have learned, and develop new theories
Frequent tests over small amounts of material allow grades to be raised if needed	Supervisors create employee improvement plans to allow you to improve your ratings if needed	Professors provide the standards and grading criteria but often allow only a few chances (through infrequent testing/assignments) to meet them

may be fired if they miss too many days. However, just showing up is only part of succeeding in college and understanding the culture. To be a successful college student, regular attendance has to be combined with maintaining a positive attitude, preparing for class, asking for help when needed, acting with integrity, and staying motivated.

If you miss a class or intend to miss a class, you should mention the absence to your instructor. Although you may not need a doctor's excuse, you should be prepared to justify your absence, especially if you have missed an exam. Most instructors, though, do not care why you missed. In fact, they don't distinguish between excused or unexcused absences. Instead, they are more interested in whether you keep up with the work.

Attitude

A good attitude will take you far in the journey to achieve your goals. Sometimes it will be hard to maintain a positive outlook because you feel overwhelmed with the challenges of college, work, and family, but if you can maintain a good attitude, your chances of success are greater. Good attitudes are infectious, and you will soon find that your professors and classmates will reflect the good attitude you have.

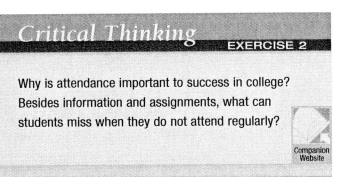

The other side of a positive attitude is a negative one, and at some point in your college career, you will feel as though the world is out to undermine your success. You may feel overwhelmed with the responsibilities of going to school and working, or you may feel frustrated that you have not progressed in your classes the way you hoped. There are numerous reasons that you may, temporarily at least, have a pessimistic outlook on your college education or your life. Bringing a bad mood into the classroom, however, can make your attitude worse and your outlook gloomier. Even though you may feel anonymous most of the time, instructors do notice when students are disgruntled and unwilling to learn. Although instructors may not know why a student is upset, they are still affected by the student's bad attitude. At the very least, they may see negativity as a sign of immaturity.

Common "bad attitude" mistakes that students make include

* acting as if they know more than the professor.
* rolling their eyes or shaking their heads when an instructor is presenting material or making an assignment.
* making negative comments out loud about the class, the instructor, or other students.
* resisting or refusing to do an assignment.
* slouching down in the seat, looking bored.
* getting angry about a low grade.
* walking out of class because of anger or boredom.

Presenting a good attitude in class is easier than you think. In fact, it just takes a little attention to the messages you send with your face, body, and language. Tips for presenting a good attitude include

* coming to class prepared with the appropriate books and materials.
* paying attention.
* demonstrating an effort to master the material and to complete assignments.
* providing positive or constructive feedback in class or privately.
* smiling and being friendly!

The belief that instructors only like students who make As or students who gush with compliments about the course is false. The truth is that professors like students who show a genuine interest and demonstrate effort in

Inside image:

Critical Thinking   EXERCISE 2

Why is attendance important to success in college? Besides information and assignments, what can students miss when they do not attend regularly?

Companion Website

the course, regardless of the grades they earn. It is the student with the good attitude, then, who gets the most from the instructor because he or she realizes that a student with a good attitude is someone who is willing to learn.

Effort

Gone are the days of an A for effort. In high school, students who merely complete work are usually rewarded with a passing grade. However, in college, effort must be coupled with quality. Putting forth the effort to write a paper and turn it in is only part of the requirement. You also have to adhere to the standards of the course. If the instructor asks for a 10-page paper that argues a contemporary topic and uses 5 sources, you must follow those guidelines. Although a high-school teacher may have given you credit for submitting a 7-page paper on a contemporary topic that used only 3 sources and contained numerous grammatical errors, a college instructor will not. Usually, you will not receive any credit for an assignment if you did not follow the guidelines or requirements.

Peter Finger/PH College

Students who are well-prepared for class improve their chances of success.

Also gone are the days when spending more time studying or writing a paper equals a higher grade. Students who complain about low grades by saying, "But I spent two weeks writing the paper" will not get any sympathy from the professor. Does this mean that you should not spend time working on assignments or studying? Definitely not. This means that you should pay attention to the quality of the work you produced given the time you spent. The quality of work is what you are graded on, not the number of hours you spent.

You will also find that you must increase your effort to get the grades you used to get in high school. You will have more reading, writing, and critical thinking to do each week, and most of the work will be done outside of class. Professors view class time as a small fraction of the course. A common rule for calculating how many hours you have to devote to a course is to study three hours for every hour you are in class. Therefore, if you are taking a 3-hour class, you should study 9 hours a week for that one course. If you are taking 12 hours a semester, you should devote 36 hours a week to studying. That means 48 (36 hours to study and 12 hours to attend class) hours of your week will be occupied with schoolwork—in class and outside class.

Honesty

It can be said that student learning is not possible without honesty and integrity. For example, if a student cheats on all the exams in a class, what has she learned about the subject? Student learning, therefore, relies on integrity.

In addition to being honest about doing the course work, you must be honest with yourself about your progress. If you do not understand the material and are making poor grades, take the time to honestly assess your preparation for the course or your abilities. Maybe you are not spending enough time studying and reviewing for the class, or maybe you need to take a lower-level course so that you can brush up on any skills you lack. It is better to admit that you need help or need better preparation than to spend valuable time performing poorly.

Instructors' Expectations

In addition to attendance, attitude, and effort, there are a few other expectations when you take college classes. For instance, when an instructor hands out a written assignment to be turned in at a later date, the assignment must be typed. In fact, unless otherwise stated, assume that all out-of-class writing assignments should be typed—they are easier to read and look more professional. If you do not know how to type or use a word processor, either find someone to type your assignments for you, or better yet, learn how to use a computer with word-processing software. The sooner you learn, the easier future assignments will be.

When you handwrite an assignment, the instructor also expects your handwriting to be legible. Handwriting that is messy or incomprehensible or is written with anything other than blue or black pen on white paper makes the instructor's job more difficult. Some instructors will ask you to rewrite the assignment or will lower your grade if your work is unreadable. If you have a disability that prevents you from writing legibly, be sure the instructor is aware at the beginning of the semester.

Another expectation instructors have is preparation—yours. Be prepared *before* you get to class by reading the assigned pages or completing the homework. Too often, students think the instructor will provide a complete overview of the material and that preparing for class is a waste of time. Nothing could be further from the truth. Instructors who assign reading or homework expect students to prepare—they may even administer quizzes to ensure that students are prepared—and to ask questions about anything they do not understand. It may be assumed that if you do not ask questions or participate in a discussion, then you understand the assignment. Professors often hold students accountable for the assigned reading on exams even though it was not discussed in class.

It is a common belief among seasoned students that instructors think that their classes are the only ones being taken, and studying for them is the only activity students do all week. More realistically, college professors expect that your first priority is your college classes. At a community college, you may find instructors who are more understanding about your multiple responsibilities, but remember their first concern is that you learn the material and meet course objectives.

Location

Where you sit in the classroom is just as important as being prepared to meet instructors' expectations. If you arrive early enough before class, you should be able to sit up close, which is where you want to be. Sitting in the back of the class where you can barely see or be seen or heard is the least advantageous place because you can be distracted easily or tempted to do other things. Sitting in the front row or as close to the front as possible maximizes your chances of success.

Students who sit up front are usually more engaged, more willing to answer questions and discuss topics, and more likely to get positive feedback from the instructor. Professors like students who sit up front and seem interested, even if they don't speak up during class. Moreover, students who sit close to the front (within the first few rows if the room is large or in the front row if the room is small) are more likely to pay attention, take good notes, and get good grades.

Maturity

Maturity is the foundation for many of the other components of college culture. Without a mature attitude and outlook, the other parts are unattainable. There are, however, less obvious actions that can help you present yourself as a dedicated, mature student. The first one is paying attention during lectures, presentations, guest speakers, and films. Although this sounds like an obvious suggestion, it is often forgotten after the first few weeks of the semester. Work on looking at the front of the room and avoiding distractions.

A common barrier to paying attention, besides staring out the window, is doing homework in class. Instructors frown on students who use class time to study for other classes or complete assignments that were due at the beginning of class. Just remember that the instructor sees you, acknowledges that you are not paying attention because you are working on other classes, and remembers everything, especially when you need a favor.

Some colleges have policies about cell phone and pager use. If your college does not, turn your cell phone and pager off in class. Unless you work in a field that requires your immediate attention in the event of an emergency or you have a gravely ill family member, turn off all electronic devices while in class. In some cases (e.g., chemistry lab), the distraction can be potentially dangerous. In most cases, however, it is annoying at best, rude at worst. Students who answer social calls in class appear immature and unconcerned about their education—or anyone else's.

An important way to demonstrate maturity in college is to understand and appreciate constructive criticism from your professor. When you receive advice or comments about your work or progress in the course, look at it as an opportunity to learn more about yourself and the expectations of college. A professor's job is to educate you and help you learn more about the world; it is not her job to undermine those efforts by putting you down.

Some students feel any feedback that is not positive destroys their self-confidence. The opposite should be true—positive feedback does not help you learn, nor does it necessarily challenge you to do better. Of course, we all want to hear something nice about ourselves, but we also should be open to the challenge of receiving criticism about the quality of our work. It takes a mature person to value constructive criticism and learn from it.

Dealing with diversity, conflict, and controversy takes a certain level of maturity. Effectively meeting any challenge to your belief system or values demands that you act with integrity and openness. Because the purpose of getting an education is to stretch your mind and expand your ideas, maturity helps you put all that new information into perspective.

Responsibility

No doubt you already juggle numerous responsibilities, and going to class and studying are just more tasks you must complete each week. Handling your responsibilities skillfully takes a positive attitude, respect for yourself, and maturity. Obviously, as a student you are responsible for taking notes, studying for tests, and attending classes regularly. But you also are responsible for asking questions when you do not understand or when you think you are being treated unfairly.

The University of South Carolina developed and adopted a creed it expects all of its students to follow while enrolled in the university. Here are two of the tenets of the Carolinian Creed that emphasize the student's responsibility:

I will practice personal and academic integrity.

I will respect the rights and property of others.

In addition, you are also responsible for taking control of your education if it is not going the way you want. As Laura Thomas, a community college freshman, admits, "I realized after my first semester of college that my instructors work for me. It is my responsibility to tell them what I need. They can't help me if they don't know what I am struggling with."

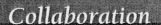

Collaboration
EXERCISE 3

Working in a group, write a five-minute scene in which a student demonstrates maturity and responsibility in the classroom. Perform the scene for the class, and ask your classmates to determine which actions demonstrate maturity.

Companion
Website

The Right Stuff

Ever since kindergarten, you've been expected to bring your supplies with you on the first day of school. Crayons, glue, and No. 2 pencils have now been replaced by computer disks, laptops, and ink cartridges. The computer has changed the landscape of education by providing students with word processing and access to research databases and the World Wide Web. Most colleges provide computer labs, e-mail accounts, and printing capabilities for student use. Because college campuses offer access to computers, your professors expect you to have a working knowledge of how to use one. Instructors may require you to word-process assignments or correspond in a chat room.

If you do not have the necessary computer skills, seek help from computer lab technicians, special computer classes, and classmates.

Other "right stuff" items include paper (for taking notes and printing papers), pens, a dictionary, writing handbook, and thesaurus. As you take more classes, specialized reference books and supplies may be needed to help you study and complete assignments.

College Culture Shock

The preceding discussion listed only a sampling of college expectations and experiences. You will encounter many other aspects of college culture, some of which may be uncomfortable or even shocking to you. As stated previously, all colleges value diversity, whether in the student body population or the backgrounds of its faculty. You will find diversity in ideas and theories among the offered subjects. Some ideas and theories may challenge your beliefs and values. Still others may contain material you find disrespectful, distasteful, or disturbing (See Exhibit 2 for some examples).

EXHIBIT 2   *Samples of possibly controversial subjects and topics.*

SUBJECTS

Art	Music	Philosophy	Theatre	Literature	Composition
Cultural Studies	Gender Studies	Political Science	Religion	Sociology	Economics
Anthropology	Law	Biology	Chemistry	Astronomy	History

TOPICS

The existence of God, higher being

Conservatism and liberalism

Nudity in art, photography

Profanity and adult situations in music, theater, literature

Sexuality, including homosexuality and adultery

The creation of the universe

The theory of extraterrestrial life

Evolution

The beginning of life

Scientific investigation and experimentation (stem cells, cloning)

Socioeconomic theory

Besides reading and discussing controversial or uncomfortable issues, your college may produce student and faculty work that contains language, images, or situations you find offensive.

What should you do if you encounter college "culture shock"? First, remember that the purpose of higher education is to provide you with a wider worldview and understanding of diversity—even if that diversity involves different ideas, theories, and methods of representing those ideas and theories. Second, remember that you have the right to an opinion and a feeling about what you encounter in college. There is no reason you should hide your feelings or attitudes about what you are learning and encountering. With this said, the third point to remember is that with your right to an opinion, you also have an *obligation* as a college student to examine your previously held beliefs and evaluate how they are being challenged in your courses or as you participate in college activities. You also have an obligation to appreciate that there is more than one way to view an "offensive" idea or presentation.

Types of Learning Experiences

Some learning experiences involve one-to-one support, such as peer mentoring and tutoring.

In addition to *what* you learn at a community college, you should consider *how* you learn. Colleges and universities frequently use learning communities, sometimes called "cohorts," to group students together so

BananaStock

they can cultivate a supportive learning community. For example, 20 students have the same weekly class schedule and possibly a scheduled study session with smaller groups. Students who participate in learning communities build an instant support and study group because they are all going through similar experiences adjusting to college life and course workload.

Two other learning experiences you may encounter involve one-to-one support: peer mentoring and peer tutoring. New students are paired with students close to finishing their degrees in a mentor relationship. The peer mentors provide orientation, advice, and support during the new students' first semester or year. They may also help with time management skills, goal setting, and degree planning. Peer tutors, on the other hand, are not usually paired with an individual student. Instead, you will encounter peer tutors at a tutoring lab or at certain times during the week. Peer tutors provide students with help in specific academic areas. The benefit of both peer mentors and tutors is that you have others to help you who are not too far removed from the college experience. They are more likely to understand your needs and goals, and they can provide insight that faculty and administrators may not be able to share.

Service learning opportunities are community service projects that are integrated into your academic experience. You may take an Introduction to Education course where part of your class work takes place at a local elementary school. As part of your work in the community, you may be required to find a solution to a common issue in the community and keep a reflective journal about your experiences.

Grades

Grades are an important part of your education, and at the same time they are unimportant. How can that be? How can something be both important and unimportant? Grades are important because they often reflect your level of achievement on an assignment or in a course; they are also important for obtaining and maintaining scholarships and financial aid. In addition, grades are important to family, friends, and employers who may be supporting you financially and emotionally. Many people view grades as a reflection of a particular level of success. For instance, most people view a student who has straight As as someone who is smart and successful.

Although most people, especially students, place great significance on grades, they are what educators call "non-measures" of student learning. For example, an A in an algebra class does not necessarily indicate a student knows how to solve quadratic equations. Likewise, an A in a literature course does not automatically mean that a student knows how to explicate a poem. Grades, in these instances, may not reflect what a student has learned in a course. Instead, they may reflect that a student merely turned in all his homework on time or that he is a good test taker.

If grades sometimes indicate a level of success in a course and sometimes don't, what are you to do? How will you ever know when to worry about your grades and when to concentrate on learning the material? The purpose of this section is to help you answer these questions by explaining how professors grade and how you can make good grades in college. This section also discusses what you can do to de-emphasize making a good grade and emphasize mastering the course material. This is not to say, however, that grades are never important. They are important because they describe the work you have done in a class. However, grades alone are not the magic carpet to college success; they are only part of the story of your achievements. Your goal should be to strike a balance between caring about your grades and caring about improving your skills and increasing your knowledge.

Grades can be indications of

* a certain level of success on an assignment or in a course.
* the time and work you put into an assignment or a course.
* the knowledge and skills you obtained.

Grades are not indications of

* your worth as a person.
* your educational and career potential.
* an inability to learn.

Banner and Cannon (1999), in their book *The Elements of Learning*, define grades as "evaluations of your work, not of your character or intelligence. You may be a wonderful person but a failure as a biologist. You may find it impossible to do satisfactory work in history but may excel in all other subjects" (p. 160). They assert, therefore, that grades have limitations. Certainly, they are a necessary part of evaluation, much as you are evaluated on your job. However, as Banner and Cannon point out, grades do not show the whole picture of who you are. Grades, then, are only part of the story of your education.

How College Professors Grade

As stated earlier, college professors grade a student on his or her ability to meet the standards of the course or of a particular assignment. The following box shows a potential set of grading criteria, or standards, for a college-level paper. In this case, the criteria are for an A paper.

Grading Criteria for an A Paper

* An excellent introduction with engaging hooks, setup, plan, and main idea
* An original, significant thesis that offers insightful interpretation or thought
* An inventive and logical organizational plan
* Smooth and varied transitional expressions, phrases, and sentences that provide unity and coherence
* Strong conclusion that ends the essay effectively
* Expressive, clear style with sophisticated sentence structure and word choice
* No more than three major grammatical errors

The Family Educational Rights and Privacy Act (FERPA) is a federal law that protects students' educational records. Under this Act, professors and other college officials cannot discuss your academic record with anyone who is not authorized by you to receive that information.

Grading Scales

Knowing how your college assesses student performance is a start to improving your overall outlook on grading. The following is a typical grading scale in college:

90–100 = A   80–89 = B   70–79 = C   60–69 = D   0–59 = F

Some colleges may use a + or − next to a letter grade such as A− or C+. Usually, colleges that allow for pluses and minuses also alter the grading scale to designate the different grades; for example:

94–100 = A   90–93 = A−   87–89 = B+   84–86 = B   80–83 = B−

Calculating Your Grade Point Average

Each semester, the registrar calculates your grade point average, or GPA, and posts it to your transcript. Because the calculation requires a little mathematical skill, it is important to know how your registrar determines it. Hours are the number of hours you are in class each week. Classes are usually three credit hours. Science classes that have labs usually carry four credit hours. Depending on the course and the program, credit hours can be as many as six or as few as one. To know how many hours a course carries, check the description in the college catalog because some classes meet for more hours a week than they are worth in terms of credit.

Letter grades carry a point value called quality points. The following example shows how many quality points each letter grade is worth.

LETTER GRADE	QUALITY POINTS
A	4
B	3
C	2
D	1
F	0

Courses that are designated developmental or remedial usually do not figure into your GPA, so they do not carry any quality points. If you audit a course or receive AP or CLEP credit for a course, you will not receive quality points. In other words, although you receive credit on your transcript for taking the course or taking a course equivalent, the grade will not factor into your grade point average. Before you figure your GPA, determine your grade points for each class by multiplying the quality points for the grade you received by the number of hours the class is worth. For instance, if you took a four-hour class and you made a B, multiply 4 (hours) by 3 (quality points for a B).

If you took 15 hours (5 three-hour courses) during the semester, and you received an A, B, and three Cs, then calculate your grade this way:

HOURS	GRADE	(QUALITY POINTS)	GRADE POINTS
3	A	(4)	3 × 4 = 12
3	B	(3)	3 × 3 = 9
3	C	(2)	3 × 2 = 6
3	C	(2)	3 × 2 = 6
3	C	(2)	3 × 2 = 6
15 Hours			39 Grade Points

Practice

EXERCISE 4

Angela has an A in English Composition I, Bs in both College Seminar and Algebra, and a C in her Biological Science class. What is her GPA for the semester? (Assume the biology class is four credit hours and the other classes are three credit hours.)

Companion Website

Finally, divide the grade points total by the hours total (39/15). Your GPA is 2.6.

What Does Your College Look Like?

Now that you have a better understanding of how your college works and what is expected of you, it is time to examine how your college looks. Getting to know the campus layout and the people who work there is important to understanding the culture.

The Campus

Find a map of your campus and study it for a few minutes. How many buildings does it have? How much parking space? How much "green" space or landscaping? Are there any unique features to your campus that make it an inviting and exciting place? Familiarizing yourself with the campus is probably the first activity you did when you enrolled. If you have not taken a tour or simply walked around campus, you should do so within the first few weeks of the semester. You should be able to locate the library, the student center, student parking, the bookstore, the business office, and the registrar's office—just to name a few destinations.

BUILDING OR AREA	AT MY COLLEGE
Student center or union	
Library	
Bookstore	
Administration building	
Theater or auditorium	
Snack bar or food court	
Athletic training facilities (indoor or outdoor)	
Science labs	
Technical and industrial training facilities	
Computer labs	
Separate divisions (e.g., technical and industrial, computer information systems, allied health, business, general education)	
Individual departments (e.g., accounting, drafting, welding, natural sciences)	
Student parking	
Benches and tables for meeting outside	
Quiet study space inside	

The more you know about your campus layout, the easier it will be to find what you are looking for when you need it most. Using your campus map or your memory, complete the campus checklist activity by checking off the types of buildings or departments within buildings that you know are present at your college.

If your college has more than one campus, familiarize yourself with the layout of the other college property. You may have to travel to a satellite campus to take a test or pick up materials for a class. If you have the time, and the other campus is not too far away, ask for a tour.

The People on Your Campus

Equally important to understanding where buildings and services are located is knowing who does what on your campus. Exhibit 3 shows basic titles and job descriptions for college officials (your college may use different titles or may have more positions than those listed).

EXERCISE 5   *Critical Thinking*

What would the ideal college campus look like? What buildings would it have? How would it be organized? Draw or describe a model college campus.

Companion Website

19

EXHIBIT 3 *The titles and responsibilities of campus officials.*

POSITION	WHAT THEY DO	WHY YOU SHOULD KNOW THEM
Board of Trustees	A group of people charged with overseeing the college operations and planning	The board of trustees is the last stop along the way to making a major change on campus. Controversial issues such as censorship, demonstrations, and firing faculty may be addressed to the board directly, depending on the circumstances.
President	The head of the school	Like the board, the president is one of the last stops for concerns about campus issues if attempts to resolve them are not successful.
Dean of Students	Sometimes called Vice President for Instruction; takes care of matters concerning curriculum, classes, degree programs, and instructors	If you have concerns about a grade, and all attempts to address the matter with the instructor and the department dean are fruitless, the dean of students can intervene. Potentially volatile issues, such as sexual harassment, should be brought to her immediate attention.
Dean of Student Services	Sometimes called Vice President of Student Services; oversees all student-related services such as contacting prospective students, enrollment, and counseling	You may actually meet the dean of student services when you enroll, and he will be an important contact person if you need assistance with any aspect of your classes.
Registrar	Handles registration and transcripts	You may visit the registrar if you recently applied for admission or if you transferred. Also, you may contact her if you receive a grade that is not correct or have to apply for an incomplete grade.
Director of Disability Services	May have other titles; handles the services provided to students with documented disabilities	If you need assistance with learning difficulties or disabilities, schedule an appointment with him. The more contact you have, the more information and help you will receive.
Career Counselor	Helps you discover what career you may be interested in and are best suited for; may also help you plan your academic career so you are prepared to enter the workforce	Stop by her office as soon as you get enrolled. You can take a skills and interest inventory that will help you think about the classes you want to take and the degree you want to complete. A career counselor can also help you with building a resume and provide tips for interviewing.
Director of Financial Aid	Handles financial aid for students and has access to scholarship information	If you need financial aid, the earlier you can see someone in this office, the better. Time is the key to getting what you need—apply early and follow up on the application. The financial aid office is usually very busy the week classes start, so plan ahead.

EXHIBIT 3   *Continued*

POSITION	WHAT THEY DO	WHY YOU SHOULD KNOW THEM
Library Director	Manages the library services for students and faculty	Talk with the director or any library staff when you need help finding a source. They can help you with the research process.
Director of Distance Education	Provides oversight for courses delivered to students at a distance; a new position at some schools	If you are interested in taking a course online or through compressed video, see her for information about how the courses work and what to expect.
Director of Campus Safety	Maintains a safe environment on campus, issues tickets, takes reports of incidents on campus, and reports annual crime statistics	If you ever become involved in or witness a crime on campus, you will need to talk to a campus officer. Because the officer's job is to maintain a safe environment, be willing to alert him to potential problems on campus.
Dean	Manages a group of departments or, if the division is small, a group of individual instructors	A dean is the next stop when you have an issue concerning a class or instructor. After you have talked with the instructor, you may see a dean to get more advice or help. Deans should be notified immediately of potentially volatile situations such as verbal threats from or physical assault by another student.
Department Chair	Oversees a department's instructors and curriculum	You may visit a department chair when considering a major in the department or if you need to talk about a certain class or instructor (after you have already talked to the instructor).
Professor, Instructor, or Lecturer	Is responsible for teaching you	There are many different names and ranks for the people who deliver content, motivate you to think critically, and assess your progress. They are the people you will have the most contact with on campus and the first people you should talk to when you have a problem.
Advisor	Helps students plan their schedules and their degrees before registration and during the semester	An advisor is another key person to your success in college. Consider the advisor the personal trainer who sets goals with you and helps you achieve them.

You should make a list of those administrators and faculty you may have to contact during your college career. For example, write down the names, titles, phone numbers, and e-mail addresses of your professors, department chairs, advisors, financial aid officers, and deans you have encountered. Keep the list in a safe place so that when you need to ask a question or get advice, you won't spend a lot of time searching for it.

When a Problem Arises

time may come when you have a problem in one of your classes. If it does, be assured that the college's employees will work with you to resolve it. There are, however, rules and procedures regarding how to resolve a problem at a college. Knowing and following these procedures will ensure that a problem is handled appropriately and quickly.

The first step to resolving a conflict in class is to define what the problem is. Is it a communication problem? Is it a problem with the course material? Is it a problem with the course standards? Once you have defined the problem, your next step is to discuss the problem directly. If the problem is with your instructor, make an appointment during her office hours to discuss the issue. If you are emotional—angry, upset, nervous—wait until you have calmed down to discuss the problem. Your goal in meeting with the instructor is to resolve the conflict.

In order for the conflict resolution process to work, you must complete the first two steps. If you are not satisfied with the result or if you feel the problem has gotten worse, not better, move to the next step: talking to the department chair or dean. You will no doubt be asked if you have met with the instructor. Again, your goal at this step is to resolve the issue. Occasionally, the instructor may be called in to help resolve the issue. Staying calm and focused on resolving the conflict will be to your advantage. In the event the problem is not solved at this level, your last stop is with the dean of students or vice president for instruction. Starting at the top will only delay resolution.

College Communications

ommunicating in and out of class with instructors and students is a major part of the college experience, but don't forget that the college communicates with you in a variety of formats. College communications, in fact, are a great place to find information about courses, programs, scholarships, activities, and policy changes. It is important that you regularly read those publications the college produces in order to stay up to date with what is going on.

College Catalog

The college catalog is one of the most essential documents you will receive during your academic career. All of the information you need to apply for financial aid, to choose courses, and to graduate is contained in the catalog. It also sets forth what you are required to do to complete a degree. The academic calendar is usually placed at the beginning of the catalog. There you will find the dates for registration, dropping courses, and final exams.

Another important reason to read and keep your college catalog is that if the college changes any requirements of your degree program, you will be able follow the guidelines that were published the year you began the program. For instance, if you are working on an office management degree and you have taken three semesters so far, you will not necessarily have to adhere to new requirements made at a later date.

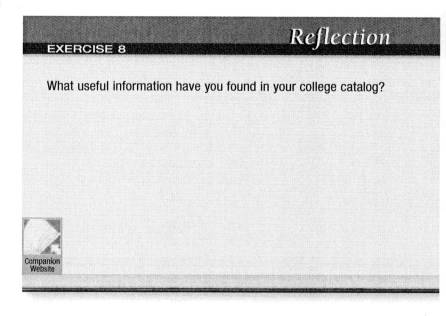

EXERCISE 8

Reflection

What useful information have you found in your college catalog?

Companion Website

Student Handbook

The student handbook is another valuable publication because it provides you with specific information about student conduct, academic standards, and student services. Usually, the handbook describes the career services, bookstore, computer labs, and financial aid offices. Academic information, including probation and suspension for misconduct and qualifications for making the dean's list, is found in the student handbook. Most schools view the student handbook as a legal document that outlines what students can do in certain situations, so be sure to read the handbook closely and keep a copy at home or in your book bag.

Campus Safety Brochure

A smaller, but equally important, document that your college publishes is the campus safety and security brochure. Information found in the brochure includes policies on handling sexual assault, substance and drug abuse, and harassment. Also, you can find contact numbers for campus police as well as campus crime statistics, which is a federal requirement.

College Newspaper

College newspapers differ from the college catalog and student handbook in that students are usually the ones responsible for the content. Within a college newspaper, you will find articles announcing upcoming events, reports on changes on the campus, editorials on important student issues, profiles of programs, and advertisements for used books, musical groups, and anything else that students want to announce. The college newspaper is also a forum to explore controversial topics and to discuss sensitive issues.

Newspapers always need students to interview, write, edit, and publish. If you have any interest in working for the newspaper, contact the editor or visit a journalism or composition professor.

Literary Magazine

One of the more entertaining and creative publications is the literary magazine. Some colleges produce a booklet or journal of students' creative endeavors; short stories, poetry, essays, art work, and photography are just a sample of the items literary magazines publish. Unlike the newspapers that are printed every day or every week, literary magazines are usually published once or twice a year.

Bulletin Boards

Even with the increased use of the Internet, the bulletin board is still an important way to get a message to students. Found all over campus, bulletin boards usually advertise used books, needs for roommates and part-time jobs, and upcoming campus events. Within academic buildings, bulletin boards often announce four-year college programs, summer workshops, and other types of academic activities.

Classroom Materials

Anything that professors hand out in class is a communication tool. The syllabus is one of the most important documents you will receive in class, so be sure to read it carefully. Exhibit 4 shows the information typically found in the syllabus.

EXHIBIT 4   *Components of a syllabus.*

- Instructor's name, office location, office phone number, office hours, and e-mail address
- Prerequisites for the course
- Course description from the catalog
- Textbook information
- Course objectives (what you will accomplish by the time you finish the class)
- Course content (what topics will be covered throughout the semester)
- Assignments and due dates
- Grading criteria
- Attendance and late work policies
- Academic integrity statement
- Disability policy
- General policies for classroom conduct

Even though the syllabus is considered a contract between the instructor and the student as to what to expect during the semester, some students do not read the document thoroughly. By reading the syllabus closely, you can ask questions about how the course will be conducted. Remember to reread the syllabus around midterm to refresh your memory of important dates and assignments.

Other important information handed out in class includes directions for assignments, photocopied readings, study questions, and notes. Regard anything given to you by the instructor as important, even if you are told the information "won't be on the test."

Although grades and feedback are discussed further in a later chapter, consider the grades and written comments you receive as communication from your instructors; in fact, it may be the most important information you receive from them. Be sure to read any comments or suggestions written on papers and exams, ask questions if you don't understand them or cannot read the handwriting, and save all feedback until the semester is over.

College Website

The college's website is a place where you can go to access the most current information about classes, academic programs, and instructor contact information. Because it is easy to update information on a website, you are more likely to receive the most accurate information.

In addition to general information about degrees and departments, your college's website may also give you access to professors' syllabi and assignments. Use this information to investigate which courses you want to take based on what the course objectives are and what papers are assigned.

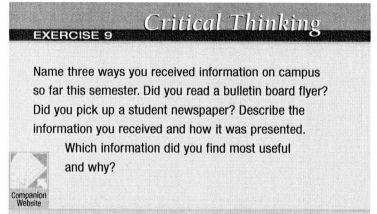

EXERCISE 9   *Critical Thinking*

Name three ways you received information on campus so far this semester. Did you read a bulletin board flyer? Did you pick up a student newspaper? Describe the information you received and how it was presented. Which information did you find most useful and why?

Companion Website

Learning Styles Application

This chart lists the four learning styles and tips based on the chapter's main ideas. Locate your learning style and read the corresponding tips to maximize your success in college.

VISUAL

Visual learners will enjoy the new sights and meeting new people in college. You may think the campus is attractive and inviting. Where your classes are, where you hang out, and who you meet will affect your experience in college.

AURAL

The new sounds at a college campus—whether the silence of the library study rooms or the noise in the student center—will pique aural learners' interest and imagination. You will enjoy talking with new people and listening to lectures.

READ/WRITE

Read/write learners will find many things on a college campus to interest you. There will be plenty to read for class, but there will also be a student newspaper or newsletter, literary magazine, and flyers that will grab your attention.

KINESTHETIC

Those whose learning style preference is kinesthetic will find a variety of programs that will satisfy the need to be active. Whether it is welding, dental assisting, or office technology, you will be able to do more than listen to lectures, read textbooks, and write papers.

Path of Discovery

Journal Entry

What is your experience so far with the college culture? What is the biggest difference you have experienced so far between high school or work and college?

FROM COLLEGE TO UNIVERSITY

The changes in culture and college services

If you are moving from your community college to a larger, more diverse university, you may experience a slight culture shock despite the semesters you already have under your belt. In addition to a bigger campus with more buildings to find and more students to meet, you may also find that a university seems more impersonal. Many students who transfer from a smaller community college complain that professors do not seem to care about them personally and that they lack the support and guidance they received at their previous school. Transfer students also note that expectations are higher—and their grades are lower—especially as they move into their majors and begin working toward a career.

Culturally, you should expect that your new university will offer more activities and groups than your smaller community college. You also should expect some kind of adjustment period as you get used to what your new professors expect of you. Statistically, transfer students do experience a slight drop in their GPA. This drop, however, is not necessarily an indication that they were not properly prepared by their community college.

All in all, the culture shock you experience when transferring to a four-year university will depend on how much bigger than and how different the school is from your community college. Just remember that whatever differences you notice, you will have similar resources at your disposal. Seek out counselors, advisors, faculty, and students who can help make your transition smoother. There are people at the four-year school to help you. Take your campus map and faculty and administrator list and find them.

FROM COLLEGE TO CAREER

How the culture will change again

Just as you adjusted to the college culture, you will have to make a new adjustment to the workforce if you have never held a full-time job. When starting your first job after college, you will experience a period of getting used to the way the office or business works. You will encounter new terms, new methods of doing things, and new people. In addition, you will experience working in groups or teams to accomplish tasks, and you will be expected to communicate orally and in a written format. You may also rely more heavily on e-mail and computers to get your work finished. Integrity will be an important part of your working experience. There will be less supervision and more expectation that you do the work you say you will do.

Any anxiety you may feel can be alleviated by paying attention to how others act on the job. Just as you made friends and found mentors in college, you should look for others who can offer guidance and help as you learn the ropes of a new career. Also, think about how you adjusted to college and use the same strategies to make the new environment seems less foreign and more comfortable.

Chapter in Review

1. Name and describe five different characteristics that professors will expect from you as a college student.
2. How will you use what you learned about grades to prepare yourself for earning grades in college?
3. What differences exist between high school and college or a full-time job and college?
4. Grades are limited because an A cannot fully express what was achieved. Describe other ways that students can mark their success in a class.

Case Scenarios

Read the following case scenarios and determine what each person should do. Refer to the information in this chapter as you write a description and plan of action for each student.

1. In Jennifer's literature class, she is reading Tim O'Brien's *The Things They Carried*. Although she understands the book is about the Vietnam War, she doesn't know why she has to read a book that contains so much profanity and graphic images of death. She made an appointment to speak to her professor about the reading assignment because she wants to avoid reading a book that is so depressing and discomforting. What advice would you give Jennifer before she speaks to her professor? Predict the outcome of the talk and what the consequence of the discussion will be on Jennifer's college career.

2. Ja-Ling is taking a biology class, and one of her assignments is to create a group presentation on an assigned topic. Her group's topic is the theory of evolution, a theory that Ja-Ling finds fascinating; however, when she meets with her group to prepare for the presentation, two of her group members express deep concern they are being asked to study something they don't believe in. They refuse to help with the project even though they know their lack of participation will lower the whole group's grade. What should Ja-Ling do?

Research It Further

1. Find the University of South Carolina's (USC's) Carolinian Creed on the Internet. Try the website www.sa.sc.edu/creed/index.htm. Using USC's creed as a basis, write your own creed that fits your college's values. Is there anything you would revise or add to USC's creed?

2. Find a map of your college and determine what building or landmark is the geographical center of the campus. Then, write a short paper on how that building is an appropriate "center" of your college. Questions you may want to consider include the following: What does the building house—a library, a classroom for the engineering department, a student center? What does the building symbolize? If you were to design a display or piece of art that reflects the college's "center," what would it look like?

3. Choose one of the job descriptions listed in Exhibit 3. Find out who on your campus fulfills that role. Interview that person about his job and how it fits into the college's structure. Present the information you obtained to your class.

4. Working in groups or individually, choose a campus building to research. As part of the research, learn as much as possible about the building, including the square footage, operating hours, points/rooms of interest, history, interesting or unusual stories about the building, what departments or areas it houses, and which college officials occupy the building. Then, make a presentation, complete with visual aids, about the building.

References

American Association of Community Colleges. "Community Colleges Past to Present." Retrieved July 26, 2005, from http://www.aacc.nche.edu/ Content/NavigationMenu/AboutCommunityColleges/ HistoricalInformation/PasttoPresent/Past_to_Present.htm.

Banner, J. M., & Cannon, H. C. (1999). *The elements of learning.* New Haven, CT: Yale University Press.

Who Are You?

2

Stockbyte

PhotoDisc

Who Are You?

L arry learned as he took courses and planned for his degree that considering values and evaluating goals are important first steps to being a successful college student. To assist you with this process, the chapter provides information to help you understand yourself better. This chapter also answers questions you may have right now:

- What is "self-awareness" and why is it important?

- What will I gain from college? How will I understand myself better?

- What are mission statements, goals, and values?

- Why is goal setting so important?

- What are learning styles and personality types?

Student Profile

NAME: *Larry Lemmons*   AGE: *33*

MAJOR: *Physical Therapy*

1. **What are your values?**

   I value helping others, honesty, education, and being true to myself.

2. **What are your long-term career goals?**

   I want to be a physical therapist who helps low-income patients. I also would like to be a philanthropist.

3. **What are your short-term goals?**

   I want to do well in all my classes and learn as much as possible. Making As and Bs is a short-term goal as well.

4. **What is your VARK learning style?**

   Kinesthetic.

Who Are You?

The question "Who are you?" sounds easy to answer. You may start by listing a variety of characteristics: male, age 25, married, father of a son, electrician, and a Native American. Or, you are a single female, age 19, part-time sales assistant, full-time student, and mountain climber. But what are you beyond those labels? Where have you been? What are you doing now? Where are you going and where do you want to be? Now the questions get a little more difficult to answer, and they take more time and thought. The point is that you need to have some idea of who you are, or at least an idea of where you want to be, when you begin college.

Maybe you don't know who you are yet, but you hope that enrolling in classes and pursuing a degree will help you come to a better understanding. Don't worry, though, if you cannot immediately articulate the essence of you. This question and the possible answers have intrigued human beings for thousands of years. In his book *Who Are You? 101 Ways of Seeing Yourself*, Malcolm Godwin (2000) explores the ways people try to answer the question "Who am I?" From body types, to ancient Indian mysticism, to workplace dynamics, there are numerous ways you can learn more about what and how you think. Understanding yourself is called self-awareness and its purpose—or the reason you should be concerned with self-awareness—is to know yourself and your environment well enough to reach your goals.

Of course, who you are will change, maybe even dramatically, as you take classes, encounter new subjects, and research interesting topics. But taking the time to think and reflect on yourself will help you map a course throughout your community college experience and beyond—back to work, to raising a family, to another college, or to a satisfying career. This chapter helps you to understand who you are by identifying where you have been, what you know, what you want to become, and how you learn. This will also help you make decisions about who and what you want to be. Think of the following information as a road map for understanding where you came from and for directing you to where you want to go. Remember that enrolling in college means you have taken the first step on a journey to knowledge and self-discovery. And each journey, as the Chinese philosopher Lao-Tzu said, begins with that first step.

Keys to Self-Awareness and Personal Fulfillment

- Background: Where you come from, what you have experienced
- Values: What you believe in
- Priorities: What is important to you at a given moment
- Motivation: What makes you do what you do, what keeps you on track to reach your goals
- Mission: What you say about what you believe in and what you want to do
- Goals: Where you want to go, what you want to achieve
- Personality Types and Learning Styles: What you are like and how you like to learn

Where Have You Been?

Before you answer the question "Where are you going?" you should consider the question "Where have you been?" How, you ask, will your past experiences help you understand where you want to be in the future? Without acknowledging where you have been and what you have learned along the way, you will have a difficult time understanding yourself completely. Although the old adage "Those who do not know their history are doomed to repeat it" may seem trite, not acknowledging that your past helped shape who you are today may stand in your way of eliminating bad habits and negative behavior and continuing positive behavior. Take, for instance, one student's statement about where she has been:

> I couldn't understand why I thought I would never go to college and earn a degree until I realized that my father used to tell me that I wasn't very smart and would never amount to anything. I learned in one of my classes that I was internalizing his expectation of me rather than listening to myself as to what I think I am capable of. Once I realized this, I could put those thoughts behind me and think positively. Sometimes when I am stressed, I start doubting myself, but I have learned some techniques to help me stay focused on my goals.

As this student points out, she acknowledges why she felt insecure about her abilities in the past, but she uses that knowledge to keep herself on track to reach her goals.

What Do You Value?

Understanding and accepting your past allows you to honestly explore your values. Values are part of your belief system and are what make you unique—your values will not be exactly the same as someone else's. A value of yours may be honesty, which means you try to be truthful and straightforward in most situations and you expect others to be honest with you. If you value hard work, then you strive to do your best in life. Values can be learned from your parents, or they can come from what your culture, religion, or ethnicity regard as important. For example, your family may value loyalty, which is shown when your father sticks by his sister no matter the bad choices she made in the past. Or, your family may value the elderly, which is shown by listening to the advice of parents and grandparents.

Values can also be formed in reaction to a negative experience. If you were discriminated against in the past, you may strive to be open-minded and value that in others. Likewise, if you grew up with family members who did not value their health and did not take care of themselves, then you may have watched them go through painful illnesses or even death. Your determination to take care of yourself and stay healthy was shaped by the negative experience of living with those who did not have the same value. Whether developed through positive or negative experiences, your values make up the belief system that underlies any decision you make even if you don't consciously realize it.

The importance of understanding your values is that this knowledge can help you set realistic goals. If you value a satisfying career, for instance, you

Your Values Do Affect Your Everyday Life

IN BOX

VALUES	REFLECTIONS OF THESE VALUES IN EVERYDAY LIFE
Honesty	Telling your best friend the truth even if it hurts her
Loyalty	Sticking up for your brother even if he made a bad choice
Family	Making time to visit relatives even if it means spending less time with friends or participating in a hobby
Financial stability	Forgoing weekend trips with friends to save money for a special purchase or retirement
Spirituality	Setting aside time to attend religious services or meditate even if it takes time away from other activities

will set goals that support that value. Therefore, you will probably investigate challenging and interesting careers and fields. If you value a stable financial future, you will set goals that enable you to earn enough money to provide for your needs and wants. If you value your family, you will make spending time with them a priority. The box above lists examples of values reflected in everyday life.

Regardless of what ultimately shapes what is important to you, your values should be a true reflection of who you are and what you believe. If they are not, you will have trouble attaining your goals because your real values will conflict.

For example, a student's parents want her to be a doctor because they value financial success and career prestige or perhaps because they are doctors. What if the student values, instead, meeting new people and traveling? What if she wants to study ancient cultures? If she decides to adopt her parents' values and ignore her own, what kind of future can you envision for her? Although her parents' intentions may be well meaning, she will have to compromise herself in order to meet their goals for her, and she will probably suffer some regret in the future.

Does this example mean that you should ignore others who try to help you figure out what you want to be? Certainly not. But you should pay attention to what you want when you do get help with your educational and career goals. Be open to others' suggestions, but make sure you feel comfortable with your final decision. Those who truly want you to succeed will be proud when they know you have achieved your heart's desire, not theirs.

Practice

EXERCISE 1

Write down five things that you value in yourself (e.g., honesty, work ethic, appreciation). Then, briefly answer these questions: Where did the values come from? Who or what influenced the development of these values?

Companion
Website

What Are Your Priorities?

As you reflect on your values, also consider what your priorities are as you begin college. Simply stated, a priority is something that is important at a particular moment. Although priorities, by their very nature, can change weekly if not daily or even hourly, you also have "big picture" priorities that remain fairly constant. For example, before you enrolled in college, your priorities may have been something like the following:

STUDENT 1

1. My *job.* I have to get to work on time, work effectively during the day, and leave when my work is finished.

2. My *family.* I need to arrive home early each evening to help with child-care duties and housework.

3. My *health.* I quit smoking two years ago after a health scare, and now I regularly exercise and watch what I eat.

STUDENT 2

1. *High school.* I have to study and complete my work so I can graduate and get into college.

2. My *family.* I need to help my parents care for my grandmother after school so they can tend to their other priorities.

3. My *friends.* Because I won't see some of my high-school friends until they return home from college next summer, I want to spend time relaxing and having fun with them.

Now that you are enrolled in college, your priorities may have changed order or you may have replaced one of your top priorities with college. If you have not replaced one of your top priorities with college yet, then you should seriously consider how you will handle the demands of higher education if you have other, more important activities demanding your attention. This bears repeating: In order to meet your educational goals (which you will learn more about later in the chapter), you have to make college a top priority most of the time. Yes, there will be times that you have to put in extra time at work or take care of an ill family member, taking time away from studying, but if you consistently place your college education at the top of the list, you will more likely be successful in your educational pursuit. Here are one student's changed priorities:

STUDENT 3

1. My *education.* I waited a long time to get a degree, and it is my top priority. The majority of my energy and time will go toward making my dream a reality.

2. My *family.* I waited until my family can handle my change in priorities. I worked out a plan with my spouse so we can both take care of our children and our household. There may be times when I need to rely on other family members and friends to take care of errands.

3. *My job.* I moved from a full-time to a part-time job so I can spend more time taking classes. My employer is supportive of my educational goals and promised to work with me as my priorities change.

What Motivates You?

Determining your values and priorities are essential first steps to learning more about yourself so you can set realistic, achievable goals. The next step is to reflect on what motivates you. Motivation is often defined as the driving force that helps you achieve a goal. What is your driving force? What motivated you to enroll in college? What motivated you to consider completing a certificate or degree? What will motivate you to enroll next semester and the next? For some students, the driving force is knowing that to get a better job, they have to get a degree. Seeing their family and friends successfully complete a degree may motivate others. Still others are motivated by the fact that they are learning more about the world around them and how they fit into it.

Reflection

EXERCISE 2

How have your values changed over the years? Compare what you valued 10 years ago with what you value now and discuss why that change occurred.

Companion
Website

Motivating Factors for Enrolling in College

- Pride
- Increased income, better job
- Opportunity for self-improvement
- More respect at home, at work
- Meet new, diverse people
- Become independent
- Experience change
- Intellectual stimulation
- Personal challenge
- New career
- Friends/family are going to college
- Certification/degree requirements for current job

Not all motivating factors are positive, and negative motivators often result in undesirable outcomes. Consider, for instance, a student who enrolls in college classes because her father informs her that he won't support her if she doesn't get a degree. If the student doesn't have any motivating factors other than her father's threat to "cut her off" financially, then she has little to keep her in college if her financial situation changes. She may also feel pressured to choose a degree or major to please him. Now consider a student who enrolls in college only to receive grant money or a scholarship in order to pay bills and purchase a new stereo and has no intention of completing a degree. This may be an extreme example of a student being motivated by the wrong reasons, but you can well imagine that once the money is deposited, there is no other motivation to attend classes and complete the work.

Before you get to the next step, goal setting, consider what motivates you. What motivated you to apply to this college? What motivated you to register for classes, choose a degree plan? What motivated you to take this class? You may have been motivated by many factors, some positive and some negative. Does this mean that even though you enrolled in this class, for example, for the wrong reasons (e.g., it sounded like an easy A; I won't have to study at all) that your action cannot have a positive outcome? Definitely not. Some of us make choices for the wrong reason, but in the middle of the action or experience, we realize the importance and worth of the choice and become motivated by something positive.

Take the example about enrolling in this class again. What if you were negatively motivated to enroll in the class, but when you bought your book and started reading about how to succeed in college, you realized that what you are learning is exactly what you needed to know? Or what if your instructor really impressed you the first day as a caring, giving, encouraging individual? It would then be likely that you would experience a positive outcome from your action, even if your initial motivating factor was not positive. The key, then, is to look for positive motivators along the way to replace the negative ones because there may be times that you need those positive motivators to get you through a class, degree, or other life experience.

What Is Your Mission Statement?

Your past experiences, values, priorities, and motivators all work together to form your mission, or purpose, in life. Considering your purpose in life, especially for those who have never thought about the reason they exist, can be a very powerful experience. All it takes is some time to think about what you have done in the past and what you believe is the right journey for you to take now.

Once you have determined what your mission is, you can write your mission statement. A mission statement is a declaration of what a person or institution believes in and what she or it hopes to accomplish. A mission statement, then, usually contains the broad strokes of the overall picture of what you want to accomplish. Values are the foundation of a mission statement. If you are unsure of your values, your mission statement will not be easy to understand and follow. You also need to have a good understanding of your priorities and motivators.

Consider how understanding your personality style or learning preference can help you through challenging situations.

You strongly believe that abortion is wrong. You were raised with the value that all life, at any stage, is precious. While studying the human life cycle in a biology class, your professor spends a class period discussing the biological effects of abortion. You are outspoken about your beliefs and you learn best by debating ideas, so you challenge the professor during class. When he asks to talk to you after class, you worry that you made a wrong move. You didn't intend to come across as disrespectful, but you do feel strongly about your viewpoint. What do you think your professor will say? What should you tell him about your actions in class?

*PERSONALITY + LEARNING STYLE = UNDERSTANDING SITUATIONS

In order to better understand and articulate your values, take a look at your college's mission statement, which reflects what it intends to do for its students. Likewise, your mission statement will reflect your intentions. As you meet your goals and learn new things, your mission may change and your mission statement should be revised.

SAMPLE COLLEGE MISSION STATEMENT

Northern County College provides high quality, accessible educational opportunities at the freshman and sophomore level in associate degree and technical certificate programs, a college-transfer curriculum, continuing education, and industry-specific training to support individual and community needs in the state. The College's mission is to enable individuals to develop to their fullest potential and to support the economic development of the state.

Practice

EXERCISE 4

Using your values as a guide, write a mission statement you can use during your college experience.

Companion Website

Keeping in mind your values, complete Practice Exercise 4. More than likely, you will need to revise it as your values and goals change and become more specific. Here is a sample mission statement you can use as a model.

SAMPLE PERSONAL MISSION STATEMENT

My mission is to have a fulfilling personal and professional life that allows me to meet new people, take on new challenges, and have flexibility in my schedule. As a mother and wife, I want to have a close relationship with my family, acting both as a caregiver and a role model. As a teacher, I am dedicated to providing students with an education that will prepare them for a four-year university curriculum and the demands of the world of work.

What Are Your Goals?

To fulfill your mission in life, you must have a plan. Setting goals and achieving them puts you on the path to fulfilling your mission. If you are not used to writing down daily tasks or voicing your future plans, then start making lists and talking about what you want to be and do.

Using your list of values and your mission statement, you can formulate goals that support both what you believe in and what you want for yourself. The fact that you are reading this book is evidence that you are someone who has set a goal and is working toward achieving it. Also, the fact that you are in college says that you value education as a means of improving your life. You may have overcome many obstacles to get where you are today. You may have faced pressure from your family and friends to go straight to work from high school rather than go to college, or you may have gotten negative feedback from others when you decided to stop working, or stop working as much, to get a degree.

Nonetheless, realize that setting and achieving goals is not as easy as writing them down and crossing them off. You will encounter obstacles, some of which may threaten to knock you off course. Flexibility and determination, then, are the keys to achieving your goals despite setbacks.

Writing Down Your Goals

Even with the loudest cheerleaders and most supportive friends and family, you still need some well-defined goals to give you direction as you chart your course in college. A goal is something you work toward—it may be to learn how to cook macaroni and cheese, to quit a bad habit, or to write a novel. Whatever your goals, they should be reasonable and attainable in the time frame you assign. For instance, if you want to lose 10 pounds in one week, you may have to rethink the time in which you want to achieve your goal. A more reasonable goal for losing weight might be to lose 10 pounds in four months. Just like a slow weight loss, a reasonable goal is more likely to be met.

As you begin to think about your goals, consider dividing them into long-term and short-term goals. Certainly, one of your long-term goals is to get an education. This goal may take a year or more, depending on how many degree requirements you need to complete and how many other responsibilities you may have. A short-term goal that contributes to achieving the long-term goal of earning a degree is to complete your classes successfully.

When making a list of your goals, consider the following guidelines:

* Make your goals attainable and reasonable.
* Break larger goals into smaller goals that will lead to fulfillment.
* Think of setting goals in these time frames: one week, one month, one semester, one year, five years, and ten years.
* Review your goals regularly and make changes as necessary.

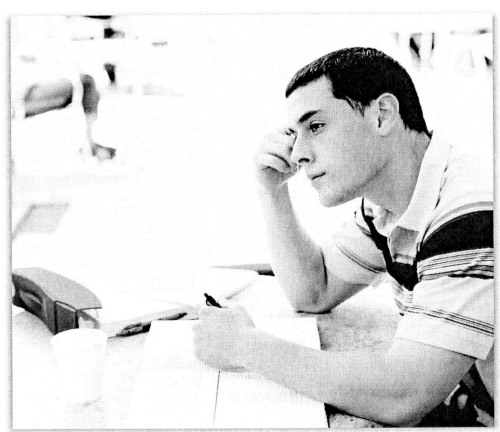

Stockbyte

Take time to reflect on your goals and write them down.

Because it is difficult to plan 10 years into the future, make a list of goals tied to the near future. For instance, if you want to own your own business in ten years, think about structuring your short-term and long-term goals this way:

LONG-TERM GOALS (10 YEARS)

Run a successful landscape design firm

Provide landscaping for low-income properties

LONG-TERM GOALS (5 YEARS)

Work for a landscape design firm

Continue community service and encourage coworkers to participate

LONG-TERM GOALS (3 YEARS)

Complete my associate's degree in landscape design and management

Continue community service work

SHORT-TERM GOALS (9 MONTHS)

Complete two semesters of landscape design classes

Continue working at the garden center

Plant and maintain my own flower and vegetable garden

Participate in community service project landscaping low-income properties

SHORT-TERM GOALS (1 SEMESTER)

Complete classes that count toward my degree

Look for community service project landscaping low-income properties

SHORT-TERM GOALS (1 MONTH)

Help friend plant new trees

Attend local lecture on seasonal planting

Begin research for final paper on plant diseases

SHORT-TERM GOALS (1 WEEK)

Study for classes

Apply for job at a garden center

Weed and fertilize yard

Take a hike in the park

No matter what you want to achieve, write down all of your goals and review them every few months to assess your progress. Henriette Anne Klauser (2001) made a career of helping people write their dreams and goals on paper so they can finally realize them. In her book, *Write It Down, Make It Happen: Knowing What You Want and Getting It!*, she states, "Writing down your dreams and aspirations is like hanging up a sign that says 'Open for Business.' . . . Putting it on paper alerts the part in your brain known as the reticular activating system to join you in the play" (p. 33). According to Klauser, the process of writing down your goals tells your brain to start paying attention to your ambitions and makes you aware of opportunities to achieve them.

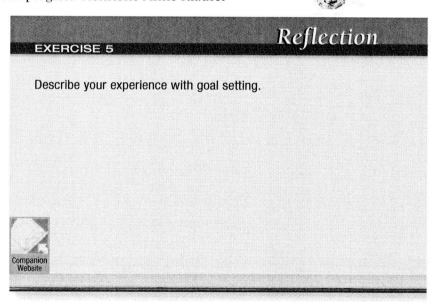

Reflection

EXERCISE 5

Describe your experience with goal setting.

Companion Website

Being Realistic About Goals

Some of us set goals that sound great on paper, goals we sincerely want to achieve, but we don't always consider the whole picture. We get excited about the end result, but we don't consider the challenges we will have to overcome to reach a goal. A world-class athlete who dreams of a gold medal around his neck also envisions the countless practices, the changes in his lifestyle, which may restrict his other interests and time spent hanging out with friends and family. He may also have to travel extensively, which will leave him little time at home. He may have to sacrifice an enormous amount of time, effort, and other personal interests to reach his goal. It would be foolish of him to assume that he can reach his goal of athletic glory without changing his priorities, without monitoring his goals closely, and without pushing himself to his limit, both physically and mentally. Eating chocolate bars on the couch every day does not contribute to an athlete's goals.

Although you won't be asked to put your body through the paces a world-class athlete does to train for an event, you will have to be realistic about your expectations as you work toward a certificate or degree. The following is an extreme example of a student with a realistic goal but unrealistic expectations.

- *Student A's goal:* I want to get a degree in psychology and become a high-school counselor.
- *Student A's expectations:* I don't like to read anything that doesn't interest me, so I skip any chapters in my textbooks that are boring. I don't like to write and I am not familiar with the library, so I will avoid any professor who assigns a research paper. I don't have a lot of time to devote to studying, so I am going to take classes that are easy and require very little outside work.

Do you think Student A will successfully reach her goal if she maintains these expectations? Although Student A demonstrates excessively unrealistic expectations, it is worth noting that we all have moments when we do not consider all the hard work required and possible challenges when faced with a large goal. Sometimes we get so excited about the end result we forget to think about what it takes to get there. What can Student A do to change her expectations and reach her goal? What can you do if you feel you have unrealistic expectations?

The following is a checklist to keep your expectations realistic and keep you on track.

- Visualize, write down, or talk through the possible steps to achieving your goal, including those that may be unpleasant (e.g., staying up late to finish a paper, saying "no" to social activities because you need to study).
- Acknowledge that there may be unforeseen obstacles that will stand between you and your goal.
- Determine a plan of action if you encounter an obstacle to your goal.
- Enlist the help of friends and family as backup support as you work toward your goal.
- Talk to an advisor or professor if you feel your expectations are not realistic or if you have any difficulty reaching your educational goals.

As these steps suggest, a little planning and a review of your expectations will help you set realistic goals you can attain.

Reaching Your Goals and Considering New Ones

In addition to writing your goals down on paper, make sure you do at least two activities a week that contribute to your long-term goals. For example, if you want to get a job writing for a newspaper, then read a newspaper or magazine each day, or write in a journal for 10 minutes a day. Once you have accomplished some of the short-term goals that contribute to a long-term goal, keep adding new short-term goals. If you successfully read newspapers and write in your journal for a month, then add another part of your long-term goal; for instance, check your career counseling center for internships at newspapers or publishing houses. Each time you achieve a short-term goal, create a new one or move to the next one on your list. Before you know it, you will reach your long-term goals and will be ready to create new ones.

When making lists of goals, remember that your free time is just as important as the time you spend working on your goals. Downtime to rest and relax is essential to refueling your energy reserves. A car stops running if you don't refuel and take care of it, and you will too if you don't give yourself the care that is needed to keep you healthy. One method of making sure you get the relaxation and rest you need is to make it a goal. Just as you have work and college goals, you should write down when you plan to do nothing and be committed to meeting that goal.

Eliminating Negative Influences

As you work toward your goals, make an effort to eliminate anything that keeps you from focusing on them. If you think you don't have time to accomplish two short-term goals during the week, then examine where you have spent your time and get rid of any activity that does not contribute to your goals or that does not reflect your values.

If you watch seven hours of TV a week, and you aren't achieving a short-term goal of becoming more informed, then replace the hours spent watching TV with something that does contribute to your goal. In addition to activities that don't contribute toward your goals, anyone or anything that distracts you and is unnecessary in your life should be eliminated: a gossipy neighbor or a destructive or dangerous habit.

If you are unsure of whether or not your activities contribute to your goals, take a few minutes to list what you did this week and determine how each activity supported or did not support one of your goals.

ACTIVITIES THAT CONTRIBUTE TO YOUR GOALS

- *Car maintenance:* Allows you to get to school and work safely
- *Exercise:* Allows you to remain healthy and reduces stress
- *Eating and sleeping:* Keep you healthy and reduce stress
- *Reading the newspaper:* Keeps you informed, helps you improve reading skills, contributes to learning

ACTIVITIES THAT MAY DISTRACT YOU FROM YOUR GOALS

- *Excessive socializing:* Takes away time and energy from other goals
- *Mindless TV watching:* May not contribute to learning
- *Using drugs and alcohol:* Keeps you from focusing on goals, is dangerous
- *Irregular sleeping and eating:* Creates stress that inhibits your ability to reach goals habits

Although you cannot remove all of the people in your life who don't support your goals, you do have the power to reduce the effect of their negativity. If you have someone in your life, a friend or a family member, who belittles your efforts to go back to school and earn a degree, try to limit your time with that person or try to focus on conversation topics that are not related to you. Lillian Glass (1997), in her book *Toxic People: 10 Ways of*

Dealing with People Who Make Your Life Miserable, recommends limiting contact with people who make you feel hurt, stressed, dumb, or unworthy. Dr. Glass refers to people who stand in the way of being your best as "toxic" because they "are hazardous to others' mental, emotional, and physical health" (p. 12). Dealing with toxic people reduces the time and energy you have to work on your goals and to benefit from the positive influence of those who support you.

Collaboration

EXERCISE 6

Working within a group, create your own list of activities that may distract you from reaching your goals. Then, determine what can be done to eliminate these activities or to turn them into more productive pursuits (e.g., watching TV can become an activity that supports a goal if you limit what and how much is watched).

Companion
Website

Staying Motivated to Achieve Your Goals

One of the hardest parts of reaching goals is maintaining the momentum necessary to achieve them. There will be times in your academic career when you will feel overwhelmed by the responsibilities you have and unsure of your ability to handle it all. When you feel weighed down by all you have to accomplish that week or that day, take the time to calm yourself first. If you can, talk with a friend, an instructor, or counselor and explain your frustration and stress.

Sometimes, if an instructor knows you are feeling overwhelmed by the expectations of a course, he will help you by giving you more time to complete an assignment. A friend may also volunteer to help out by studying with you.

To stay motivated and to resist the temptation to give up because of the stress, review your short-term and long-term goals. Is there anything you can change that will make your goals more reasonable or attainable? Have you allowed enough time to achieve them? Revising your goals or your time line may be necessary to keep you on track.

Lastly, think positively about yourself and your progress. Many students before you successfully juggled a job, classes, and a family. That is not to say that they did not doubt themselves along the way or suffer small setbacks. The difference between them and those who were not successful is that they persevered because they believed in themselves. Tell yourself that you can get through stressful times.

Critical Thinking

In what ways will goal setting affect your college experience?

Companion
Website

Personality Types and Learning Styles

So far in this chapter, you have been asked "Who are you?" and "What do you value?" but there is still a question that remains: "What are you like?" What is your personality type? Do you like to sing karaoke in front of a group of strangers? Do you like to participate in group sports? Do you enjoy bungee jumping or mountain climbing? Would you rather read a book than go shopping? Do you believe in love at first sight?

Describing personality types has been an activity for thousands of years, and all cultures have some way to describe different types of people. One example from hundreds of years ago is known as the four "humors" or "tempers": sanguine, choleric, melancholic, and phlegmatic. Malcolm Godwin, in his book *Who Are You? 101 Ways of Seeing Yourself* (2000), describes the four personalities:

1. *Sanguine:* "Carefree, easy-going, extrovert, lively, sociable . . . ."
2. *Choleric:* "Tends to react very quickly to situations and becomes easily over-excited, impulsive . . . ."
3. *Melancholic:* "Quiet and often withdrawn, pessimistic, sad, reserved . . . ."
4. *Phlegmatic:* "Detached, aloof, nonchalant, thoughtful, careful . . . " (pp. 46–47).

Our tendency to classify personalities is likewise seen in the descriptions of the zodiac signs. The person who asks, "Hey, baby, what is your sign?" is not just interested in knowing what month another person celebrates her birthday. He wants to know if her personality will be compatible with his. Finding potential mates is not the only reason we want to learn more about ourselves and others. Body types (pear or apple, endomorph or mesomorph) and the body mass index (BMI) system are two examples that give us information about how healthy we are or should be depending on our height and weight. We classify all aspects of our lives in order to better understand them, to improve *self-awareness* and, ultimately, to improve ourselves.

Being aware of yourself and knowing your personality type are ways to better understand how you learn. Most personality tests provide feedback on what motivates you and how you best work with others. Learning styles inventories, likewise, provide feedback on how you learn best depending on your personal preferences or strengths. Information about what you like and dislike, how you relate to others, and how to work productively will help you achieve your goals and, as Gordon Lawrence (1995) states in his book *People Types and Tiger Stripes*, help you make "dramatic improvements in the effectiveness of [your] work" (p. 5).

There are many different personality tests and learning styles inventories. Although this chapter discusses the Left-Brain/Right-Brain, Neil Fleming's VARK, Howard Gardner's Multiple Intelligences, and the Myers-Briggs Type Indicator, it is worthwhile to know there are others out there you may want to investigate on your own.

Left-Brain/Right-Brain

Based on scientific research done in the 1960s and made popular in the classroom by Betty Edwards' book *Drawing on the Right Side of the Brain* (1979), descriptions of left-brain and right-brain processes help teachers adapt their teaching styles to different types of learners and help students adapt their note-taking and study habits. Nancy Lightfoot Matte and Susan

Hilary Green Henderson (1995), in their book *Success, Your Style! Right- & Left-Brain Techniques for Learning*, describe left-brained people as "analytical, taking things and ideas apart to comprehend something" and right-brained people as "holistic, looking for patterns and relationships" (p. 3). Matte and Henderson further state that left-brained people "respond to facts while right-brained people respond to feelings" (p. 3). The purpose of determining which side of the brain you rely on most when processing information is to help you determine which learning methods you prefer and recognize which teaching types work best for you and which will be a good workout for the other side of your brain.

Left-Brain/Right-Brain Learning Style Inventory

Matte and Green Henderson (1995) provide the following learning style inventory.* To get a sense of your preferred learning style, for each of the following statements, circle the letter corresponding to the response that describes you best. Scoring instructions are provided at the end of the exercise.

1. I prefer to spend my weekends and free time:
   a. Doing what I want to do whenever I want to do it.
   b. Making a list of what I have to do and checking things off as I do them.

2. When an instructor gives an assignment, I prefer:
   a. To know the exact requirements for completing the assignment—when it is due, how long it should be, how to format it, and so on.
   b. To have some freedom to set the standards, figure out different ways to do it and turn it in when I please.

3. When planning a party, I:
   a. Make lists of whom I'll invite, what food and drink to serve, and what I need to do before the party.
   b. Think about the type of party mood I want and then invite the right people to create it.

4. When I move into a new place, I:
   a. Mentally visualize how the furniture can be arranged.
   b. Draw a floorplan before arranging the furniture.

5. When talking with a friend, I:
   a. Understand what my friend is telling me mostly from the words spoken.
   b. Get the message from my friend's facial expressions and gestures (i.e., nonverbals) as well as his words.

6. When thinking about how I talk and write, the statement that describes me best is:
   a. I use very precise language to describe and explain what I am talking about. I am very conscious of and careful with grammar and the meaning of words.

---

*From *Success, Your Style! Right and Left Brain Techniques for Learning*, 1st Ed., by Matte/Henderson. © 1995. Reprinted with permission of Wadsworth, a division of Thomson Learning: www. thompsonrights.com. Fax 800-730-2215.

   b. When talking or writing, I use metaphors, similes, and other figurative language. My communication style is descriptive, and maybe even poetic or emotional.

7. When solving a problem or learning a new concept or process, I:

   a. Prefer to look at the parts and put things in step-by-step order.

   b. Prefer to get a sense of the whole problem or concept first.

8. When I try to determine how I feel about an issue, I:

   a. Look at the facts, think about the issue logically and rationally, and then come to my conclusion.

   b. Often make up my mind based on emotion or intuition.

9. It is easy for me to see how things fit in a pattern or relationship.

   a. Yes.

   b. No.

10. Generally, I know what time it is.

   a. Yes.

   b. No.

SCORING

Assigning the following number values for each of the responses for items 1–10, total up your score and divide by 10.

  1. a=7   b=1
  2. a=1   b=5
  3. a=1   b=5
  4. a=5   b=3
  5. a=3   b=5
  6. a=1   b=7
  7. a=3   b=5
  8. a=1   b=7
  9. a=7   b=1
10. a=3   b=5

A score between 1 and 3.4 indicates you function primarily in a left-brained mode, while a score between 3.5 and 4.9 suggests you use a combination of left- and right-brain functions. A score between 5 and 7 indicates you are more of a right-brained processor.

VARK

Although the left-brain/right-brain learning styles inventory gives you only two descriptions of how you may learn best, there are other learning styles inventories that provide more choices. VARK, which stands for Visual, Aural, Read/Write, and Kinesthetic, is a system developed by Neil D. Fleming that helps you determine what type of learner you are and provides study strategies based on your strengths. If you have strong preferences in more than one mode, you are considered MM, or multimodal. You can determine what your learning style is by answering questions similar to the following.

1. When getting directions to someone's house, what do you need to do to remember them?

    a. Write them down.

    b. Recite them.

    c. Look at a map.

    d. Drive or walk to the person's house.

If you answer A, you fall into the read/write (R) category. If you answer B, you are an aural (A) learner. If you answer C, you learn better with visual (V) information. And if you answer D, then you are a kinesthetic (K) learner. Fleming developed a focused learning styles questionnaire that helps you understand how you may respond in certain situations. However, as Fleming states on his website:

> VARK deals with only one dimension of the complex amalgam of preferences that make up a learning style. The VARK questions and results focus on the ways in which people like information to come to them and the ways in which they like to deliver their communication. The questions are based on situations where there are choices about how that communication might take place. It is important to say what VARK is not, so that other components are not perceived as being a part of it. VARK has little to say about personality, motivation, social preferences, physical environments, intraversion–extraversion.

VARK Learning Styles Inventory

The following information comes from Neil Fleming's website, www. vark-learn.com.*

This questionnaire aims to find out something about your preferences for the way you work with information. You will have a preferred learning style, and one part of that learning style is your preference for the intake and output of ideas and information.

Choose the answer that best explains your preference and circle the letter. Please select more than one response if a single answer does not match your perception.

Leave blank any question that does not apply.

1. You are about to give directions to a person who is standing with you. She is staying in a hotel in town and wants to visit your house later. She has a rental car. You would:

    a. Draw a map on paper.

    b. Tell her the directions.

    c. Write down the directions (without a map).

    d. Collect her from the hotel in your car.

2. You are not sure whether a word should be spelled "dependent" or "dependant." You would:

    a. Look it up in the dictionary.

*Used with permission.

    b. See the word in your mind and choose based on the way it looks.

    c. Sound it out in your mind.

    d. Write both versions down on paper and choose one.

3. You have just received a copy of your itinerary for a world trip. This is of interest to a friend. You would:

    a. Phone her immediately and tell her about it.

    b. Send her a copy of the printed itinerary.

    c. Show her a map of the world.

    d. Share what you plan to do at each place you visit.

4. You are going to cook something as a special treat for your family. You would:

    a. Cook something familiar without the need for instructions.

    b. Thumb through the cookbook looking for ideas from the pictures.

    c. Refer to a specific cookbook where there is a good recipe.

5. A group of tourists has been assigned to you to find out about wildlife reserves or parks. You would:

    a. Drive them to a wildlife park.

    b. Show them slides and photographs.

    c. Give them pamphlets or a book on wildlife reserves or parks.

    d. Give them a talk on wildlife reserves or parks.

6. You are about to purchase a new stereo. Other than price, what would most influence your decision?

    a. The salesperson telling you what you want to know.

    b. Reading the details about it.

    c. Playing with the controls and listening to it.

    d. It looks really smart and fashionable.

7. Recall a time in your life when you learned how to do something like playing a new board game. Try to avoid choosing a very physical activity (e.g., riding a bike). You learned best by:

    a. Visual clues—pictures, diagrams, charts.

    b. Written instructions.

    c. Listening to somebody explaining it.

    d. Doing it or trying it.

8. You have an eye problem. You would prefer the doctor to:

    a. Tell you what is wrong.

    b. Show you a diagram of what is wrong.

    c. Use a model to show you what is wrong.

9. You are about to learn to use a new program on a computer. You would:

    a. Sit down at the keyboard and begin to experiment with the program's features.

    b. Read the manual that comes with the program.

    c. Telephone a friend and ask questions about it.

10. You are staying in a hotel and have a rental car. You would like to visit friends whose address/location you do not know. You would like them to:

    a. Draw a map on paper.

    b. Tell you the directions.

    c. Write down the directions (without a map).

    d. Collect you from the hotel in their car.

11. Apart from the price, what would influence your decision to buy an optional textbook?

    a. You have used a copy before.

    b. A friend was talking about it.

    c. Quickly reading parts of it.

    d. The way it looks is appealing.

12. A new movie has arrived in town. What would most influence your decision to go (or not to go)?

    a. You heard a radio review about it.

    b. You read a review about it.

    c. You saw a preview of it.

13. Do you prefer a lecturer or teacher who likes to use:

    a. A textbook, handouts, and readings.

    b. Flow diagrams, charts, and graphs.

    c. Field trips, labs, and practical sessions.

    d. Discussion and guest speakers.

SCORING

QUESTION	A CATEGORY	B CATEGORY	C CATEGORY	D CATEGORY
1	V	A	R	K
2	R	V	A	K
3	A	R	V	K
4	K	V	R	
5	K	V	R	A
6	A	R	K	V
7	V	R	A	K
8	A	V	K	
9	K	R	A	
10	V	A	R	K
11	K	A	R	V
12	A	R	V	
13	R	V	K	A

CALCULATING YOUR SCORE

    Total number of Vs circled _____

    Total number of As circled _____

    Total number of Rs circled _____

    Total number of Ks circled _____

Multiple Intelligences

Harvard psychologist Howard Gardner is well known for his theory of multiple intelligences, which is another term for "what we know, understand, and learn about our world" (Lazear, 1991, p. xiv). Gardner identified eight intelligences that describe how we know and learn. *Verbal/linguistic* intelligence is evident in people who use language with ease. People who demonstrate the verbal/linguistic intelligence enjoy reading and writing and may be journalists, novelists, playwrights, and comedians. The *logical/mathematical* intelligence is demonstrated by an ease and enjoyment with numbers and logic problems. People who have a strong leaning in the logical/mathematical intelligence like to solve problems, find patterns, discover relationships between objects, and follow steps. Career choices for logical/mathematical people include science, computer technology, math, and engineering.

Collaboration

Complete the VARK inventory individually. Then, form small groups in which someone with each learning style is represented (at the least, include one other learning style in the group). Discuss the different ways each person likes to learn and determine if there are similarities or differences among the different learning style strengths.

Companion
Website

Dana White/PhotoEdit

Your career choice should take into account your personality type, your intelligences, and many other factors.

Visual/spatial is an intelligence characterized by anything visual— paintings, photographs, maps, and architecture. People who have a strong visual/spatial sense are usually good at design, architecture, painting and sculpture, and map making. *Body/kinesthetic* is an intelligence that focuses on body movement. Body/kinesthetic people enjoy using their bodies to express themselves. Obvious career choices for this intelligence include dancing, sports, and dramatic arts. *Musical/rhythmic* intelligence encompasses the mind's proficiency with the rhythms of music and hearing tones and beats. People who have strong musical/rhythmic intelligence may use musical instruments or the human voice to express themselves. Career choices for this intelligence include all types of musical performers.

How you relate to others and yourself is part of the interpersonal and intrapersonal intelligences. People with strong *interpersonal* intelligence relate well with others. They read others' feelings well and act with others in mind. *Intrapersonal* intelligence centers around the ability to understand oneself. People who possess intrapersonal intelligence know how and why they do what they do. *Naturalistic*, the eighth intelligence, refers to people who enjoy and work well in an outdoor environment. Naturalistic people find peace in nature and enjoy having natural elements around them.

Myers-Briggs Type Indicator

The Myers-Briggs Type Indicator, or MBTI®, is a popular personality test that was developed in the 1970s by Isabel Briggs Myers and Katharine Briggs. The "four dimensions of type" the MBTI uses are:

Extraversion (E) / Introversion (I)
Sensing (S) / Intuition (N)
Thinking (T) / Feeling (F)
Judgment (J) / Perception (P)

* *Extraversion:* Likes to focus on people, is active in the world
* *Introversion:* Reflective, thinks before acting, attuned to inner world
* *Sensing:* Observes using all five senses, in touch with physical realities
* *Intuition:* Imagining, thinking about possibilities
* *Thinking:* Using logic, being objective and skeptical
* *Feeling:* Employs personal feeling, sensitive to people's needs, dislikes conflict
* *Judgment:* Goal-oriented, planning, controlling
* *Perception:* Curious and open-minded, taking in information

Sixteen personality types can be identified using combinations of the four dimensions; for example, ENFJ, ISTP, ESTJ, and INTJ.

Knowing your MBTI type is one way to understand who you are and what your strengths and weaknesses are. However, there

Critical Thinking
EXERCISE 9

If a friend wants to be a nurse because he thinks he can make a good living but has no interest in the field other than financial, what would you tell him? What if you know his true dream is to write?

Companion
Website

are many more ways of understanding you, and no test can accurately measure exactly what you want out of life and how you will get it.

Many other learning styles and personality types questionnaires will allow you to explore what ways of receiving and giving information work best for you. The goal is to realize your personality and learning style strengths and use them when you are studying new or difficult material or considering a career. However, don't forget your weaker areas. You can improve them with a little work, but you may want to wait until the material you are learning is easier before you begin experimenting with different learning styles.

What Else Do You Want to Know?

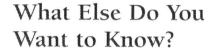ow that you realize that you know much more than you thought, take some time to make a list of what you want to know more about. No doubt, you are in college because you want to learn more about a particular topic or field, which may be your major and your career goal.

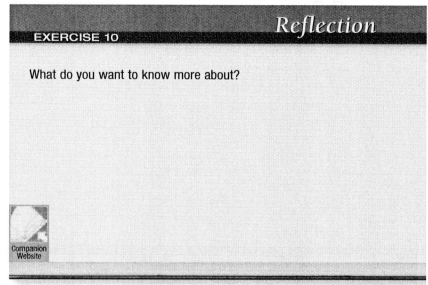

Reflection

EXERCISE 10

What do you want to know more about?

Companion Website

Learning Styles Application

This chart lists the four learning styles and tips based on the chapter's main ideas. Locate your learning style and read the corresponding tips to maximize your success in college.

VISUAL

Visual learners find meeting goals easier if they can see a visual representation of the goal. If you want a degree so you can start your dream job, cut out a picture of someone in your dream job role and place it in a prominent place. Whenever you need some extra motivation, look at the picture for inspiration.

AURAL

Those who learn better by hearing may need to talk to a close friend or mentor to keep the momentum going to reach their goals. You may even want to record your own motivational words to play when you need reassurance that you can make it.

READ/WRITE

Writing down goals is a comfortable activity for read/write learners. Spending some time each day or every other day checking off to-do lists and rearranging daily priorities will keep you on track to reaching your goals.

KINESTHETIC

Kinesthetic learners feel best when they are engaged in activity. You will achieve short-term goals more easily if you limit your list to items you can do within a couple of days. The act of completion will keep you motivated to add to your short-term goals list and to achieve them.

Path of Discovery

Journal Entry

Name and describe three people or situations that changed your life. What did these people or situations teach you about your values, priorities, motivators, or goals? How have they changed you?

FROM COLLEGE TO UNIVERSITY

What you know and how you learn will change

If your beliefs, goals, and values remain relatively unchanged during your community college experience, then your move to a four-year university should be easy, right? The transition can be relatively smooth if you are willing to apply some of the ideas in this chapter to your new environment. Chances are good that your new school will present a variety of challenges that will require you to adapt.

First, your definition of who you are may have changed, perhaps dramatically. You will be more confident in your abilities and better able to handle the stress of juggling numerous responsibilities. Your values may also change after your semesters at a community college; if you were unsure of what you valued before, you may finally have a clearer picture of your belief system. On the other hand, you may be more confused than ever about what you believe after studying different religions, psychological theories, and social ideas. Because higher education values inquiry and research, no matter what shape your values are in when you transfer, you will find support as you struggle to make sense of it all at the four-year university.

Just as your knowledge of yourself and your values will change, your goals will go through a transformation. Although your main goal of graduating with a four-year degree will still be in sight, you will notice that you have already met some of your smaller goals. Perhaps you successfully completed an associate's degree, or you just became more organized. Just the fact that you are ready to transfer credits means you accomplished some necessary steps to fulfilling the rest of your goals.

In addition, you can revise your list of what you know because what you know changes after taking classes at a community college. You may even be able to include in your "What I Know" list a career choice. Also, you may know yourself better, through the application of the learning styles. However, you have to be prepared to adapt to different teaching styles and new pressures after you transfer.

Now, to prepare for the next step, revise, preferably on paper, your list of what you know. Recognize that the learning styles you felt most comfortable with may have to be adapted—or new styles explored and used—at your four-year school.

FROM COLLEGE TO CAREER

Goals and a mission will help you succeed

Many businesses rely on creating mission statements, strategic plans (long-term goals), and operational plans (short-term goals) to chart a course for their success. Because you have experience writing your own mission statement and goals, you are able to contribute to your company's planning. You can do this because you understand how the company's values underlie its mission and how its goals create its road map to success. Your experience in goal setting will help you write departmental or personal goals. Because you understand how values, mission, and goals fit together, you can create goals that are explicitly linked to the focus of your workplace.

Chapter in Review

1. Create a list of your values and priorities at this time in your life.
2. Using what you learned from this chapter, explain why you think some people have difficulty reaching their long-term goals.
3. Design a plan to help you reach three short-term goals.
4. Evaluate two of the personality tests/learning styles inventories and determine which one is more helpful for college students to know. Explain why you think the personality test/learning styles inventory is the best one for students.

Case Scenarios

Read the following case scenarios and determine what each person should do. Refer to the information in this chapter as you write a description and plan of action for each student.

1. Ahmed has started college, but he is not sure what he wants to do. In fact, he is afraid to tell his parents that he wants to be a dental hygienist because his parents want him to take over the family business. Neither of his parents went to college, and they don't understand why any of their children would want to work outside the family business. Ahmed values loyalty to his family—he has been through many challenges that strengthened his relationship with his parents—but he also has a strong interest in the health field. Ahmed's ultimate goal is to be a dentist, but he thinks that working as a hygienist first is a way to make sure that he has what it takes. What advice would you give Ahmed? What should he do to make sure his goals are met?

2. Serena, a single parent, has started her first semester in college, but she also works full-time in a law office. Her sister keeps her twin boys while she works, but she sometimes has to miss work when her sister is unavailable. Serena wants to get a four-year degree and eventually go to law school, but she feels it will take too long if she doesn't start now. She is motivated by time and money. She wants to hurry and get her degree, and she wants to be financially independent so she can take care of her boys. She works very hard, but she doesn't have any other family or friends who can help her. To add to her obstacles, her sister is not supportive of her desire to get a degree and improve her life. Serena's sister thinks that she has all she needs and shouldn't "mess it up by going to college and getting all kinds of crazy ideas."

What advice would you give Serena? What have you learned about setting goals and managing priorities that would help Serena? What have you learned about overcoming challenges that would help Serena?

Research It Further

1. During the Middle Ages (500–1500 A.D.), the terms *sanguine, phlegmatic, choleric,* and *melancholic* were used to describe people. Research these descriptions further and have the class determine which category each student falls into.

2. Choose a long-term career goal and research what qualifications are necessary to accomplish it. For example, if you would like to be a network administrator, check your college catalog for degree requirements and look on the Internet for job descriptions that include the kind of degree and work experience required. List any other skills necessary for the career.

3. Using the keywords "mission statements," search the Internet for college and business mission statements. Print out at least three different mission statements and identify the similarities and differences. Report your findings to the class.

References

Edwards, B. (1979). *Drawing on the right side of the brain.* Tarcher.

Fleming, N. D. "VARK: a guide to learning." Retrieved 20 Sept. 2003, from www.vark-learn.com/english/index.asp.

Glass, L. (1997). *Toxic people: 10 ways of dealing with people who make your life miserable.* New York: St. Martin's.

Godwin, M. (2000) *Who are you? 101 ways of seeing yourself.* New York: Penguin.

Klauser, H. A. (2001). *Write it down, make it happen: Knowing what you want and getting it!* New York: Simon & Schuster.

Lawrence, G. (1995). *People types and tiger stripes* (3rd ed.). Gainesville, FL: CAPT.

Lazear, D. (1991). *Seven ways of teaching: The artistry of teaching with multiple intelligences.* Palatine, IL: Skylight.

Matte, N. L., & Green Henderson, S. H. (1995). *Success, your style: Right- & left-brain techniques for learning.* Belmont, CA: Wadsworth.

Managing Your Time and Stress

3

PhotoDisc

Photolibrary.com

Managing Your Time and Stress

tuart's time management practices are similar to many college students'—they write down only the important activities. In this chapter, your goal is to find the method that works best for you to help you keep time and stress under control. This chapter presents you with different methods and ideas for increasing your chances of success. Specifically, you will be able to answer the following questions once you have completed the chapter:

* *What is time management and how will it help me in my life?*

* *How do I manage my goals and priorities?*

* *How do I get organized?*

* *How do my energy levels relate to time management?*

* *What can I do to stop procrastinating?*

* *How can I minimize negative stress at work, home, and college?*

Student Profile

NAME: *Stuart Dixon* AGE: *24*

MAJOR: *Criminal Justice*

1. How do you manage your time?

   I actually manage my time pretty well. I don't really write down what I need to do; I keep up with it mentally.

2. What do you do as a stress reliever?

   To relieve stress, I write, draw, listen to music, and box.

3. What have you learned about your ability to handle stress?

   I have learned that I handle most things better than the people I work with.

4. What is your VARK?

   Kinesthetic.

The Next Step

Now that you have a better understanding of college culture and have read and thought about values, goals, and priorities, it is time to figure out how to make it all fit together. In order to connect your educational objectives with your college's demands of you as a student, you must develop good time and stress management skills. Without them, your goals will be harder to achieve; with them, you will find the path to realizing your dreams a little easier and your steps along the journey more stable. This is not to say that attaining your educational goals will be simple—there is no way to predict what obstacles lie in your path—but the ability to plan your time and reduce stress effectively will keep those goals in focus and give you the confidence to meet them.

Managing Your Time

Despite our many differences, we all have the same number of hours each day and the same number of days each week. Why, then, does it seem as though some people are more accomplished than others? Are they able to magically extend the day by a few hours or sneak eight days into a week? Do they forgo all sleep, meals, and personal needs just to get things done? Although we would like to believe that high achievers have superhuman strength, the truth is they usually do not do anything to achieve their goals that we cannot do as well. When you talk to very productive people, they usually tell you that the secret to their success is that they learned to manage their time efficiently. Effective time management is not a talent; it is a skill, one that gets better as you practice over time.

Analyzing Your Time

If the first step is recognizing that we all have the same amount of time to work with, then analyzing your time is the second step to effective time management. Tim Hindle (1998), in his book *Manage Your Time*, suggests keeping a time log of your day that is divided into 30-minute increments (p. 9). The purpose of a 30-minute time log is to raise your awareness of what you are doing throughout the day. Make your own time log like the one in Exhibit 1 for one day's worth of activities. Keeping an eye on how you spend your time helps you make realistic time management goals and keeps you from wasting too much time or miscalculating how much time it takes to complete tasks.

Asking the questions "Where did the time go?" and "What do I do with my time?" is a start to analyzing your time. You should also analyze your time management skills—or how well you use your time wisely to meet your goals and stay healthy in the process. The following assessment asks 10 questions about time management abilities.

Practice

Complete the Personal Time Assessment worksheet to determine how well you manage your time.

Companion
Website

EXHIBIT 1 *Time log example.*

TIME	WEDNESDAY'S ACTIVITIES
7:00 A.M.	Get ready for classes; eat breakfast
7:30 A.M.	Review notes for business class
8:00 A.M.	En route to school
8:30 A.M.	Business Communications
9:00 A.M.	Class, continued
9:30 A.M.	Class, continued
10:00 A.M.	See advisor to plan next semester's classes

You may already be a good manager of time. Certainly, if you are able to work, take care of your family, and attend your college classes without getting confused or overwhelmed, then you can already manage your time. Nonetheless, what causes students the most stress is trying to schedule enough time to prepare for classes, study for exams, write papers, and

ACTIVITY *Personal Time Assessment*

Circle the number (1-Never, 2-Sometimes, 3-Usually, 4-Always) that best describes your experience.

STATEMENT	NEVER	SOMETIMES	USUALLY	ALWAYS
1. I arrive to class prepared.	1	2	3	4
2. I review my notes within 24 hours of class.	1	2	3	4
3. I spend my time on campus taking care of personal business, talking with professors, studying, or doing research.	1	2	3	4
4. I have study goals, and I achieve them each week.	1	2	3	4
5. I feel prepared for tests.	1	2	3	4
6. I spend enough time on writing assignments.	1	2	3	4
7. I get enough sleep each night.	1	2	3	4
8. I spend some time each week doing something I enjoy.	1	2	3	4
9. I have enough time to take care of most of my personal needs.	1	2	3	4
10. I get support from others to help me meet my educational goals.	1	2	3	4

Score each column.

Add each column's total.   Total

(continued)

SCORE RANGE	MEANING
32–40	You do a good job managing your time. For the most part, you are satisfied with how you manage your time and what you accomplish each week.
26–31	You do a good job managing your time for most activities. Identify your weaker areas and create a plan to improve time management in those areas.
19–25	You may be dissatisfied with your time management and find only a few goals are met each week. Review what you are doing right with some of your time and make a plan that will draw upon your time management strengths.
Below 18	You may feel as though you are not meeting most of your goals during the week. An honest look at your goals, necessary activities, and priorities is needed.

participate in various extracurricular activities. Good time management skills include knowing your goals and priorities, being aware of how much time you have and how you are spending it, and making adjustments along the way. We all are given the same number of hours in a day, but how we use those hours differs greatly because of the way we manage our time.

Multitasking

One way you can manage your time more effectively is by multitasking or doing more than one activity at once. If you have the ability to focus on more than one activity at a time, then multitasking may be a good way to manage your time wisely. If, for example, you're talking on the phone, you may be able to fold clothes or sweep the floor at the same time. There may be times when you can take your reading material with you while waiting at the doctor's office or getting your car's oil changed, generate ideas for a paper as you listen to the news on the radio, or listen to lecture recordings while riding a bicycle at the gym. You can multitask most effectively if both tasks do not require your complete attention. For instance, you shouldn't read a textbook while driving or chopping vegetables! Be prepared for multitasking opportunities by carrying along reading material, notes, and paper and pen for writing ideas down. Then, take advantage of those times when you can complete two or more tasks at once.

Getting Creative

You cannot create more time, but you can get creative with how you use it and manage it.

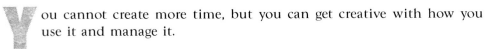

- If you have children, consider setting up a "babysitting co-op" where classmates, friends, or neighbors watch each other's children while you study or take care of personal errands.

- Use the Internet to automate tasks that take considerable time to do. Your bank may provide automatic bill payments that will save you time and stamps each month. Consider browsing and shopping online for items that may take several trips to different stores to find.

- If you need to save time running errands, find out whether local businesses offer deliveries—some do for free—and take advantage of them. Think about the time you will save having your cleaning, groceries, and medicine delivered.

- Create a monthly newsletter for family and friends to replace hours on the phone talking to individuals and on the computer sending e-mail.

Managing Your Priorities

Managing your time and priorities when you are in college can be a game of strategy, action, and patience. In the activity on the following page, consider what should be top priority; what can be completed if there is time; and what can be delegated, modified, or rescheduled for another day. It is Monday morning, and you have 10 items on your to-do list to accomplish today, but you don't have time to complete them all. Determine which activities are top priorities and which are not. Then, list those you eliminated and explain why you decided to make them low-priority items. Finally, describe how you will accomplish the low-priority items the next day.

Before you can begin to manage your time and monitor your stress levels, you have to make sure that your goals and priorities are clear. Writing down your goals and setting your priorities, which may change frequently, are the first steps to realizing your dreams; they are also the first steps to figuring out how much time you need to spend on each goal. Before thinking about time management, take time to review what you have written down as your short-term goals and priorities.

If you listed your priorities right now, college would be near the top. Certainly, enrolling in college and reading this book mean you are committed to furthering your education. Nevertheless, you have to figure out where the priority of going to college fits in with your other priorities. Perhaps attending classes is your only priority because you live alone and do not work; more likely, however, college competes with other priorities. If you are going to succeed in college, your education must be a top priority most of the time.

In addition to college, you have to consider your family as a priority. Depending on your situation, you may have family members who need you for emotional, physical, and financial support. You may even be the only one they can rely on. Because family is often a first priority for many students, it is important to manage your time with them wisely and effectively.

If you have not yet done so, talk to your family about the new responsibilities you have. Be honest in your descriptions of what you are doing and what you need from them. If you think time will be limited for family trips and weekend activities, let them know. If you think you will need to cut out some basic duties such as planning meals, cleaning the house, and running errands, be sure to communicate this to your family. The more they know about what to expect, the better able they will be to support your decision to enroll in college.

MONDAY'S TO-DO LIST—FOURTH WEEK OF CLASSES

- Pick up sister at airport at 7:30 P.M. (Airport is 15 minutes away.)
- Attend two classes, one at 2:00 P.M. and one at 4:00 P.M. (You have a one-hour break in between.)
- Complete paper for 4:00 class. (You will need an hour to finish.)
- Prepare dinner for family at 6:30 P.M. (It will take at least 30 minutes.)
- Study for Tuesday's psychology exam. (You would like to spend two hours.)
- Take children to school at 7:45 A.M. (School is 10 minutes from your house.)
- Get up at 6:00 A.M. and go to gym for an hour workout.
- Call your cousin who had surgery last week. (Spend 20 minutes.)
- Help children with homework. (Spend 1 hour.)
- Meet study group at noon to start working on final project for business communications class.

From the list above, identify which three items should be top priority.

Top priority

Top priority

Top priority

Why did you identify these to be the most important?

With the time remaining, determine what else you can accomplish in the same day.

Additional activity

Additional activity

Additional activity

Additional activity

Why did you decide that those activities could be completed if time allowed?

What items can be low priority, modified, or rescheduled?

Low priority

Low priority

Low priority

Why did you choose these items as low priority?

How might you modify the low-priority items so that they can be completed in the same day?

Another priority you may have is your job. Most community college students work as well as attend classes. For some, their jobs supplement their household income and are not necessary for survival; for many others, their jobs are more important than college because they provide the primary or sole income for the family. If your job is your top priority, then you should know where the other priorities must fall, and you should be prepared to make sacrifices in other areas to ensure that your job remains at the top.

With all the other responsibilities you have, it is easy to overlook the priority of relaxing; without it, the other priorities can run you down. Don't forget that you can have fun while in college, and you certainly should participate in activities you enjoy. Without them, your college career will seem stressful and dull. Scheduling downtime to play and rejuvenate is an important part of effective time management. Get outside, read for pleasure, or participate in those activities you enjoy. Relaxing and having fun will recharge your body and mind to concentrate on the demands of your other priorities.

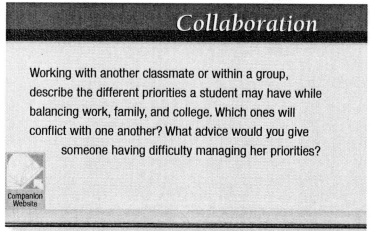

Collaboration

Working with another classmate or within a group, describe the different priorities a student may have while balancing work, family, and college. Which ones will conflict with one another? What advice would you give someone having difficulty managing her priorities?

Companion Website

Managing Your Goals

You will see this suggestion throughout this book: In order to accomplish anything, you must set goals and write them down. Even something as simple as spending two hours preparing for class should be written down as a goal for the day or week. The goals must be manageable, however. Having too many goals for the week may make you feel overwhelmed at the thought of meeting them all or like a failure for not accomplishing them all. Avoid the temptation to over-schedule, and be realistic about how long it will take to complete your goals for the day or week. Setting too few goals for the week may make you feel like a rudderless ship, which makes it easier to get off track.

Once you have them written down, communicate the goals to your coworkers, family, and friends. Enlist their help to meet your goals, especially if you need to schedule time to study and complete assignments. Tell them that you must have the evenings free of distractions, or make arrangements with them to have a weekend or weekday to yourself to study. Don't assume that because they *know* you are in school that they will also *know* you need extra time and personal space to get your work finished. Managing time is much easier if your priorities and goals are concrete, realistic, and communicated to those around you.

Managing Your Energy

Just as important as managing your time is managing your energy. Think about this scenario: You have all weekend off from work and your spouse took the kids to visit the grandparents. Therefore, you have 48 hours of complete solitude to write a research paper that is due on Monday. Sounds ideal, doesn't it? But what if you have the flu for those two

Time is valuable only if you plan and use it well.

Dana Stephen Derr/Getty Images Inc.-Image Bank

days? Does the time mean anything when you don't have the energy to do any work? What if, instead of having the flu, you worked two double shifts and haven't slept more than five hours in two days? Will you be able to use your free 48 hours productively or will you need to take care of yourself?

Time is only valuable if you have the energy to use it well. Thus, you need to be aware of how you feel, how energetic you are, and how willing you are to use your time wisely. To determine which times of the day you feel the most energetic, complete the activity on the next page. In the first section, place an X in the appropriate column for each time of day. If you work nights and sleep during most of the day, create your own chart with the times you are awake.

Critical Thinking   EXERCISE 3

Looking at the third section, which shows Carla's energy levels, what times are best to schedule classes? What times are best to study? What times are best to take care of simple tasks such as organizing her notes or cleaning her study space? Why did you make your decisions?

Companion
Website

Second, assess your energy levels in another way: in addition to the time of day, your energy levels rise and fall during the week. Do you find yourself tired on Monday mornings, but full of energy on Fridays? Or do you feel worn out by Thursday evenings, but rejuvenated on Sundays? Depending on your work, school, and personal schedules, you will find that you have regular bursts of energy at certain times of the week. Use the second section to determine which days of the week you feel most energetic. Place an X in the appropriate columns.

Finally, complete Exercise 3 by referring to the third section.

TIME OF DAY	HIGH ENERGY	NEUTRAL	LOW ENERGY
6:00 A.M.			
8:00 A.M.			
10:00 A.M.			
12 noon			
2:00 P.M.			
4:00 P.M.			
6:00 P.M.			
8:00 P.M.			
10:00 P.M.			
12 midnight			

WEEKDAY	HIGH ENERGY	NEUTRAL	LOW ENERGY
Sunday			
Monday			
Tuesday			
Wednesday			
Thursday			
Friday			
Saturday			

Carla's Energy Levels

TIME OF DAY	HIGH ENERGY	NEUTRAL	LOW ENERGY
6:00 A.M.			X
8:00 A.M.	X		
10:00 A.M.	X		
12 noon		X	
2:00 P.M.			X
4:00 P.M.			X
6:00 P.M.	X		
8:00 P.M.		X	
10:00 P.M.			X
12 midnight			X

Along with managing your energy you must maintain your health. You cannot expect to experience high levels of energy and productivity without taking care of yourself. Sleeping regularly and eating small meals often help you maintain your energy levels, as does moderate exercise; sugar, caffeine, and a sedentary lifestyle zap energy reserves, making it difficult to manage energy and time efficiently. As always, though, check with your doctor first before changing your dietary and exercise habits. At the least, avoid fad diets, rigorous exercise plans, and late-night activities during the semester, all of which drain your energy reserves.

Reflection

Describe a situation in which you had the time to complete a task but had a low level of energy. How did you feel? Were you able to complete the task or did you have to reschedule it?

Companion Website

Identifying Time and Energy Zappers

Despite your best efforts to manage your time and energy, there will be times that your plans are interrupted by people and last-minute changes. A few distractions during the day can be a nice break from the mundane tasks of going to school and working or caring for a family. However, if they take so much time away from your studies that you can't seem to keep up with the pace of your classes or that you are stressed out, you will need to find ways to lessen the frequency of or eliminate the intrusions.

Although you may be able to create your own list of time and energy zappers, here are a few common ones:

- People who want your attention and time, but don't need it
- Interruptions such as unnecessary phone calls
- Fatigue and illness
- Personal problems
- Mindless television watching
- Internet surfing that serves no purpose
- Continuous "chatting" online
- Playing video or computer games
- Inability to say "no"
- Procrastination
- Poor organization

Reflection

If you need to visit the library to find sources for a paper, which day of the week is best for you? If you need to study for a math exam, which day of the week is best? What class work can you do on the days when your energy is the lowest? What class work can you do on the days when your energy is the highest?

Companion Website

* Inability to concentrate because of learning difficulty, medication, or stress

Now is the time to block out the zappers. You can't afford the time they waste, and you must be proactive in getting rid of them. Some will be easy to eliminate, such as playing video games or hanging out all day with friends, while others will be more difficult, such as learning to say "no" to people or eliminating procrastination. The key to getting rid of the energy and time wasters is to take on the easiest ones and work on, through goal setting, the others.

One way to help yourself manage your energy is by becoming aware of which activities relax you when you are stressed and which activities allow you to refill your energy reserves. Complete the activity below.

ACTIVITY   *What Relaxes You?*

In the table below, place an X in the appropriate column next to each activity. If the activity both relaxes and energizes, place an X in both columns. If the activity does neither, leave both columns blank.

ACTIVITY	RELAXING	ENERGIZING
Watching television		
Spending time with family/friends		
Pleasure reading		
Doing housework		
Exercising (light to moderate)		
Gardening		
Talking on the phone		
Writing		
Cooking		
Shopping		
Napping		
Participating in a hobby		
Surfing the Internet		
Organizing closets, drawers, files		
Enjoying a nice meal		

Getting Organized

Personal Space and Supplies

If your personal space is cluttered and disorganized, it is hard to keep your life straight. To manage your time effectively and efficiently, you must organize. First, find a place in your house or apartment that you can call your own. Make sure it is comfortable and quiet and has adequate space for books, notebooks, and other supplies. It has to be a place you *want* to be or it will be difficult to go there to stay on task. Consider starting or ending your day with straightening or cleaning your work space. Leaving it until it gets too messy may make working difficult, as you are likely to lose items and waste time looking for what you need.

To stay organized, buy two calendars, preferably one to hang on a wall and one to carry with you. How they are organized, by month or week, is up to you. Both calendars, however, should allow you to look ahead easily. Make it a habit to write your daily and weekly tasks on both calendars. Make it part of your routine every evening to write down your goals for the next day and to review each morning what you need to do during the day. As you complete each task, scratch it out. Here is an example of a typical day's activities:

Collaboration

EXERCISE 6

Working within a group or with another classmate, describe the types of activities that can zap students' time and energy, then create solutions for eliminating them.

Companion
Website

THURSDAY

* Make appointment to have oil changed
* Pick up dry cleaning
* Take kids to baseball
* Study for history quiz on Friday
* Read 30 pages for English
* Get book from library

Using a Calendar

In order to juggle all your family, work, and college responsibilities, use a calendar. Which one you choose depends on how you can best visualize your time. Once you get a calendar, write down all your planned activities and tasks. Because you have quite a few things to do for college, consider getting a separate calendar or planner just for your classes.

Exhibit 2 shows a typical wall or large desk calendar. The benefits of using a monthly calendar are that you can visualize the whole month at one time and can anticipate busy days or weeks. Drawbacks to using a monthly calendar are that it is usually not very portable and it does not provide much space to write details about your duties. They are good, however, for major activities and appointments.

Another type of calendar is weekly, whereby you can glance at each week at a time (see Exhibit 3). A benefit to a weekly calendar is that you have room

EXHIBIT 2   *Monthly calendar.*

SUNDAY	MONDAY	TUESDAY	WEDNESDAY	THURSDAY	FRIDAY	SATURDAY
					1	2
3	4	5 library w/ B.W., 2:00	6	7	8	9 picnic, noon
10	11 work late	12	13 Dr. appt., 2:00	14 play rehearsal 7:00	15 pay bills	16
17	18	19 library w/ B.W., 2:00	20 lunch w/ Rhea	21 play rehearsal 7:00	22	23
24	25 nutrition exam 10:00	26	27	28 English paper due	29	30 birthday party 2:00

EXHIBIT 3   *Weekly calendar.*

MONDAY	TUESDAY	WEDNESDAY	THURSDAY	FRIDAY	SATURDAY	SUNDAY
8:30 Work	9:00 English 11:00 Acct.	8:30 Work	9:00 English 11:00 Acct.	8:30 Work	8-10 Clean house	
2:00 Geology 3:00 Trig		2:00 Geology 3:00 Trig		2:00 Geology 3:00 Trig	3-4 Exercise	3-8 Work on paper
5:00 Pick up dinner 7:00 Study for Accounting	6:00 Help sister with painting			7:00 Movie with friend	6-11 Study	

EXHIBIT 4   *Daily calendar.*

TIME	FRIDAY, MARCH 10, 2006
7:00 A.M.	Get ready for school
8:00 A.M.	Arrive to school early and study in the library
9:00 A.M.	Algebra
10:00 A.M.	English 2
11:00 A.M.	Study for biology exam
12:00 A.M.	Eat lunch; review notes for algebra
1:00 P.M.	Biology—EXAM!!
2:00 P.M.	Drive to work; errand to return book
3:00 P.M.	Work
4:00 P.M.	
5:00 P.M.	

to note the details of each activity; a drawback is that because you can only view one week at a time, it is difficult to anticipate what you must do the next week.

A daily calendar (see Exhibit 4) works well if you are very busy during the day. However, this kind of calendar is the most difficult to work with if you need to plan ahead. Because you cannot visually see the rest of the week or month, you may overlook important events or be surprised by them. Use a daily calendar only if you are extremely organized and can plan ahead effectively, or use it in conjunction with a longer-term calendar.

Whichever type of calendar you choose, be sure that it is used every day. Write down your daily and weekly tasks and scratch them off as you complete them. Also, check your calendar each morning before you leave for work or school. Knowing what to expect for the day makes surprises less likely.

Keeping It Clean

With new calendars and a designated space at home to schedule and review your tasks, you shouldn't need much more, right? There is one last suggestion for keeping your life organized: Keep your area clean. As stated before, you will lose valuable time looking for important papers if your work area and bookbag are cluttered. Make it a point each day or week to straighten up your personal space. Get rid of unnecessary slips of paper and other items. The better you can see your calendar and your workspace, the easier it will be to reach your goals. Think about your personal space as if it were the path to your goals. If you purposely put obstacles in your way (e.g., clutter) as you work toward your goal, it will be more difficult to get to your destination. If, however, you clear the path of clutter, then your footing will be more secure, and your path will be safer, making it easier to reach your goal.

Running Low on Time and Energy

There will be times when you find yourself with daily or weekly goals still left on your list, but you don't have the time and energy reserves that you hoped to have. Sometimes life throws us a curveball, and our beautiful plans are mangled if not completely destroyed. If you find yourself in such a situation, you will benefit from changing your goals and priorities quickly and eliminating unnecessary items from your to-do list. For example, you planned to bake a friend a birthday cake from scratch, but you don't have two hours to do it. What can you do? How about buy a cake on the way to your friend's house? The outcome is still the same: your friend has a cake for his birthday. You hoped to get all the bills paid by the end of the day, but you don't have the time and energy left? Pay the bills that are due the soonest and complete the task the next day.

There will be some days that you just can't do it all. You may find that you cannot read the assigned chapter in your sociology class the night before. If this happens to you—and it will at some time in your college career—then create a back-up plan. Avoid giving up completely if you run out of time or energy; do something, even if it is just a little bit. Can't get to the library to start looking for sources for your research paper? Create an outline or a task list instead and go to the library the next day. Do something that keeps you moving forward, but don't give up. You will have more energy and time the next day to complete new tasks.

Procrastination

An example of time and goal management at its worst is procrastination, an activity that seems to be an integral part of going to college. One would think that all college students routinely participate in cramming and "pulling all-nighters." Putting off studying and completing projects certainly adds to your stress, but procrastination does not have to be a necessary part of going to college. Realistically, community college students delay starting projects and studying because they are pressed for time, not because they are wasting time hanging out with their friends or having fun.

There are many humorous sayings about procrastination:

> If it weren't for the last minute, nothing would get done. —Anonymous

> I never put off till tomorrow what I can possibly do . . . the day after. —Oscar Wilde

Kidding aside, procrastination can be, American author Elbert Hubbard remarked, "the father of failure." Postponing an activity or task because you do not want to do it or can find more interesting activities to do can have serious consequences. For example, if you put off researching your legal terminology paper until the night before, you might find that the library closed early or access to online databases is down. You may even discover that your computer won't work and your printer is out of ink.

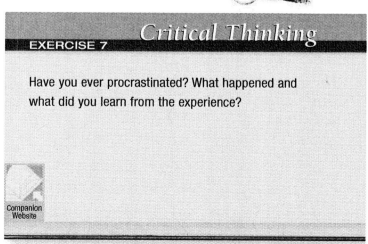

Critical Thinking

EXERCISE 7

Have you ever procrastinated? What happened and what did you learn from the experience?

Companion Website

Procrastination can, then, be a barrier between you and your goals and cause you undue stress. Managing your time and planning ahead will, however, minimize your desire to procrastinate. Writing down your tasks and goals, too, will make them visible and instill the need to cross them off your list.

FIGHTING PROCRASTINATION

* Divide the project into smaller parts. If you have a paper to write, break the task into generating ideas, drafting the paper, and completing the final draft. Do only one part at a time.

* Create a time line for when you want to complete each part. Make adjustments if needed, but try to stick to the schedule.

* Give yourself enough time to complete each part. It is easy to assume that you can find all the resources you need for a paper in one day. A more realistic goal is to find two sources during one trip to the library.

* Just do it. Start right here, right now, and don't think about finding a better time to begin.

* Recognize that behind every procrastinator is someone who fears—the unknown or failure. Acknowledge that fear by writing down what the fear is. Once you recognize your fear, you are more likely to move past it.

* Reward yourself for completing a particularly difficult or boring project.

* Write a list of consequences of *not* doing the project on time and a list of consequences for doing the project on time. Decide which list you can live with.

* Remind yourself of the reason you are in college and think about how this project supports that reason.

Managing Stress

Stress is a physical and psychological response to outside stimuli. In other words, just about anything that stimulates you can cause stress. Not all stress, however, is bad for you. For example, the stress you feel when you see someone get seriously hurt enables you to spring into action to help. For some students, the stress of an upcoming exam gives them the energy and focus to study. Without feeling a little stressed, these students might not feel the need to study at all.

Not everyone, however, handles stress the same way, and what is a stressful situation for you may not be for someone else. How we handle stress depends on our genetic makeup, past experiences, and the stress-reducing techniques we know and practice. There are ways to reduce stress or change our reaction, both physically and psychologically. First, though, it is important to be able to identify causes of stress. This list is not exhaustive, but it can start you thinking about different ways you experience stress.

POSSIBLE CAUSES OF STRESS

* Self-doubt
* Fear of failure or the unknown
* Speaking in public
* Uncomfortable situations

Taking care of your body (and mind), including taking time to relax, will help you alleviate the negative effects of stress.

Stockbyte

- Pressure to succeed (from yourself or others)
- Lack of support—financial, physical, or psychological
- The demands of a job such as a promotion/demotion, deadlines, and evaluations
- Life experiences such as the death of a loved one, having a child, getting married, and moving
- Too many activities and not enough time to complete them
- Congested traffic
- Waiting in lines

Stress Patterns

Each of us has certain triggers, such as the ones listed previously, that stress us. Usually, however, the same situation doesn't stress us the same way each time we are in it. Take, for example, waiting in line at the bank. One day, you might be extremely angry about waiting 15 minutes in line to cash a check because you are late for a job interview. The next time, though, you are in the same line waiting the same amount of time, you may be calm and relaxed because you are enjoying a little quiet time to think while your mother waits in the car. Thus, it is not necessarily the situation or action that causes negative stress, but more likely other factors that are involved.

When you suffer from lack of sleep, you may be more likely to react negatively to people and situations that usually do not bother you. When you feel unsure of your ability to be successful in college, you may take constructive criticism as a personal attack. Being aware of times and situations that cause you the most stress is one step to managing your stress better. For example, if you realize that you are sensitive to others' feedback because you feel insecure, then you may be less likely to react negatively. Complete the activity below.

Minimizing Stress in College

Because there is stress in college, at work, and at home, it is important to identify the different stressors in each environment and work toward minimizing negative stress in each area. Some weeks, you will have to contend

ACTIVITY   *Assessing Your Stressors*

Identify which situations are stressful and which are not. Consider other situations, or people, that cause you to react negatively and add them to this list. The goal is to recognize a pattern of stress and then work to overcome it. When you can tell your professor or coworker that you experience negative stress when assigned a big project, then they can help you create a plan to complete it.

SITUATION	STRESSES ME	DOES NOT STRESS ME
Starting a big project		
Paying bills		
Being in a messy environment		
Receiving graded papers and exams		
Not getting enough sleep		
Taking a personal or professional risk		
Getting out of bed		
Not getting feedback on my work		
Being distracted by other people		
Thinking about the future		
Taking tests		

with negative stress in only one area, but there will be times when it seems as though each part of your life is making you miserable. The more you know about what you can and cannot control, the more likely you will work through stressful times and stay on track with your goals.

Stress in college is inevitable, but it doesn't have to be overwhelming if you know what you can do to minimize negative stress. There are several ways students unknowingly cause stress:

* Failing to read the catalog for course prerequisites and descriptions as well as degree program requirements.
* Registering for more hours than they can handle.
* Trying to do too much at work and home.
* Missing deadlines.
* Arriving late for class or appointments.
* Keeping the same social schedule.

The information in this chapter should help you minimize stress in college by providing you with information and strategies for accomplishing your goals. Even if you avoid the listed behaviors, you may still find that things don't go your way in college. If you realize that there will be times that you or others make mistakes, then you will be more likely to bounce back from problems. Following are some suggestions for minimizing negative stress at school:

* Read all information you receive from the college.
* Pay attention to flyers on doors, bulletin boards, and tables.
* Talk to your advisor, instructor, and counselor on a regular basis.
* Check out the college's website.
* Read publications such as newspapers and newsletters the college sends to the community.
* Ask questions.
* Get involved with campus organizations and clubs.

Minimizing Stress at Home

Reducing stress at home will, no doubt, be the first step to minimize your overall stress. Because your family and friends are your most important supporters, what they think of you and the demands they place on you must be

INTEGRITY MATTERS

One way to eliminate stress and anxiety is to make integrity a top priority. Even though it may seem less stressful to take the easier path, in the long run, your negative stress will be less when you maintain integrity.

discussed. Some family members may be unsure of what you are doing or worried that your schoolwork will leave little time for them. Your friends may feel the same way, especially if they are used to hanging out with you after work and on the weekends. The key to minimizing stress at home is to communicate your needs. Talk to your loved ones about what you and they can expect when you are taking classes. Here are some other tips for making your home life a sanctuary rather than an asylum:

* Tell your family when you have exams or major projects due.
* Inform them of your breaks and vacation time. They may be excited to count down the days until you are finished with the semester.
* Explain how your responsibilities will change when you are in college.
* Be aware that you are a role model for your family. You may be inspiring other members to go to college.

Minimizing Stress at Work

For some, stress on the job can be the most difficult because of the fear of performing poorly and being fired. It can also be particularly tough to manage because you may feel uncomfortable confronting coworkers and being honest about your feelings. There are ways, though, to cope with the negative effects of stress at work. To help minimize the amount of stress you have about your job, you should do one or more of the following:

* Talk to your employer about your educational goals. Your boss may be very excited that you are increasing your knowledge and improving your skills.
* See if your employer will allow flextime to take classes. You may be able to arrive at work early, skip a lunch break, or stay late in order to take classes during the day.
* Let your boss know when you have finals or other activities that may interfere with your regular workday.
* Unless you ask permission, avoid studying on the job.
* Handle any conflict that may arise with your schedule as soon as possible. Coworkers may be jealous of your success or they may misunderstand the arrangements you made to work and go to school. Address any concerns you have about your workplace environment to the appropriate person.

There is no cure-all for stress. It is an integral and important part of life and can actually be thrilling and exciting. Nonetheless, preventing or reducing it in the first place can keep you happier and healthier, which will make you better able to achieve your goals.

Reducing the Negative Effects of Stress

Because you cannot eliminate all stress, develop methods for reducing the negative effects your body and mind experience when stressed. One of the quickest, easiest ways to reduce the negative effects of stress is to take a deep breath. You may have even told someone who was upset to breathe deeply in order to calm down. The breath is, as many cultures have known for thousands of years, an important part of life; for example, in yoga, the ability to control it is essential to controlling the mind and body and to bringing in fresh air to the lungs and other organs.

Visualization is another method for reducing the effect stress has on the mind and body. In order to visualize a more relaxed time and place, find a quiet, comfortable spot, sit down, and close your eyes. Relaxation experts suggest that you visualize a place that makes you feel warm and relaxed. Many people think about a beach because the mood there is often relaxed and the sound of the ocean is comforting. You should find your own special place.

Once you decide where you want to go mentally, start noticing the details in your place. If you are at the beach, then you should feel the sunshine's heat. Next, listen to the waves crashing on the surf and smell the salty air. Depending on how long you need to visualize this special place, you may want to stick your toe in the water or lie down on the beach and soak up the rays—leave your stress in those designated beach trash cans. The goal of this method of relaxation is to stay there as long as you need to; when you come back to your present location, mentally that is, you should feel refreshed and renewed.

Sometimes physical activity can be a better stress reliever than mental exercises. Getting outside or to the gym to work out your frustrations and stress is an excellent way of maintaining your health. Exercising eliminates the physical side effects of stress while taking your mind off your troubles. If you do not usually exercise, start slowly. Begin, for instance, with a 15-minute walk around the block or do some simple stretching exercises on the floor. Overdoing exercise can lead to more stress, so start small and increase the time you spend as you get stronger.

If you happen to exercise too much, you can look toward massage therapy to reduce all your stress. Although it is a little less conventional than other methods of reducing stress, a massage can improve circulation and alleviate muscle soreness. Seek professional massage therapy or ask a family member to rub your neck, shoulders, or feet. Massage therapy can give you the rejuvenation you need to tackle the rest of the week.

You have heard that cliché that "Laughter is the best medicine," and it is also an ideal way to eliminate stress. Have you ever been in a very stressful situation when someone made you laugh, and you thought, "Boy, I needed that." You probably felt all the tension melt away as you doubled over giggling. Surrounding yourself with people who make you laugh is one way to keep stress at a minimum. Other ways include renting comedies or reading funny books. Of course, good, old-fashioned acting silly can relieve stress and anxiety as well.

Lastly, comfort yourself with familiar favorites to eliminate the negative effects of stress. A special meal or a visit with your best friend will put you at ease. Looking at old photographs, reminiscing about family trips, and watching your favorite movies are great stress relievers. If you are in college in a new town or have moved out on your own for the first time, you may find comfort in the familiar, whether it be an old pillow or stuffed animal. Make sure, though, that your methods of reducing negative stress are healthy; drugs and alcohol may temporarily relieve stress, but they cause more problems in the long run.

Practice

EXERCISE 8

Complete the following sentences.

When I feel stressed, I like to . . .

Three activities that make me feel better after a hard day are:

1. _____

2. _____

3. _____

Companion Website

Staying Flexible

An important method of managing stress is to remain flexible. If you try to control too many aspects of your life, you will quickly discover you can't do it all. Although it is important to manage your time and mark your progress toward your goals, you must still plan for the unexpected and be willing to make adjustments. Good time managers plan for problems by keeping their schedules loose enough to make room for adjustments. For example, if you have a doctor's appointment at 2:00, you shouldn't schedule a job interview at 3:00. Delays in the doctor's office or traffic problems could keep you from your 3:00 appointment. Instead, give yourself plenty of time in between scheduled tasks, especially if you have to rely on others' time management skills.

Reflection

What stresses you? In what ways can you eliminate or reduce the amount of stress you have?

Companion Website

Knowing When to Get Help with Stress

If you ever feel as though you cannot cope with the amount of work and responsibility you have—despite attempts to reduce your stress—seek professional help. Excessive crying, difficulty breathing, inability to get out of bed, and suicidal thoughts are severe reactions to stress. Knowing when to reach out to other people is crucial to your recovery.

When asking for help, find someone you trust who will be objective about your experiences. Sometimes, close friends and family members can be your best allies to combat stress, but other times an outside party, who will listen to what you have to say without judging, can be extremely helpful. When you talk to someone, be honest about what you are feeling. Don't try to minimize any fear or anxiety. The more they know about what you are experiencing, the better able they will be to help.

You are working 40 hours a week, taking 12 credit hours for the semester, and have two children under the age of 5. You are stressed because you are having trouble managing all of your responsibilities. Although you don't have any family members who live nearby, you do have a few good friends, one of whom has children as well, and another who is also in college. When you approach them about making a plan to help you juggle all of your responsibilities, both your friends have very different ideas. The one with children thinks you all should go out to a park and let the kids play while you talk. The other offers to pick you up sometime to go out to dinner. You would prefer time alone to study and take care of errands, but you don't know how to voice your opinion without offending your friends. What do you do?

Consider how understanding your personality style or learning preference can help you through challenging situations.

*PERSONALITY + LEARNING STYLE = UNDERSTANDING SITUATIONS

Learning Styles Application

This chart lists the four learning styles and tips based on the chapter's main ideas. Locate your learning style and read the corresponding tips to maximize your success in college.

VISUAL

Visual learners find using calendars an effective time and task management tool because they visually represent upcoming events and activities. You also benefit from visualization techniques for stress management and can reduce stress by watching TV, reading magazines, or going through old photographs.

AURAL

Aural learners usually benefit from talking about their priorities and goals and how they will accomplish tasks. Talking through stressful situations is also advisable for this type of learner. They can also relax by listening to their favorite music.

READ/WRITE

Read/write learners find the act of writing down a to-do list or a goals list an effective way to manage their time and efforts. Pleasure reading, journaling, or writing to friends and family is an effective way to deal with stress.

KINESTHETIC

Kinesthetic learners deal with stress most effectively by getting out and participating in a physical activity. Exercise, even moderate activity, is a good stress reliever.

Path of Discovery

How do you feel when you have a day or a week when it seems as though you cannot achieve your goals because of unexpected challenges? What have you done in the past to get back on track after such a day? How have you used those experiences to prepare each day or week?

FROM COLLEGE TO UNIVERSITY

How your stress will change and how to handle the new pressures

There are many possible stressors awaiting you when you make that move from your community college to university. Increased tuition, higher expectations, more difficult workload, impending graduation, and goal realization are all reasons to feel anxious about the transition, but remember that you have already succeeded in college by getting this far.

To meet the challenges that await you, be honest about them. For example, your professors will be asking more from you academically. In addition, recognize the fact that you will be graduating in just a few semesters and that you should plan for life after school. These realities, while daunting, do not have to be defeating if you are honest about them. With some work—and the good habits you form at your community college—you can overcome them with the same success.

Regardless of the new challenges, once you transfer, it will be even more important to have a solid support structure at work and at home. In addition, you will be making connections with people who will hopefully help you get a job after college. All of these relationships can provide you with a system for handling the demands of a four-year university. Be mindful of the stress-reducing strategies that work best for you. Practice them regularly and seek out help with achieving your goals; you then will be more relaxed and more confident in your abilities.

FROM COLLEGE TO CAREER

Decreasing stress and improving time management on the job

If you decide to go directly from college to work, or back to work, your time and stress management skills can make the difference between a dreaded job and a life-fulfilling career. Time management is even more important on the job because your actions affect more people. Likewise, if you have difficulty managing your stress, then people will find working with you stressful. Practice makes perfect, and the more you practice good time management skills, the less stress you should have. You won't, however, be able to eliminate stress altogether. On the job, the stakes are much higher than in college.

One way to decrease stress on the job is to cultivate relationships with coworkers who can provide support. It is important to turn to colleagues for help when times get rough. A good relationship with a coworker can mean the difference between wanting to throw up your hands and getting through the challenges. Another way to reduce the stress you feel on the job is to keep the lines of communication open with your supervisor as well as your family. The more they know about what you are facing, and how you feel, the more sensitive they can be.

In addition to managing your stress on the job, be vigilant about managing your time. No doubt, you will have more tasks and responsibilities to juggle, and how well you can manage all the balls in the air will determine your future in your job. Using a calendar and writing down daily tasks will help you keep up with your work. Also, being honest about *not* meeting deadlines will keep you on top (and help minimize stress). There may be times when you won't be able to manage your time as effectively as you wish, but if you can be honest, and speak up quickly, you may be able to save others time and reduce their stress.

Chapter in Review

1. What should you consider when you begin drafting a time management plan for a semester?

2. What stresses you? In what ways can you eliminate or reduce the amount of stress you have?

3. What activities zap your time and what can you do to eliminate the amount of time they take from you?

4. Use your work from Practice Exercise 1 to answer the following questions: What did you spend the most time on? What did you spend the least time on? Are you spending the most time on activities that contribute to your goals? If not, why? What surprised you about how you spent your time?

5. Remember the last time you procrastinated. What did you learn from the situation? What would you do differently now?

Case Scenarios

Read the following case scenarios and determine what each person should do. Refer to the information in this chapter as you write a description and plan of action for each student.

1. Chaya is doing very well in her classes. She manages her time wisely and adjusts her schedule any time something unexpected comes up. However, Chaya has had a hectic week. Her boss expects her to stay late to finish a special project; she has an important exam Thursday evening; her daughter is sick with a stomach virus; and her husband has been out of town for the last two weeks. Her goal is to take care of each problem without jeopardizing her job, her grade, or her daughter's welfare. What do you recommend she do? Is it realistic to expect that she can take care of each of her problems?

2. George has a 20-page research paper for his Abnormal Psychology class due at the end of the semester. The professor asked that an annotated bibliography, an outline, and a rough draft be turned in at the same time as the

final draft. George is feeling overwhelmed. Help him map out a plan of action so he can fulfill the requirements without unnecessary stress.

3. Barbara was sick for two weeks and fell behind in her classes. She is worried that she won't be able to catch up or make up her work. What should she do?

4. Glenn's coworkers do not understand why he is going back to school to get a degree. They think he is wasting his time, and they have started leaving him out of social functions because he has canceled so many times before, saying he has to study. Glenn is usually good-natured, but his coworkers' daily negative comments are starting to take a toll, and he is contemplating quitting school after the semester is over. What advice do you have for Glenn? Can he manage his college classes and his job? What should he do about his coworkers' attitudes and actions?

Research It Further

1. Keep a journal of how you spend your time for the next seven days. Write down how long you spend on each activity. Make sure you are honest and that you write in your journal every few hours. Then, create a report for your class as to how you spend the majority of your time.

2. Create a survey that asks your classmates how they cope with stress. Once you collect your data, report the results to your class and determine which stress relievers are healthy and which are unhealthy.

3. Brainstorm the different ways students can relieve stress in unhealthy ways. Then, search the Internet or library resources for information about the effects of these unhealthy activities.

4. Create a "toolbox" for students who are plagued by procrastination. Make the toolbox creative and fun.

References

Hindle, T. (1998). *Manage your time.* New York: DK Publishing.

Listening and
Taking Notes Effectively

4

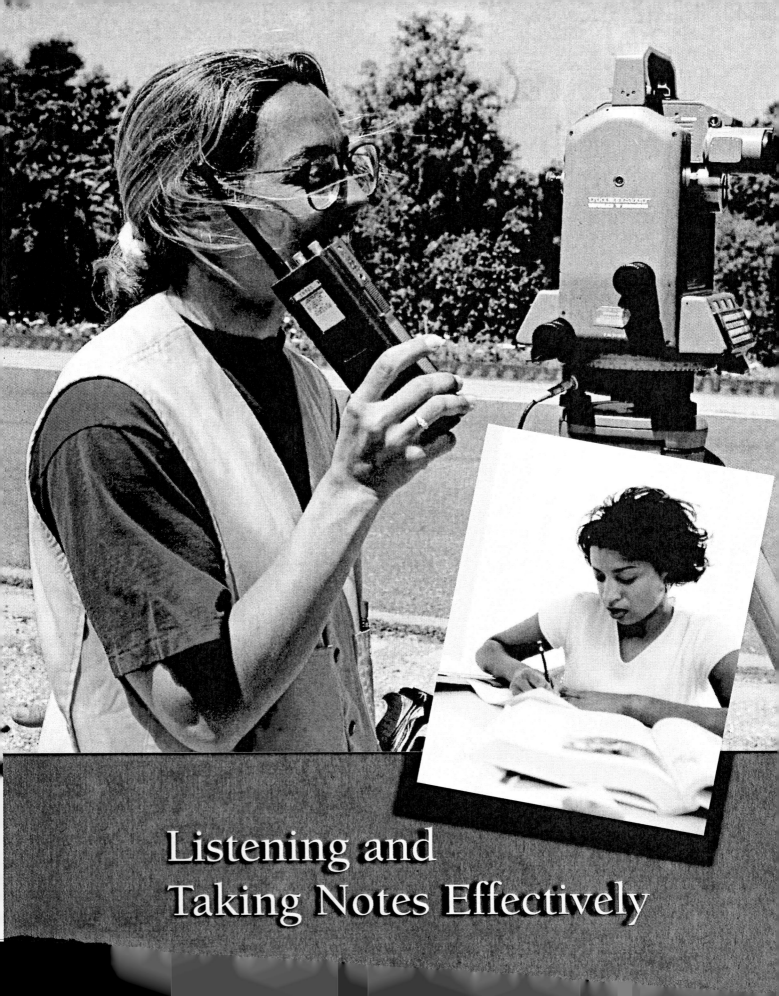

Listening and
Taking Notes Effectively

istening and taking notes effectively gives you an edge in college because you can take in more information and easily remember it. Laura can attest to the importance of developing an efficient note-taking system, especially for those students who have learning difficulties that prevent them from using just one style. This chapter discusses various note-taking strategies, including the method Laura developed. This chapter also helps you improve your listening skills. You will find answers to the following questions:

- How can I listen more effectively?

- What are the barriers to listening?

- What note-taking methods are available to me?

- How does my learning style strength affect my note-taking strategies?

- How can I still benefit from note taking if I have a note taker?

Student Profile

NAME: *Laura Thomas*   AGE: *38*

MAJOR: *Social Work*

1. **What are your college goals? What is your ultimate career goal?**

   I want to get an associate's degree and have my dad see me graduate from college. I want to work in hospice care for the Veterans' Administration.

2. **What was your biggest obstacle when learning to take notes?**

   The hardest part about note taking is figuring out what to write down. I realized I don't have to write down everything the teacher says.

3. **What advice you would give to students who are learning how to listen and take notes effectively?**

   Sharpen your pencil, have plenty of paper, and stay organized with a binder that has dividers. Use hole-punched paper and keep your notes in the binder. Remove notes that you don't need after taking an exam and keep them in a safe place.

4. **What is your VARK?**

   Visual.

The Listening and Note-Taking Connection

Listening, memory, and note taking all have something in common: They are necessary in the process of learning. You will not make it through your classes successfully without doing all three. Retaining and recalling information, however, is only part of the process. This chapter helps you receive the information, which in turn helps you turn the information into a knowledge base that you can build on for the rest of your life.

Preparing to Listen

Active listening is a term you may hear in college classes; someone who listens actively is concentrating on what is being said and is taking steps to remember the information. To be an active listener, you must decide that listening is a worthwhile activity and that important information will be shared. The following suggestions are intended to help you listen actively and effectively.

The first step is to prepare to listen before you get to class—read the assigned pages or chapters ahead of time to identify the lecture or discussion topic and to become familiar with new words and concepts. Preparing to listen also includes reviewing your assigned readings before you get to the classroom. If you have a few minutes between classes or on the bus, pull out your book and skim the major headings, bold terms, and any text boxes.

To listen effectively while in class, avoid distractions. Sit up front away from talkative people, and put unnecessary textbooks, cell phones, pagers, and other distracting items away. Your best defense against interruptions is to clear your desk of everything except your textbook, a pen, and paper. If you need to get anything during class, such as a dictionary, minimize the disruption.

If you find yourself next to a chatty classmate or one who likes to write you notes, simply move. Even if you are politely listening or reading her messages, you are still disrupting the class. Talkative classmates make it difficult for you and others to listen, and they distract you from taking good notes.

Another good way to listen effectively is by maintaining a positive attitude about the class. If you think the class is a waste of time or is boring, you are less likely to pay attention. Even if your beliefs are true—and others bemoan the class as well—pretend the class is the only one left before you graduate and that if you don't pay attention and take good notes, then you will have to stay another semester.

Minimizing outside distractions is another way to keep a positive attitude. There will be times that you have to work late, stay up all night with a sick baby, or help a friend who just had a crisis. If not handled well, these stressful experiences can affect your class performance. As much as possible, leave your personal life at the door, and concentrate on the class you are sitting in. Even if the day's lecture is overshadowed by a personal problem, remember that you *can* handle both your academic duties and your personal life.

Finally, prepare for class psychologically by preparing physically. Eat something before class so you aren't interrupted by a growling stomach. Dress in layers in case the room temperature is uncomfortable. Nothing is more distracting than being too hot or too cold. Get plenty of sleep the night before class to help you pay attention and listen effectively. Although adequate sleep may be a luxury if you work a late shift, make an effort to get a good night's

PhotoDisc

Someone who listens actively is concentrating on what is being said and is taking steps to remember the information.

sleep as often as possible. You can't maintain your concentration and information retention, or even good health, without adequate rest.

Listening Critically

As stated previously, active listening requires focusing on the task at hand and concentrating on what is being conveyed, whether it be words or sounds. Another part of listening effectively is listening critically, or the act of processing and evaluating what you hear. Listening critically helps you make decisions about what is important and what is not, what is objective and what is biased, and what should be stored for later and what should be discarded.

Listening critically is a skill, one that must be practiced regularly. Your college professors should invite you to think critically and challenge assumptions (that is learning!). As you become comfortable with listening actively and critically, you will move from merely listening and taking notes to listening in order to evaluate and ask questions about the notes you took. Here are some questions to consider as you learn to listen critically:

- *Speaker.* Is the speaker a credible source? How do I know? What possible biases does he have? What is his experience with the topic?

- *Message.* What is the speaker's purpose? What are the details he uses to convey his message?

- *Details.* Is the speaker using facts or opinions? How do I know? Which type of details works best for what the speaker is trying to convey?
- *Self-knowledge.* What do I already know about the topic? How does what the speaker is saying conflict with or support my beliefs and opinions? Have I learned something new?
- *Larger picture.* How does what the speaker is saying fit into the larger picture? How can I relate the message to something I already know about life or the world? Are there any connections between what I heard and past experiences?

Answering some of these questions will get you started on the right path to listening critically. Even though you already listen critically and mentally ask questions about what you hear, you may still have to "tune in" when you hear something you don't agree with or don't understand.

Remember, *critical* does not mean *negative.* If you find that what you are hearing is contrary to what you know about the subject, you can still ask respectful questions. Most people do not mind being politely challenged or debated.

Collaboration

Working with another classmate, take turns explaining why you are in college. Then, discuss how each of you listened critically. If there were any barriers to listening, describe what they were.

Companion Website

Potential Listening Barriers

Despite your efforts to prepare for class, you may find barriers to listening effectively, barriers that you cannot avoid no matter how prepared you are. For example, what should you do if your instructor talks too fast, uses technical jargon or an advanced vocabulary, is unorganized, digresses from lecture material (e.g., tells stories, allows too many irrelevant questions), or does not explain key concepts? Although you shouldn't coach your instructor in the art of speaking, you can ask her to slow down or define terms. Most professors do not mind repeating information or defining specialized terms and vocabulary because they want students to understand the material.

Reflection   EXERCISE 2

Think about a time when you heard someone speak and you did not agree with what was said. How did you listen? How did you react to what you were hearing?

It may, however, be a little harder to ask the instructor to be more organized or to stay on topic. One option is to ask if she would provide an outline before each class. To bring the professor back to the original subject, ask a question about it or an upcoming exam or assignment that addresses the subject.

In addition to not getting enough sleep or sitting in an uncomfortable classroom, there are other barriers to listening effectively. If you have an unaccommodated learning disability or a hearing problem, you may not be able to listen productively. Discuss any learning or hearing difficulties with a counselor and ask for help. A more common hindrance to effective listening is the students' insecurities about their ability to do well in the course. It is not uncommon for a new student to feel, at first, intimidated by the course, the instructor, or other students. The reason for the discomfort may stem from a student feeling that she is not good enough or smart enough to be in college. A student also may feel that everyone, except him, knows what to do, what to say, and how to act. This fear is actually common and it usually subsides after the first week or two.

Remembering What You Heard

Once you have prepared to listen in class and have eliminated any barriers that inhibit your ability to take in information, turn your attention to remembering

what you hear in class. Taking notes, of course, is one way to retain information; however, there are other methods that will help you recall information at a later date.

One way to remember what you hear and learn in class is to ask questions. Asking questions may be difficult if you are shy or feel out of place in the classroom—some students refrain from asking questions because they don't want to look ignorant in front of their classmates.

Then there is the other end of the spectrum— the constant questioners. These students dominate the professor's time by asking questions that sideline the discussion or questions about material that was already covered. Don't be intimidated by a predominantly quiet classroom or by

Practice

Choose something to read aloud to a classmate. Pair up with another student and take turns listening to each other's readings. See how much you can remember of the information your classmate read by restating the information.

Companion Website

those students who bother the professor with excessive questions. If you have a question, ask it. Some instructors believe there are no "stupid questions." If you don't feel comfortable asking questions during class, visit with your professor after class or during office hours. Some instructors ask students to write questions down and pass them up before class is over. Take advantage of such a practice; you will be able to ask questions without the fear of speaking up in front of classmates.

Participating in discussions and activities is an excellent way to remember key concepts. In fact, professors consider student participation a part of active learning. You are more likely to remember a concept if you can incorporate it into your own thinking. There is a reason that the most talkative students are usually the most successful—they make the material relevant to them, which makes remembering easier.

Another method of remembering, tape-recording lectures, is popular with students who have the time to listen to the tape. Listening to

Critical Thinking
EXERCISE 4

Describe the ultimate ineffective listening scenario. Write a scenario in which a student fails to use every kind of listening strategy. Present your scenario to the class.

Companion Website

INTEGRITY MATTERS

Listening with integrity means that you listen with an open mind and without judgment until the speaker is finished. Then, you can ask questions if there are points you don't understand. Listening with integrity also means that you avoid twisting the person's words to fit what you want to hear. Practicing active and critical listening will help you maintain integrity.

a tape recording works best if you have a long commute or if you go over your notes as you listen. Be sure to ask permission before you begin to tape and make sure you have fresh batteries.

How Information Is Presented

earning to listen effectively is the first step to taking good notes, but you will also benefit from understanding how information can be presented during a lecture. As you attend more classes, you will notice that professors have a certain way they present material. Some follow the textbook in the same order. Others lecture only on new material not found in the textbook or other course materials. Then, others present a combination of the two. Reading assigned chapters and materials before attending class allows you to determine which lecture information is new and which is covered by the assigned reading materials.

Information can be organized in many different ways. Recognizing these various ways helps you keep your notes organized and provides strategies for revising and reviewing your notes when you begin studying.

Chronological. When notes are chronological, details are arranged by time (first this happened, then this happened, etc.).

EXAMPLE OF CHRONOLOGICAL LECTURE NOTES

1801: United Kingdom of Great Britain is created

1803: Louisiana Purchase is made by Thomas Jefferson

1815: Battle of Waterloo signals end of Napoleon's career

Cause/effect. In this style, details are arranged by presenting a cause and then its effects or an effect and its causes.

EXAMPLE OF CAUSE/EFFECT LECTURE NOTES

Cause: Civil War

Effects: slavery ended, industrialism began, the nation was brought back together, the federal government proved stronger than the states

Compare/contrast. In this style, details are arranged by similarities and differences.

EXAMPLE OF COMPARE/CONTRAST LECTURE NOTES

Similarities between Robert Frost and Walt Whitman: were males, used nature in their poetry, considered "poets of the people"

Differences between Frost and Whitman: Frost's poetry is more structured, while Whitman's is open and loose; Whitman's speakers are more positive and upbeat than Frost's; Whitman lived during the 19th century, while Frost's life spanned both the 19th and 20th centuries

Most important/least important. In general, details are arranged in order of importance. The most important detail can come first with minor supporting details following, or the least important details start a list that works up to a major detail.

EXAMPLE OF MOST IMPORTANT/LEAST IMPORTANT LECTURE NOTES

Self-awareness (purpose of education)

Values

Goals

Mission

Personality type

Learning style

Note-Taking Strategies

There are numerous methods of taking notes, and your goal is to find the note-taking strategy that works best for you. Remember that you may have to adapt your note-taking style to each course, each teaching style, and each learning style strength. For example, outlining may work well in a history course in which the instructor writes key terms on the board and organizes her lecture around key ideas. If your professor prefers unstructured discussion, adapt your note-taking strategy to make the most of unorganized information.

Whatever you choose for a particular course, your learning style, or a specific situation, there are a few tips to remember when taking notes.

* *Listen for the main ideas.* Instructors will slow down and emphasize information, terms, and definitions. They may even use verbal signposts such as "The most important thing to remember is," "This may appear on an exam," or "Two crucial points about." If the instructor writes down or hands out an outline, you can be sure it contains the lecture's main points.

* *Leave plenty of "white space" (blank space on paper) when taking notes.* Don't try to fill your page with as much information as possible. You need the white space to add more notes later or to synthesize ideas once you have reviewed.

* *Review your notes as soon as possible after class.* Waiting two weeks to review your notes ensures that you won't remember everything you wrote or how it all fits together. Most experts suggest that you review your notes within two days of the class.

Develop a Shorthand

As you take more notes in each class, you will find yourself using some of the same words over and over again. These words are good candidates for abbreviating or denoting with symbols, creating your own shorthand. Shortened words such as *ex.* for *example*, *w/* for *with*, and *b/c* for *because* are abbreviations you may already use in notes and e-mail messages. Symbols you may already use include % for *percentage*, + for *add* or *and*, and # for *number*. If you develop a new abbreviation or symbol, make a note of what it means; for example, *TR* could mean *Theory of Relativity* in a science course and *Teddy Roosevelt* in a history course.

The following is a list of other commonly abbreviated words and symbols:

At	@
Between	betw, b/w
Decrease	decr
Department	dept
Does not equal	≠
Government	govt
Increase	incr
Equals	=
Example	eg, ex
Important	imp
Information	info
Regarding	re
Significant	sig

Developing a shorthand allows you more time to concentrate on what is being said. As you practice more, you become better at judging what information is worth writing and what is not, and your shorthand becomes more efficient. Just remember to read over your notes within a day or two so your abbreviations are fresh in your mind. It is a good idea to complete the words or concepts then so you won't struggle to remember what the shortened words mean later in the semester.

Outlining

An outline is a good note-taking method if the instructor is organized and presents information in a logical pattern. Some instructors encourage outlining by writing key words and concepts on the board or an overhead projecting device. If your instructor organizes lectures or class discussions, outlining your notes is easy. The key to effective outlines is to leave plenty of space between the items so you can add extra information. An outline for a lecture on effective listening might look like this:

I. Preparing to Listen Effectively

II. Listening Critically

III. Possible Listening Barriers
    A. External
        1. Hunger
        2. Climate discomfort
    B. Internal
        1. Feelings of self-worth
        2. Stress

IV. How Information Is Presented
    A. Chronological
    B. Cause/Effect
    C. Compare/Contrast
    D. Most Important/Least Important

Taking Notes in the Textbook

Writing in the margins of your textbook is another effective way to take notes, especially if the reading assignment is lengthy. If you don't mind writing in your textbook, you can summarize the main points you read. Writing brief summaries (two or three words) or questions in the margins helps you make sense of and remember what you read. Brief, marginal summaries also help you review material before class and after class when you start studying for an exam.

Annotating in your textbook and writing down critical questions are two methods to further reinforce what you read and to prepare for note taking in class. Move beyond your summaries or retelling the material to drawing lines to connect major ideas and concepts and to asking questions such as "How do I know this to be true?" and "What else should be considered?" Annotating the textbook with your own notes not only reinforces main ideas, but also helps you synthesize the information in new ways to produce connections between concepts, making the material more memorable and more relevant.

If you decide to write in your textbook, be sure it is not one you want to sell back to the bookstore. If you do not want to write in your book but still want the benefits of summarizing the material, write your summaries on a separate sheet of paper. Make sure to label each piece with the chapter title and page number of the book.

Highlighting in your textbook is another method students use to take notes. A highlighter pen is used to mark important concepts for review, but don't highlight too much information. Over-highlighting the text has the opposite effect—instead of making it easier to understand key terms and information, too much highlighting makes everything seem of equal importance. If you do use a highlighter, use it sparingly. For example, don't highlight more than two sentences in a row. A better method is to use highlighting and written summaries together.

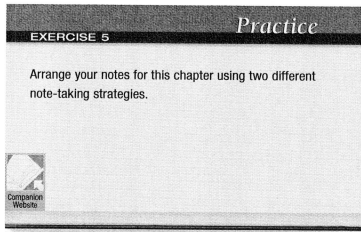

Practice

EXERCISE 5

Arrange your notes for this chapter using two different note-taking strategies.

Companion Website

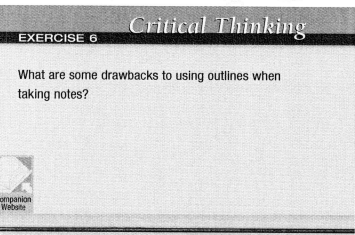

Critical Thinking

EXERCISE 6

What are some drawbacks to using outlines when taking notes?

Companion Website

Annotating in your textbook and writing down critical questions are two ways to further reinforce what you have read.

© Mary Kate Denny/PhotoEdit

Cornell System

Cornell University professor Dr. Walter Pauk developed a note-taking system that is popular with many students. The Cornell System, also known as the T System, is ideal for those who benefit from the visual impact of organized notes. The key to the Cornell System is dividing your notebook paper before you begin writing. To do so, draw a horizontal line across the paper two inches from the bottom. Then, draw a vertical line from the horizontal line to the top of the page about two inches from the left margin. The page should look like this:

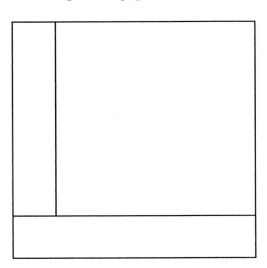

The largest area, the right column, is used for taking notes during class. The left column is used for noting questions if there is material you don't understand or if you think of possible exam questions as you write. The bottom section is reserved for summarizing your notes as you review them. The act of summarizing helps you understand and remember the information.

Note-Taking Strategies in the Disciplines

The following strategies for note-taking in the disciplines are just samples of what you may encounter in college. The following are note-taking strategies, grouped by discipline, that make reviewing and studying easier.

Art. In an art appreciation class, you have to identify eras (20th century), movements (Cubism), and artists (Picasso) as well their characteristics as seen in drawings, paintings, and sculpture. Quickly sketching the works in your notes and listing the characteristic details helps you record the information you receive through lectures. You may also notice that in the study of art there are times of intense change (usually coinciding with a world or cultural event) followed by artists who imitate or slightly modify the new style. As you review your notes, look for patterns within groups of artwork and for points of contrast.

Music. In a music appreciation class, the same suggestions for an art appreciation class work when taking notes. Instead of re-creating a painting or sculpture in your notes, write down descriptions of what you are hearing and what the sounds remind you of. Are the sounds fast or slow? Do you hear one instrument or many? Does it sound like a stampede or a trip down a lazy river? "Translating" music samples into written notes, as well as reviewing music clips on your own, strengthens your understanding of the material. As with your art notes, upon review, look for patterns across movements and eras and note contrasting ideas and elements.

Literature. Taking notes in a literature class requires that you complete the assigned readings before class and that you annotate and highlight your text. Because literature classes, even survey classes, focus more on discussion than lecture, be prepared to take notes on the analysis (how your classmates and instructor take the text apart and examine it) of the literature. As with music and art classes, being familiar with basic terminology before you get to class helps you take better notes. As you review your notes, look for ideas that pull the different readings together.

Languages. Foreign language classes center more on speaking and interacting than on listening to a lecture. Taking notes is not necessarily advantageous because you should focus all of your attention on listening actively, processing what is heard, and interacting based on what you hear. Daily preparation is essential to learning foreign languages; take notes as you encounter new material and ask questions in class to get clarification on anything you do not understand. Any notes you do take should be reviewed soon after class. As you review the notes, categorize material such as irregular verbs and include any tips for using or remembering the parts of language.

Science. Concepts and processes are key in science classes and your notes will reflect that. Prepare for class by reading the assigned material, making note of new vocabulary words, and studying diagrams and figures in the text and handouts. As with any class, ask questions if you have trouble following the steps of a process. As you review your notes, consider the different ways you can represent these concepts and processes visually and physically.

History. History class lectures are usually presented in chronological order, so using the tips for information that follows a time sequence will help you take notes in this class. However, you are also required to move beyond specific dates and events to considering overall themes, ideas, and movements.

In addition to chronological order, lectures may also use a cause/effect organization—you list and elaborate on the effects of a cause or the causes of an effect. For example, a history lecture topic is "The economic and social effects of the end of the Civil War." As you review your notes, look for major themes and recall actions that led to important events.

Math. Taking good notes in math classes requires that you prepare and attend each class meeting. As with foreign languages, studying for math should be an everyday occurrence because the skills you learn in each class build on the ones you learned in the class before. When reviewing your notes, recopy them to ensure that you understand, line by line, what you are copying. If you have any questions, write them in the margins of your notes to ask during the next class meeting.

Collaboration

EXERCISE 7

Working in a group of three or more, discuss your VARK learning style strengths and weaknesses. Decide how you would take notes for an upcoming exam based on your learning styles and relevant note-taking strategies.

Companion Website

Note-Taking Strategies with VARK

Visual Learners

Visual learners benefit from seeing the notes on the page, but they may also benefit from creating images of the material they wrote down. Take, for example, cause/effect information for the increase in electronic communication. An instructor may talk through or write down a few key ideas like this:

> In the late 1990s, electronic communication grows at home and in the workplace.
>   Effects: closer relationships with those who are far away, increased productivity, long distance costs decrease, decline in stamp sales, need for communication guidelines at work, problems with sharing too much information or sending junk, bombardment of spam and viruses.

A visual learner may take that same information and create a visual representation, as shown in Exhibit 1.

Aural Learners

Reading notes aloud, recording lectures, or recording yourself talking through material are all strategies for recording material. Although "taking notes" implies writing down words and then reading through them, there is no reason aural learners must suppress their learning style strength during the process. An aural learner can pair up with a read/write learner and talk through the material they heard in a recent class. The read/write learner can then record notes or annotate ones he already has and share them with the aural learner.

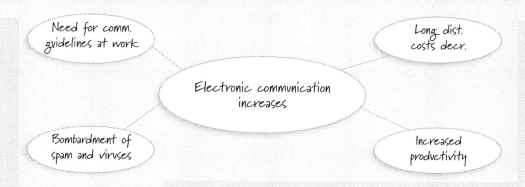

Read/Write Learners

Read/write learners are at an advantage because their learning style strength is writing down notes and reading through them. However, not all instructors present information in a format that is easiest for read/write learners. As you read earlier, highly visual, aural, or kinesthetic disciplines are challenging for read/write learners to take effective notes. The key is in "translating" visual, aural, and kinesthetic material by describing with words what you experience. For example, in a music class, describe the sounds you hear or the rhythmic pattern; in an anatomy class, write descriptions or list the characteristics of organs to accompany pictures and body maps. Rereading your notes and annotating as you review reinforces what you learned regardless of whether you originally obtained the information visually, aurally, or kinesthetically.

Kinesthetic Learners

The act of taking notes by writing or typing them provides kinesthetic learners with a physical activity that makes remembering the written notes easier. Kinesthetic learners benefit from using more physical activity or objects when they review their notes shortly after taking them. For example, if you are using formulas to calculate volume in your math class, review your notes by creating your own volume problems in the kitchen. The act of pouring and measuring water and then calculating your measurements makes it easier to remember the process when completing homework problems or taking a test.

Likewise, a good way for a kinesthetic learner to study for an art class, or any class that uses visual images, is to re-create the artwork with paper and colored pencils. No need to strive for masterpiece quality when re-creating works of art; the physical activity of drawing the wavy lines in the background of Edvard Munch's *The Scream* will help you recall the piece on an exam.

Critical Thinking

Companion Website

A friend is taking a visual arts class and is having trouble making sense of his notes because they pertain to specific artwork. The instructor did not hand out reproductions of the art, so the student tried to sketch the pieces during class, but that took too long. Do you have any suggestions for your friend on how to take more effective notes?

Finding Your Own Note-Taking Style

Laura Thomas, a student at a community college, developed a special note-taking system because of a learning disability. While taking an introduction to college course, she discovered the note-taking systems discussed in her textbook did not help her take good notes. Through trial and error, she developed a system that works for her.

Before class begins, Laura uses a pencil to date each page and leaves plenty of room to write. When taking notes, she writes on only one side of the page; in fact, most of her pages contain less than 50 words. Although she uses more paper, her notes are easier to read.

Next, she stars words that the instructor says are important. The most important part of her note-taking system is her use of arrows to make connections between ideas. By giving herself plenty of room, she can add any connections revealed later in the lecture. If her instructor reviews the material before an exam, Laura highlights what she already has and adds notes in the spaces. See Exhibit 2 for an example of Laura's notes.

One strategy Laura developed to help with her learning disability is that she doesn't worry about spelling. To make connections between ideas, she draws lines between words that relate to each other. She also makes charts for anything that is compared and contrasted. Finally, she keeps all of her notes in a binder that is divided for each class. Staying organized is an important part of her method. Although she uses only one binder during the semester, she keeps her notes organized by removing them after an exam. When she removes notes she no longer needs, she places them in labeled folders at home. She carries with her only the notes she needs at that time.

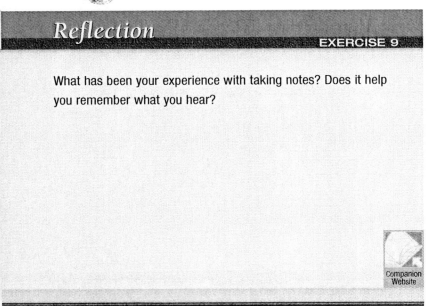

Reflection

EXERCISE 9

What has been your experience with taking notes? Does it help you remember what you hear?

Companion Website

A Note on Note Takers

There may be a time when you have to rely on someone to take notes for you, or you may have a learning or physical disability that requires someone to take notes for you all semester. Student or professional note takers help unique learners and students with a disability receive the same education opportunities as others. Whether you depend on someone every once in a while or for the duration of your education, the following are some things you should consider:

- If possible, review the note taker's notes with the note taker or other classmates. Because the physical act of taking notes helps students remember information, you should find other ways to reinforce the material.

- Stay focused when you are in class. Find ways to help you remember the material such as creating visual maps or scenes in your mind.

EXHIBIT 2 *Laura's notes.*

Ancient	Jewish Beliefs—Monotheism (1st)	Jehovah

Jews divided   all humanity
Strictly-segregated ↓   ↓

○ We (Jews)   They (Gentiles) ✡

We (Jews)	They (Gentiles)
No outside conversion	non-Jewish
convenant with God	place on earth
↓	↓
chosen people	Tempters & obstacles
family-most important	
↓	Sacred text
society revolved around	Old Testament
Patriarchal male-dominant	
↓	Jehovah (Yahweh)
more rights	share-Christianity concepts (similar)
(+) marriage-lineage	① Fall of man from grace
(−) bachelor-frowned	② Day of judgment
male married by 24	③ Immortality
prefer 20	④ 1 God (worship)
Female-13 can marry	
↓	
more children	

● Prepare for class beforehand. Because you won't be taking notes, preparation is critical.

● Don't take your note taker for granted by missing class or not preparing. The note taker is not a surrogate student, she is only a supplement.

● If your note taker's notes are difficult to read, incomplete, or missing because he does not attend regularly, talk to the disability services counselor. She can arrange for a new note taker.

Consider how understanding your personality style or learning preference can help you through challenging situations.

You are taking a chemistry class and your learning style strength is aural. The professor, however, relies on diagrams, drawings, and hands-on experiments to demonstrate concepts and processes. You are having trouble understanding the material, and it is only the third week of class. You spoke to your professor about your trouble, but because you are shy, you weren't completely honest about how frustrated and stressed you are. In fact, when you met with your professor, she suggested that you come by during office hours and go through the experiments again and again until the material sinks in. What should you do when you meet with her during office hours the next time?

*PERSONALITY + LEARNING STYLE = UNDERSTANDING SITUATIONS

Reviewing Your Notes

Notes are only as good as the extent to which you review them. If you never look at your notes after taking them, then they serve little purpose. Therefore, to make the most out of your notes, you must review them. As stated earlier, reviewing should be done within two days from the time you took them. With this said, it is easy to be lulled into a sense of "studying" by merely reading your notes again and again. When reviewing your notes, it is best to reorganize the material, make connections between concepts—even across disciplines—and ask questions about what you are learning.

If you use the Cornell System, then you have a built-in area for adding more information, summarizing, and asking questions. If you do not use a particular method, you can still benefit from filling in any blanks or holes in your notes with information you have since learned. As stated earlier, spell out any abbreviations that may cause confusion later. After filling in any gaps, you should include questions—either on the same page or a new page—to help you think about the material on a deeper level. For example, asking "Why is it important to know this?" helps you move beyond demonstrating your comprehension of the material to making it relevant and useful.

Freewriting about the material you learned is another way of remembering and understanding the information. This technique is often used as a way to generate ideas for writing, but it can also be used to take advantage of all the thoughts you have about the material. For optimum effectiveness, freewrite within a day or two of the class lecture. With or without your notes, write down (or type into a word processor) all the information you remember from the class.

The key to freewriting is continuation—do not stop writing even if you can't spell a certain word or get stuck on a particular idea. Give yourself 5 or 10 minutes to freewrite; then, go through your freewriting material and highlight or rewrite into complete sentences the information that pertains to the lecture. In essence, you learn the material in depth as you write about it.

Finally, reading your notes to a friend is a useful method for reviewing material. You can do this in person or on the phone. The benefits of reading your notes aloud and discussing them include filling in any gaps in the information and reinforcing what you learned. You can also critically question the material and take turns making connections between major concepts.

Tips for Successful Note Taking

* Prepare for class by reading *all* the assigned material before arriving. If you cannot read all of it, read as much as you can.

* Prepare to listen actively by removing distractions and bringing supplies.

* Listen actively; concentrate on what you are hearing, seeing, and experiencing.

* Listen critically by asking questions, either on paper or in class if your professor encourages class questions.

* Use a note-taking strategy that takes into account both your learning style strength and the subject matter.

* Go beyond reviewing your notes by rereading them; instead, focus on concepts and main ideas, make connections between the large ideas, and ask critical questions about processes and ideas.

* Continue the process regularly throughout the semester.

Learning Styles Application

This chart lists the four learning styles and tips based on the chapter's main ideas. Locate your learning style and read the corresponding tips to maximize your success in college.

VISUAL	Visual learners need a little extra help when preparing to listen because it is not their learning style preference. Visualizing concepts and creating visual representations of notes will help you reinforce what you heard. Also, pay attention to visual clues and nonverbal communication that signal major points, important contrasting ideas, and changes in thought.
AURAL	Listening is a strength for aural learners, but it doesn't mean you can ignore other ways to "hear" what is being said. Consider nonverbal communication as well as movement and text in order to get the full lecture.
READ/WRITE	Read/write learners work on their listening skills by practicing, writing what they hear, and reading their notes aloud to someone who can fill in any missing material. As a read/write learner, pair up with an aural learner to make sure your notes are complete.
KINESTHETIC	Kinesthetic learners benefit from lectures that include movement and activity. Hand gestures and body movements are important clues to the message being sent. You can translate a speaker's activity into your notes by recording when the speaker uses his hand, for example, to underscore an important idea.

Path of Discovery

Journal Entry

Have you ever experienced a time when you did not listen? What happened and what did you learn from the experience?

FROM COLLEGE TO UNIVERSITY

Improving your listening and note-taking skills when there are more distractions

When you transfer to a four-year university, the good habits you practiced at your community college will help you succeed. However, you may find that you have more distractions. There may be more people on campus and in your classes, more organizations and associations to join, more activities to participate in, and more stress when deciding on a major and getting ready to graduate.

In addition to distractions, you may also find that professors at four-year universities lecture less and rely more on student discussion and presentations. Your ability to organize the material into coherent parts is critical to making sense of the course. If you have trouble taking good notes, talk to others who have been at the university longer than you—they may have some tips. It is also a good idea to join a study group or at least find a "study buddy" to review your notes with. Although you may have done well studying by yourself at the community college, you may now realize that group interaction and work is not only encouraged but is also necessary for success.

FROM COLLEGE TO CAREER

Practicing critical listening skills gives you an edge at work

Most of the communication you do on the job involves listening: listening to clients' urgent needs, your employer's plans for the next six months, coworkers' explanations, and subordinates' questions. Being a good listener involves practicing the critical listening tips outlined in this chapter. Why do you need to listen critically on the job? Because you will be bombarded with information at all levels: above you from your boss, at the same level as you from your coworkers, and below you from those who work for you. Critical listening skills enable you to filter what you hear so you can act appropriately and avoid making errors in action and judgment. Consider, for example, a coworker who comes to you to complain about a company policy. By not listening actively and critically, you may disregard what the speaker is saying because you don't have time to do anything about it. However, if you take the time to analyze the speaker (Is she credible?), the message (Is its purpose to vent or change something?), what you know about the situation (Is the policy flawed and in need of change?), and the larger picture (How will this proposed change affect others?), then you are more likely to act appropriately and confidently.

On the job, as in life, you will not—and should not—respond to all messages you receive the same. Practicing critical listening skills makes it easier to determine which messages are critical and which can be acted upon later, making you a more efficient and effective employee.

Chapter in Review

1. List and describe the different note-taking strategies.

2. In what situations might taking notes distract you from learning? What other methods of remembering should you employ in those situations?

3. Describe the ultimate ineffective listening scenario. In a group or individually, write a scene in which a student fails to use any kind of effective listening strategy.

4. Using the information in this chapter, create note-taking guidelines for one of your classes. Keep in mind how the nature of the class determines how you take notes and how your learning style affects your strategy.

5. Which of the note-taking methods are the most effective for you? Which are the least effective? Explain your answers.

Case Scenarios

Read the following case scenarios and determine what each person should do. Refer to the information in this chapter as you write a description and plan of action for each student.

1. Theo borrowed Jon's notes for his algebra class and promised to return them before the next exam. However, Theo lost them, and with only two days left before the next test, he is not sure what to do. Jon is a good student and probably doesn't need them very much, but Theo wants to be able to borrow future notes from Jon. What should he do?

2. Karla has a learning difficulty, and she struggles with taking notes. The counselor assigned a note taker to takes notes for her in each class. Now that Karla is getting this help, she stopped preparing for class and listening closely. Sometimes she doesn't get the notes from her note taker until a week later. If you are Karla's friend or counselor, what advice would you give her about using a note taker?

Research It Further

1. Survey the students in one of your classes as to which note-taking strategies they use the most. Create a table from your results and present it to your classmates.

2. Using the keywords "note-taking strategies," search the Internet for websites that offer note-taking guidance. Choose two or three and review the information to determine which site offers the most practical and complete tips. Present your findings to the class.

3. Create your own note-taking or listening strategy and present it to the class, highlighting the benefits of your method over another method.

Reading Skills

5

PhotoDisc

BananaStock

Reading Skills

an says, "You have to do the reading" in college, and he is absolutely right. Whether you love to read or you find the activity to be a challenge, reading is an integral part of your education in college. Can you imagine getting a degree and not reading a page? Technology changed the way we read and how we incorporate written information, but it did not change the importance of reading to being educated individuals. This chapter discusses different reading strategies for sharpening your reading skills, whether you are reading books, magazines, e-books, or Web articles. More specifically, you will find answers to the following questions:

- *What is the importance of reading effectively in college?*

- *How can I break down a long reading assignment so I can comprehend it and remember what I read?*

- *What is active reading, and what is the difference between skimming and scanning?*

- *What methods can I use to sharpen my reading skills?*

College Reading Expectations

f death and taxes are unavoidable parts of life, then reading is an inevitable part of college and lifelong learning; fortunately, reading is more enjoyable and more profitable than death and taxes. The bottom line is that you will not be a successful student if you do not read assigned and supplemental material regularly. Likewise, it will be difficult to practice lifelong learning after college without reading on a regular basis. Reading class handouts, college publications, and your textbooks is essential to success in college. The reasons that reading is important to your college education and lifelong learning are many, but here are just a few incentives for making reading an integral part of your daily college work:

* Reading provides you with basic information you can use to create knowledge of a subject.
* Reading improves your understanding of others and the world around you by exposing you to new viewpoints, ideas, and cultures.
* Reading helps you understand yourself, which helps you make better life choices.

Having said that, it must be acknowledged that some students just do not enjoy reading because of bad experiences in school or learning difficulties. Thus, for some college students, reading is a challenge to academic fulfillment. Professors would be ecstatic if all of their students read well and enjoyed the assigned reading material. Realistically, students find some reading dull and difficult to comprehend, and they long to read something "exciting." The not-so-good news is that until you get into those classes that pertain to your major or career choice, you may very well feel that the assigned reading is uninteresting—the good news is that there are ways to improve your comprehension *and* enjoyment of the reading assignments.

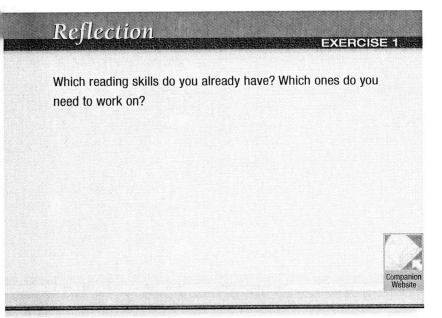

Reflection

EXERCISE 1

Which reading skills do you already have? Which ones do you need to work on?

Companion
Website

In addition to the different subject matter you encounter in college reading, you will also find the reading load is heavier than in high school or for your job. If you are taking 4 three-credit-hour classes, you can expect to read over 100 pages a week if each professor assigns a textbook chapter. This number does not include full-length novels, supplementary articles, required periodical subscriptions, reserved library materials, online resources, and your own notes from class—all of which may be part of your weekly reading load. The truth about college reading is that there is plenty for you to read and you are accountable for reading, comprehending, and thinking critically about the material.

What to Do with a Reading Assignment

When you first get a reading assignment, spend a little time preparing to read to help you maximize the time you have to complete it. No doubt, the first week of classes, you will be given handouts and syllabi and assigned chapters to read in your textbook. How do you manage it all without getting behind and becoming overwhelmed? First, all written material from your professors must be read. You will be held responsible for it at some point, so create a process for reading and remembering what you read.

Regardless of the assignment size, treat it seriously—make a conscious effort to read and remember important information. A positive attitude toward the reading assignment makes the other steps easier to complete. Before you begin reading, organize the assignments according to size, importance, and date due, starting with the most important documents. A shorter assignment can be completed first unless its due date is far off.

BananaStock

The reading load in college is heavier than in high school.

To increase your chances of reading effectively, establish a definite time and place to read. Just as you set a time to study or go to work, schedule time to read, preferably the same time each day. Finding a comfortable, quiet area to read is also important because it puts you in the mood to focus on what you are reading. Equally important to setting a definite time is establishing routine breaks. Get up, walk around the room, get a drink of water, and get the circulation going in your legs again. Taking breaks in which you physically move around helps your concentration and keeps you from falling asleep.

In addition to finding the right place, consider setting a purpose for reading to make the assignments easier to comprehend and complete. For example, if your reading purpose is to improve your understanding of networking, then when you sit down with your computer networking textbook, you are in the right frame of mind. Conversely, if your reading purpose is to be entertained when reading a chapter in economics, you may be disappointed and less receptive to remembering what you read.

Writing down your goals is the first step to realizing them. The same is true for reading. If your goals are to increase your reading speed, vocabulary, and understanding of the material, you should do more than give them passing consideration. Set specific, concrete goals for individual assignments or the whole semester. A reading goal example might be to increase the number of pages you can read in one sitting or to learn five new words a week and use them.

Finally, take care of yourself throughout the semester as you do the assigned work. You can't read effectively if you are tired, hungry, or sick. Don't force yourself to read if physical or psychological issues distract you. Too much sugar and caffeine and too little sleep make reading more difficult, as can certain medications and emotional distractions. If you cannot concentrate, return to the material when you feel better.

Another way to prepare to read effectively is to start a reading log to help focus your reading goals. A sample reading log appears at the end of this chapter for you to photocopy and use.

Active Reading

Active reading, a term you may hear often in college along with active listening, means that you become fully engaged in reading by focusing your mind and body on the activity. Many first-time students read passively, rather than actively, and do not fully concentrate on the material. Just reading the words is not enough for college classes. Instead, you must be a part of the process by using some or all of the following reading strategies: skimming, scanning, breaking down material, building vocabulary, taking notes, checking comprehension, and reviewing and recalling what was read. The information that follows will help you become an active reader.

Skimming and Scanning

You may already be familiar with the terms skimming and scanning as they pertain to reading. *Skimming* is reading material quickly and superficially, paying particular attention to main ideas. This activity is used when you first get a reading assignment because it helps you get a feel for what the material is, how long it is, and how difficult it will be to read. To skim a text effectively, read the first and last paragraphs, the main headings of each section, and the first and last sentences of each paragraph. Of course, if time is a factor, delete some of the steps. Ideally, skimming is done before in-depth reading; however, sometimes skimming may be the only chance you have to read the material. If this is the case, pay attention to the major headings of each section and the first and last paragraphs of the material. Don't be surprised, though, if you miss major ideas sandwiched in the middle.

Although it now has a meaning similar to skimming, scanning is a reading method that traditionally meant "examining a text closely." Nonetheless, some reading experts define *scanning* as looking quickly for a specific item or topic as you would scan a phone book for someone's name or a dictionary for a particular word. Scanning also includes examining the table of contents and index to narrow your focus and prepare you to find what you are looking for. Similar to skimming, scanning requires that your eyes move quickly over a page. However, the difference is that you know what you want to find and will slow down once you find it. Scanning is particularly useful when reviewing sources to use for a paper. You can determine rather quickly if the source pertains to your topic or not. After scanning, you then skim or read the text actively.

Breaking the Material Down

As stated earlier, part of scanning a text is examining its parts. Certain pages hold valuable information for deciphering its purpose. Students who want to "hurry up" and read the meat of the assignment often overlook some of the most important parts: The title, author, table of contents, chapter titles, introduction, section headings, headnotes, bibliography, and index are wonderful and revealing components of a piece of writing.

Title. The title of an article or book gives you a clue as to what it is about. For instance, the title to this book is *The Community College Experience* because the information in it reflects the unique needs of community college students, not students at other types of institutions of higher education. When reading any material, take time to think about the title's significance and go back to it to look for additional meaning once you complete the whole text.

Author. Who the author is can be just as important as what she has to say. Authors' reputations can lend credibility to their words or instantly make readers suspicious. If you recognize the author's name, then you should have a good idea what the text is about. The more you read, the more you encounter writings by certain people, and you will expect certain viewpoints from them.

Table of contents. Most books have a table of contents that shows how the book is organized. A table of contents lists the chapters as well as many subsections. The table of contents also contains the beginning page number for each chapter or section. Familiarize yourself with the table of contents to make it easier to find information when you need it.

Introduction. Sometimes overlooked, the introduction can provide all the information you need to determine whether a particular book is what you want. When researching a topic, you can decide whether or not a book is a good source for you by reading the introduction. Introductions typically tell the reader what the book is about, what unique features it contains, and what viewpoint is supported.

Chapter titles. Chapter titles are a good indication of what you can expect to read. They also help you locate information quickly. Can you imagine trying to find information from this text about taking notes without any chapter titles? You would have to scan each chapter until you found it.

Section headings. Section headings work the same way as chapter titles— they indicate how the material is organized and give you a sneak peek of what is to come.

Headnotes. Headnotes appear at section beginnings or before essays and explain or briefly summarize what you are about to read. Headnotes can provide biographical information about the author or indicate the essay's main points.

Bibliography. A bibliography, or list of references or works cited, usually appears at the end of an article or a book, right before the index. Literally, a bibliography is a list of books the author has read or used to prepare his text. This section of a book or article is often overlooked, but it actually contains a wealth of information for the reader. If you want to learn more about a topic the author mentions briefly, look at the bibliography to see what other books are listed about the subject. Also, if you are doing research and need instant access to a list of more sources, an author's bibliography can supply you with that information.

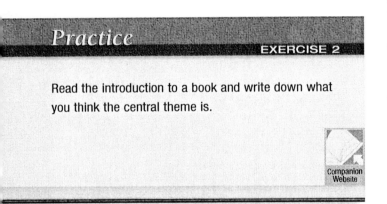

Index. One of the last elements of a book is its index, which is an alphabetical list of major ideas and concepts that are keyed to the pages on which they appear. If you need to find information on note taking, for instance, use the index to pinpoint the exact page where it appears. Indexes (or indices) are especially helpful when evaluating research sources for whether or not they contain material about your subject. For example, if you locate a book on African American playwrights and need some information on Lorraine Hansberry, look for her name in the index to see if she is mentioned in the book. If she is not listed, then you know the book is not a good resource for you.

You may think that breaking the material down is time consuming and unnecessary, especially if you do not have much time to spend reading anyway. Yes, at first it takes more time, but the more you do it, the less time it takes because you know what to look for. Also, your reading speed and comprehension will improve, which means you can complete your assignments quicker.

Building Your Vocabulary

Increasing your vocabulary is another benefit to reading regularly. Some students get sidelined when they read because they encounter unfamiliar words. Few students take the time to look up words they don't know and subsequently miss out on learning new ideas or understanding the author's intent. Although it is well worth your time to look up words when you read, there are some methods you can use to decrease the time you spend flipping through a dictionary.

The first method is to look for context clues in the sentence. Many times you can figure out what the word means by how it is used in a sentence or by the words that surround it. Consider the following sentence:

Students often use context clues to *decipher* the meaning of unfamiliar words.

If you didn't know that *decipher* means to figure out, you can still understand the sentence by considering that students are using something (context clues) in order to do something to (decipher) unfamiliar words. You might deduce, then, that students are making the unfamiliar words more familiar by using context clues. Now, try this sentence:

> It was not until we traveled to Beijing that we realized how *ubiquitous* American fast food is. On every street corner, we saw a McDonald's or a KFC.

If you are not familiar with modern-day Beijing, you may not know that American restaurants are plentiful. Thus, to understand the meaning of *ubiquitous*, the second sentence provides the context clues. With the phrase "On every street corner," you should realize that *ubiquitous* means *everywhere*.

Although context clues allow you to make sense of most unfamiliar words, there will be times you cannot rely on the other words to help you. For example, can you tell what the words *amenable* and *obsequious* mean in the following sentence?

> Charles was *amenable* to going out to eat with Sheila's *obsequious* mother.

In this case, if you don't know what the words mean, the sentence offers little assistance. Does Charles want to go out to eat or doesn't he? Is Sheila's mother someone who is enjoyable to be around or isn't she? To answer these questions, you may need to look the words up. Here is what you find if look them up in *Webster's New World Dictionary*:

> a·me·na·ble (əme′nə bəl) *adj.* [[<Ofr , L *minare*, to drive (animals)]] 1 responsible or answerable 2 able to be controlled; submissive—a·me′na·bil′i·ty *n.*—a·me′na·bly *adv.*

Now, look up *obsequious* for yourself and see if you can decipher the sentence.

Another way to figure out what words mean is to know some common Latin and Greek root words, prefixes, and suffixes (see Exhibit 1 for examples). For example, if your professor calls astrology a *pseudoscience*, and you know that the Greek root *pseudo* means false, then you can understand that your professor is claiming that astrology is not a true science. In order to learn the common roots of everyday words, study words' origins. Taking a college reading class or using a dictionary regularly will help you learn to recognize the roots in other words.

TIPS FOR BUILDING VOCABULARY

* Purchase or borrow discipline-specific dictionaries that contain a large amount of terminology (e.g., medical or scientific dictionaries, foreign language dictionaries, and glossaries for literary terms).

* Before asking your professor or classmate what a word means, look it up.

* Don't be afraid to look up words, even the same word multiple times. You will eventually recall the meanings.

* Use new words in conversation to "try them out." Using them regularly helps you remember what they mean.

EXHIBIT 1 *Common Latin and Greek root words.*

ROOT	MEANING	EXAMPLE WORD	DEFINITION
Ante	Before	*Antebellum*	Before the war, specifically referring to the American Civil War
Anti	Against	*Antibiotic*	Against life, specifically against microorganisms
Auto	Self	*Autobiography*	Writing about the self
Biblio/Bibl	Book	*Bibliography*	A list of books
Cede	Go, leave	*Secede*	Leave an organization or alliance
Chrono	Time	*Chronological*	Events ordered by time in which they occurred
Cogn	Know	*Recognize, cognizant*	To know from before; fully informed
Graph	Write	*Autograph*	Person's own signature
Inter	Within, between	*Intermission*	The period between performances
Phil	Love	*Philanthropy*	Love of humankind
Photo	Light	*Photography*	Producing images using light in the process
Pseudo	False	*Pseudonym*	False name

* Write a new word on a 3x5 index card along with a sentence using the word. Look up the definition when you have time and add it to the card. Take the cards with you and review your new words while waiting in line or stuck in traffic.

* Buy and browse a thesaurus, a book that contains synonyms for words. A thesaurus is handy when you are searching for a word that is similar to another.

* If you have an e-mail account, subscribe to a word-a-day service that sends you a new vocabulary word each day, or buy a word-a-day calendar.

* Subscribe to magazines that challenge your reading skills: *The Atlantic Monthly*, *The New Yorker*, and *Harper's* are examples of print magazines that contain interesting and challenging material.

Practice

Rewrite the following sentence using synonyms for the words *amenable* and *obsequious:*

Charles was amenable to going out to eat with Sheila's obsequious mother.

Companion
Website

Taking Notes While You Read

If it is not too distracting, take notes as you read, either in the textbook or a notebook. Writing down any key ideas, terms to look up later, and questions you have as you read is an excellent way to stay focused and improve comprehension—taking notes helps you remember what you read.

Questions to consider and answer as you read include the following:

* What is the reading's main idea?
* How would I summarize the main idea of each paragraph in two or three words?

ACTIVITY   *Calculate Your Reading Speed*

Knowing how quickly you read is helpful when planning reading time and marking your progress. The goal is to increase your speed *and* your comprehension. To calculate your reading speed, time yourself while you read the following article from *The Chronicle of Higher Education.**

COMMUNITY-COLLEGE STUDENTS' REASONS FOR DROPPING OUT ARE FAMILIAR ONES, STUDY FINDS

David Glenn

Community-college students drop out at much higher rates than do students in four-year colleges, but for similar reasons, according to an ambitious new study that was described here on Tuesday at the annual meeting of the American Sociological Association.

The study's central finding—that the dynamics of dropping out of community colleges and four-year colleges are essentially the same—might not sound like heart-stopping news. But the study's author said that her work should dispel any suspicions that community-college students are so different from their four-year counterparts—in age, ability, and life circumstances—that the traditional explanations for dropping out don't apply to them.

Indeed, community colleges probably should follow some of the same dropout-combating advice that has been given to four-year colleges during the past decade, said the author, Regina Deil-Amen, an assistant professor of education at Pennsylvania State University at University Park. In particular, Ms. Deil-Amen said, community colleges should pay attention to their students' levels of academic integration (how frequently they interact outside of class with teachers, librarians, and other staff members) and social integration (their participation in campus clubs and friendship networks).

The terms "academic integration" and "social integration" derive from the work of Vincent Tinto, a professor of education at Syracuse University who during the 1970s developed a widely-used model of how students decide to drop out. Students who face identical intellectual and financial obstacles can vary widely in their propensity to drop out, Mr. Tinto observed—and the difference often has to do with how well students believe that they fit at a particular college.

Many recent studies have empirically supported Mr. Tinto's basic insights, Ms. Deil-Amen said, but few of them have looked specifically at the community-college context. In her project, Ms. Deil-Amen drew on a large-scale federal research project known as the Beginning Postsecondary Longitudinal Study, which followed students who first enrolled in college in 1995. From that study, Ms. Deil-Amen took data concerning 3,300 students who entered four-year institutions and 3,600 students who entered community colleges.

Ms. Deil-Amen's analysis found that, among community-college students, "participation in clubs or arts activities, study groups, and frequent interaction with faculty and advisers outside of class were all significantly negatively associated with dropout." This appeared to be true even for students who attended part-time, who had low grades, who had children, and who worked many hours outside of college.

Participating in study groups turned out to be one of the most powerful variables in Ms. Deil-Amen's analysis. All else being equal, joining study groups appeared to reduce a community-college student's odds of dropping out by approximately 28 percent.

Among four-year students, study groups had no statistically significant effect. That was one of the few strong differences Ms. Deil-Amen found between the two groups.

Along with her quantitative analysis, Ms. Deil-Amen conducted detailed interviews with community-college students and dropouts in the Chicago area. In her paper—titled "Do Traditional Models of College Dropout Apply to Non-Traditional Students at Non-Traditional Colleges?"—Ms. Deil-Amen quotes one of those students on the value of study groups and social networks: "When you doubt yourself, your intelligence, everything . . . you feel as though you can't make it, you're not going to make it, it's a horrible feeling. . . . When you find a student who says, 'Yes, I know what you're talking about. Yes, I have that same problem'—even if she's never solved it and you're still experiencing add it, you're not alone anymore."

This article is 580 words long. To calculate your reading speed, divide the number of minutes it took to read the passage into 580. For example, if it took you 2.5 minutes to complete the passage, then you read at a rate of 175 (580/2.5) words per minute.

Number of words   580   580/ ___ (number of minutes) = ___ WPM

Number of minutes   ___

Average readers read between 200 and 250 words per minute, but that does not reflect their comprehension of the material. Techniques for improving speed are worth learning and practicing. Your college may offer a speed reading class, or you may be able to read about methods for improving speed through books or websites.

Practice

Without referring to the article, answer the following questions:

- What is the article's main idea?

- What do the terms *academic integration* and *social integration* mean?

- According to the article, what is the one overwhelmingly consistent factor in the retention of community college students?

Companion Website

Checking Your Comprehension

The most important aspect of reading is comprehending and remembering what you read. If your textbook has questions after each chapter to help you reinforce what you learn, get in the habit of answering them when you finish a reading assignment. Even mentally answering the questions helps you understand the material. If your textbook does not have questions, create your own or write a short chapter summary. To reinforce what you learn, trade summaries with a classmate.

A high reading speed means very little if you do not remember anything you read. Your goal is to improve your reading speed to help you keep up with the reading demands of college and to improve your retention and comprehension of the material.

Reading in the Disciplines

he following are strategies for reading in the disciplines you may encounter in college.

Math. Take your time to read the written information and explanations as well as the visual representations of problems and steps to solving them. Reading assigned chapters *before* you get to class helps you check your reading comprehension.

Literature. You may find you have more reading in literature classes—novels, short stories, plays, and poetry. Start early on these long reading assignments, and take notes along the way. Depending on the literature's complexity, you may have to read it a few times, especially poetry. Sounding out individual words, or subvocalization (see the Reading Difficulties section in this chapter), is often considered a reading difficulty, but it may be necessary to slow down and read short pieces of literature aloud. Also, pay attention to details when reading fiction and poetry.

Languages. The goal of reading in a foreign language is to improve your comprehension. Use a dictionary the first time you encounter new vocabulary and work on improving your speed.

Sciences. Reading in the sciences takes time and focus as you encounter new concepts and processes. Look for visual representations of the content in your textbook.

Social Sciences. Large amounts of assigned material are part of any social science class. Start reading early and look for key ideas. People and their theories or their actions (in history) are key components of the reading. Learning the who, what, when, and where of the material makes it easier to remember.

One definition of integrity is doing what you say you will do even in the face of adversity. Acting with integrity in college includes making a commitment to complete reading assignments in all your classes even if you face challenges. Reading in college is not optional; rather, it is crucial to success. When you make the commitment to enroll in college, you must also follow through and tackle the reading that is part of the experience.

Improving Your Reading Attention Span

Each semester gets more demanding in terms of reading because you are advancing in your degree program and are encountering new, more challenging content. Therefore, the more practice you have reading effectively, the easier it is to complete larger reading assignments. If you find that your reading attention span is not long, then work on lengthening it.

First, determine how many pages you can comfortably read without getting distracted or tired. Record the number in your reading log, a notebook, or a calendar. Each time you read an assignment, note how many pages it is. See if you can "beat" the number from the previous reading session. The more you read and the more you challenge yourself with reading, the better you will get. Just be patient.

Thinking Critically When Reading

In addition to all you learned about preparing to read and improving your reading skills, you must also consider reading critically. As stated earlier, critical thinking is required in college classes. Your instructors not only want to impart basic information to you through the lectures, class discussions, and assigned readings, but they also want you to think critically about the information in order to add to your understanding of yourself and the world around you. It is not enough to know that Lincoln's Emancipation Proclamation was delivered on September 22, 1862; instead, you should think critically about

Taking notes while reading will help you remember, understand, and think critically about the text.

Rachel Epstein/PhotoEdit

why the speech was given, the effect the speech had on its audience, and the far-reaching implications of its message long after it was given.

How can you begin to think more critically about your reading? First, make sure that you understand what you are reading. Improving your vocabulary and reading comprehension is essential in understanding the material. Second, get comfortable taking notes whenever you read. Writing in the margins or a designated notebook is the foundation for remembering what you read so you can think critically about it.

The next logical step is to question what you read. Reading critically means that you question everything from the author's background and expertise to the information she presents and how she organizes it. You may think that published authors are always right—or they wouldn't be published—so you may find questioning an authority on a subject uncomfortable at first. "Who am I to say this person is wrong?" may be a question that runs through your head as you begin to read and think critically. The answer is that you are the perfect person to question the author because you are his audience, the person for whom he is writing. If you have questions about his ideas, then others may as well.

The following are some standard questions you should ask of every reading:

* Who is the author? What is her background? What makes her knowledgeable on this subject? Does she have any bias toward the subject?
* Who is the audience for this material? Are the length, vocabulary, and organization of the information appropriate for the audience?
* Are there any factual errors? Does the author misrepresent information or oversimplify it?
* Does the author say anything that seems confusing?
* Do the author's examples support her overall point? If not, which ones do not? Why don't they support it?
* Does the author omit anything from the information?
* What else do you want to know about the subject?
* What questions do you have about the information that the author did not answer?
* Overall, how do you rate the reading?

When you first start thinking critically about your assigned readings, answer as many of these questions as you can. You don't have to answer all of them each time you read, but the more you read with a critical eye, the more questions you will have.

The OK5R Reading Strategy

Many different reading strategies have been developed to help students read critically and effectively. What most methods share in common is a multiple-step process that involves spending time reading, writing, and thinking about the text.

Critical Thinking

SQ3R, which stands for survey, question, read, recite, and review, is another popular reading strategy. Compare these five steps with those of the OK5R method and determine which method might be easier for you to use.

Companion
Website

Devised by Dr. Walter Pauk (1984), the OK5R method divides the process into seven steps—notice that actually reading the text is in the middle.*

* (O) Overview: Chapter by chapter, look at the titles, headings within the chapters, and the subheadings. This sampling gives you an idea of the book's overall emphasis. According to Pauk, there is no need to read whole paragraphs; instead, "taste" the text.

* (K) Key Ideas: To find the key ideas, read the beginnings and endings of each chapter. You should have a good grasp of the key ideas from your overview.

* (R1) Read: Now, read your text more closely, stopping frequently to ask yourself how each paragraph, with its details, supports the book's main idea.

* (R2) Record: For each paragraph or page, write a one- or two-word summary of the key ideas. Mark any sentences or words that do not make sense, and note any questions you have.

* (R3) Recite: To improve your ability to remember the material, stop to recite, or say aloud, what you learned. Do not look at the book or your notes when reciting. When you are finished, check your notes and the book to see how well you remembered what you read.

* (R4) Review: Look back over your notes and see if you can fit all the "jigsaw" pieces, as Pauk refers to them, of ideas together into one picture. Review your notes soon after you read and make a point to review them later.

* (R5) Reflect: Take some time after you read to think about how the ideas fit into your life. The more you understand how your life is affected by the main ideas, the more likely you will remember the reading and create knowledge from it.

Reflection

EXERCISE 6

What do you enjoy about reading? What kinds of writing do you like to read and why?

Companion
Website

Putting the Pleasure Back into Reading

One of the most difficult reading obstacles every college student faces, no matter how well he reads, is generating interest in the material. A common student complaint is that the reading is boring. True, some college material is dry and dull, but you can change how the reading affects you by changing your attitude about the reading itself. Sometimes, you just need to trick yourself into enjoying what you read, and one way to do that is to tell yourself that you will learn something new and useful.

---

*From W. Pauk, *How to Study in College*, Third Edition. Copyright © 1984 by Houghton Mifflin Company, p. 192. Used with permission.

Another way to put pleasure back into reading is to seek out pleasurable reading yourself. If you have favorite authors or types of writing, go to a bookstore or library and get a copy of a book or magazine that may spark your interest. Make an effort to find reading material that is interesting, stimulating, and even fun. Reading or browsing through a magazine or newspaper each week helps your reading skills. A habit of reading also makes it easier to stick to the schedule you set for reading class material. If you have a good book waiting, it serves as a reward for completing those less exciting reading assignments. Once you develop good reading habits, you will find yourself reading—and enjoying it—even after classes are over. You will soon discover you have a curiosity to learn new things and reading will satisfy your thirst for knowledge.

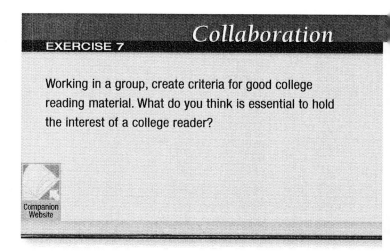

EXERCISE 7

Collaboration

Working in a group, create criteria for good college reading material. What do you think is essential to hold the interest of a college reader?

Companion Website

Reading Difficulties

For some students, no matter how much they want to read well, the activity is difficult. Having to deal with reading difficulties makes a short reading assignment seem like climbing Mount Everest and makes it hard to stay motivated. This section describes some common reading difficulties students experience. It is not intended as a comprehensive list, nor is it intended as a diagnosis of problems you may experience. If you think you may have a reading difficulty or a learning disability, see your college counselor for a proper diagnosis. Your college's counseling services can also provide you with resources to help alleviate any problems you have because of a learning difficulty.

Some reading difficulties are more bad habits than disorders. Subvocalization, or pronouncing each word in your mind as you read, is one type of bad habit that some readers experience. Reading the same words or sentences over and over again, or regression, is another. Improving your reading speed, or the rate at which your eyes move across the page, often eliminates the reading habits that slow you down. Moving a finger, pen, or pencil across the page as you read slows down your reading speed. Unless you are stopping to take notes along the way, eliminate the use of an instrument to keep your eyes moving. Finally, poor concentration negatively affects how quickly you read. In some cases, poor concentration is part of a larger issue that may be diagnosed by a health professional. If poor concentration is just a bad habit, work toward improving it by eliminating distractions and following the suggestions outlined in this chapter.

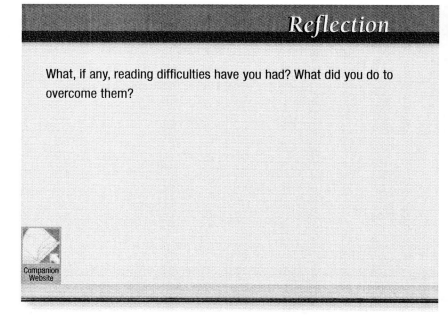

Reflection

What, if any, reading difficulties have you had? What did you do to overcome them?

Companion Website

Consider how understanding your personality style or learning preference can help you through challenging situations.

You have right-brain and aural learning style preferences and a large reading load this semester. In your economics class, you will read over 800 pages during the semester. You also have four novels to read in your American literature class, and a biology textbook and lab manual for your biology class. You don't consider yourself a strong reader because it often takes you a long time to complete even short assignments. You love to listen to mystery novels on tape, but when it comes to reading through textbooks that contain unfamiliar terminology and abstract concepts, you are discouraged. What can you do to successfully complete the reading assignments and improve your reading skills?

*PERSONALITY + LEARNING STYLE = UNDERSTANDING SITUATIONS

Dyslexia is a neurological disorder that makes it difficult for people to comprehend and recognize written words; they may also have trouble writing and spelling. According to the International Dyslexia Association, (2004), 15–20 percent of all students are dyslexics and most dyslexics have average or above-average intelligence. The good news about dyslexia is that many - students learn to cope with the disorder and succeed in college and careers.

Attention deficit disorder (ADD) and attention deficit hyperactivity disorder (ADHD) are behavioral disorders in which a person has difficulty paying attention. Reading becomes just another obstacle that someone with ADD or ADHD must overcome. To work through any difficulties that ADD/ADHD may cause, contact your counseling center. As with dyslexia, ADD/ADHD can be managed so that your reading skills get sharper.

Some reading difficulties are actually the result of vision problems. A regular eye exam can determine if your difficulties are caused by the need for corrective glasses or contacts. If you think your eyes are the reason you have trouble reading words, get your eyes checked by a doctor. You may want to stop first at your college's health clinic, if one is available, for a screening. Also, take advantage of any health fairs offered on your campus where you can get a free screening that may pinpoint the problem.

Title of text or chapter _____

Number of pages _____

Author _____

Class _____

Instructor _____

Date reading should be completed _____

Estimated time to complete _____

Reading goals _____

Actual time to complete _____

Reading goals achieved   YES   NO

Skimmed   YES   NO   PARTIALLY

What is the reading about?

What did I learn from the reading?

What questions do I still have about the reading?

What difficulties, if any, did I have while reading?

New Vocabulary Words

_____   _____   _____

_____   _____   _____

_____   _____   _____

_____   _____   _____

Learning Styles Application

This chart lists the four learning styles and tips based on the chapter's main ideas. Locate your learning style and read the corresponding tips to maximize your success in college.

VISUAL

Students with visual learning preferences often find reading a stimulating activity because it involves visual processes. You may also appreciate diagrams and drawings that represent key concepts.

AURAL

Those with aural learning preferences may benefit from reading some material aloud, especially material that requires you to slow down and pay attention to detail. One word of caution: subvocalization can slow reading speed, which may inhibit you from reading large amounts of material in a short amount of time.

READ/WRITE

Students with read/write learning preferences often enjoy taking in information in a written format. You may find it easier to remember what you read by taking notes as you read.

KINESTHETIC

Students who prefer to learn kinesthetically may need to work through processes and problems in order to grasp the material. You will retain what you read if you incorporate some movement during the reading process.

Path of Discovery

Journal Entry

How do you plan to improve your reading skills in college?
What do you hope reading well will do for you?

FROM COLLEGE TO UNIVERSITY

How the reading load and expectations will change

You may have noticed that with the ongoing discussion of college to university, the demands become greater—the reading expectations are no exception. The reading load will increase significantly—you may find you have hundreds of pages to read and comprehend each week. You may also find you are expected to do more than just recall the information. You have to think critically about the reading by asking questions of the author and of yourself. Professors in upper-level classes require you to discuss the readings in class, and the discussion will move beyond the reading's content to the formulation of new ideas and opinions about the topic. The more you can contribute, the more you will learn from the reading and the class.

FROM COLLEGE TO CAREER

How reading skills help you succeed

There are very few, if any, careers that do not require some level of reading—jobs in computer programming and networking require constant reading to stay on top of new developments and trends in the field, as do industrial careers that require you stay abreast of the latest regulations and laws. No matter how hard you try, there is just no escaping a career that requires reading.

The good news is that after completing your certificate or degree, you will be a better reader and will understand the importance of reading regularly. A better vocabulary, an improved reading comprehension, and a faster reading speed will help you do your job better. An employee who reads well is an asset to a company because she is usually more attuned to the latest trends and ideas. An employee who reads effectively also knows what is happening in the company and can handle challenges more efficiently.

Chapter in Review

1. Which reading skills are essential to success in college?
2. What, if any, reading difficulties have you had? What did you do to overcome them?
3. What do you enjoy about reading? What kinds of writing do you like to read and why?
4. How do you evaluate a text?

Case Scenarios

Read the following case scenarios and determine what each person should do. Refer to the information in this chapter as you write a description and plan of action for each student.

1. Daicki hates to read, and he will do anything to keep from reading in college. He does, though, like to read home improvement magazines. He is working on his associate of arts degree. What can he do to read, read well, and enjoy reading?

2. Meghan thinks she may have a reading difficulty, but she has never been diagnosed. Instead, she works extra hard to keep up with and understand her reading assignments. However, as her classes get more difficult, she worries that she won't be able to keep up. What can she do to stay on top of her reading assignments?

3. Wilson can't remember anything he reads for class, even though he reads for hours the night before. He also has difficulty remembering what words mean. Although he is building his vocabulary slowly, he still finds himself looking the same word up several times before he can remember. What should he do?

Research It Further

1. Interview three people about their reading habits and preferences. Find out what kinds of reading they do for their job and what kinds of reading strategies they use to complete the reading. Also, ask if they read for pleasure and what types of reading they enjoy most. Write down your findings and present them to your class.
2. The National Adult Literacy Survey (Kirsch, et al., 2004) found that over 40 percent of Americans are functionally illiterate, which means they can function in society but cannot perform complicated reading tasks. Most of these Americans are at a disadvantage socially and economically.

Do your own research as to what challenges people who cannot read or cannot read well face.

3. Create a survey that asks members of the campus community what can be done to encourage students to read more. For example, are they willing to participate in a book club or host a local author on campus?

References

Glenn, D. (2005)."Community-college students' reasons for dropping out are familiar ones, study finds." *The Chronicle of Higher Education*, August 17, 2005. Retrieved August 22, 2005, from http://chronicle.com/temp/email.php?id=fowli7bl7ngbg247gi98ku57kxkareq2.

International Dyslexia Association. (2004). "Dyslexia basics." Retrieved May 18, 2004, from www.interdys.org.

Kirsch, I.S. (2004). "Executive summary of adult literacy in America: A first look at the results of the national adult literacy survey." National Center for Education Statistics. Retrieved March 13, 2004, from http://nces.ed.gov//naal/resources/execsumm.asp#econ.

Pauk, W. (1984). *How to study in college* (3rd ed.). Boston: Houghton Mifflin.

Study Skills
and Test-Taking Strategies

6

Dynamic Graphics

Study Skills
and Test-Taking Strategies

tudying and school share more than the letter "s." For some students, the words invoke both fear and anxiety when spoken in the same sentence. Although going to college and studying do go hand in hand, studying doesn't have to be a dreaded activity. In fact, you may learn to look forward to studying, especially as you take classes that interest you and apply to your career. This chapter's purpose is to help you improve your study skills, which will in turn help improve your test-taking strategies. No matter what you have heard, successful students study frequently and effectively. If you have never been "good" at studying, you can improve by following the steps that work best for you.

This chapter provides you with study strategies and tips for making the test-taking process easier. Specifically, this chapter addresses the following questions:

- How much time and effort should I spend studying?

- How do I make studying in groups worth my time?

- What tips are there for improving the outcome of studying?

- What kinds of test questions will I encounter and how can I best answer them?

- What are the best strategies for taking tests?

151

How Much Time Should You Spend Studying?

How much time should you devote to studying? For first-time students, this question is hard to answer because they have not experienced the rigors of college classes before. Many first-time students seriously underestimate the amount of time needed to study for a class. A common formula used to teach students how to predict the amount of study time is to spend three hours studying for each hour you are in class each week. For example, for a class that carries three credit hours and meets three times a week for one hour, you should study 9 hours a week. Now, if you add 40 hours of work on the job to 12 hours of schoolwork and class, you get 52 hours that you are working, either for your job or your classes.

Exhibit 1, a sample weekly calendar of someone who works a typical 40-hour week and spends 10 hours in class each week, will help you better understand how much of your time should be spent studying.

Given the schedule shown in Exhibit 1, will this student be able to reach the 48 hours of study needed for her college classes? In order to reach 48 hours, this student would need to study at least 5 hours each day during the week and 11 hours on Saturday and Sunday. In other words, every waking moment that she is not at work, in class, or taking care of herself and her other responsibilities, she should be preparing for class, completing homework, writing papers, and studying for exams. If she could not devote that much time to her college classes, she would need to take fewer classes, ask for help with home responsibilities, or cut back on her hours at work.

Many students opt to cut back on studying because other activities, such as running errands, exercising, and socializing, are necessary parts of their lives. Although you may be able to reduce your study time for a few classes, that won't be possible for most classes. Taking college classes is a tremendous time commitment and you have to work in your other responsibilities (except maintaining your health) as best you can. To be successful in college, you have to make a conscious effort to put studying near the top of your priority list most of the time.

Reflection

EXERCISE 1

What are your study habits now? How do you manage your study time and what time of day do you study most effectively?

Companion Website

When and Where Should You Study?

The best time to begin studying is when the semester starts and you have notes to review. Even though you are not in class every day, you have to study every day. Studying the night or day before an exam may be too

EXHIBIT 1   *Sample weekly calendar.*

MONDAY	TUESDAY	WEDNESDAY	THURSDAY	FRIDAY	SATURDAY	SUNDAY
6:30–7:30 Get ready	6:30–7:30 Get ready	6:30–7:30 Get ready	6:30–7:30 Get ready	6:30–7:30 Get ready	7:00–10:00 Clean house, shop	7:00–10:00 Study
7:30–7:45 Travel	7:30–7:45 Travel	7:30–7:45 Travel	7:30–7:45 Travel	7:30–7:45 Travel	10:00–11:30 Soccer	10:00–11:00 Church
8:00–12:30 Work	8:00–12:30 Work	8:00–12:30 Work	8:00–12:30 Work	8:00–12:30 Work	11:30–12:15 Lunch w/ team	11:15–12:30 Lunch w/ parents
12:30–1:15 Lunch, errands	12:30–1:15 Doctor's appointment	12:30–1:15 Lunch w/ friend	12:30–1:15 Lunch, walk 1 mile	12:30–1:15 Lunch, study	12:15–2:00 Errands	12:45–3:45 Study
1:15–4:45 Work	1:15–4:45 Work	1:15–4:45 Work	1:15–4:45 Work	1:15–4:45 Work	2:00–6:00 Library, do research	3:45–5:45 Yard work
4:45–5:00 Travel	4:45–5:00 Travel	4:45–5:00 Travel	4:45–5:00 Travel	4:45–5:00 Travel	6:00–7:00 Dinner	6:00–7:00 Dinner
5:00–5:45 Dinner, study	5:00–5:45 Dinner, study	5:00–5:45 Dinner, study	5:00–5:45 Dinner, study	5:00–7:00 Dinner w/ friends	7:00–9:00 Study	7:00–8:00 Walk 3 miles
6:00–9:00 Classes	6:00–9:00 Classes	6:00–9:00 Classes	6:00–9:00 Classes	7:00–9:30 Movie	9:00–10:00 Answer e-mail, watch TV	8:00–10:00 Laundry, get ready for next week
10:00 Bed	10:00 Bed	10:00 Bed	10:00 Bed	10:00 Bed	10:00 Bed	10:00 Bed

late to review and remember all the material covered over the past several weeks. Start reviewing your notes within 24 hours of taking them. If possible, you should start studying for future exams right now, today.

If you are a typical community college student, then your time is limited. You may not have the luxury of large blocks of time, so be creative about studying. Because it is more effective to study for short periods of time, you can study in between classes, during breaks at work, and on the way to work and school (provided you are not driving). One way to ensure that you study during the day is to bring notes or a book with you whenever you anticipate waiting for long periods of time. You may decide to get up earlier or stay up later to get some studying in before starting or ending your day.

If you have the luxury of choosing when you study, pay attention to the *time of day* you are most alert and receptive to learning. The best time for you to study is dependent on your energy levels and your regular daily activities. Some people know that they are "night owls," while others claim to be "morning people." If you know when you are at your best, study your hardest subjects or most difficult concepts at that time. If you have a predictable schedule all semester, plan to study at the same time each day.

The environment in which you study is just as important as the time of day and the length of time you spend. Again, consider the kind of environment that works well for you. Some people need complete silence with no visual distractions, while others need a little background noise to stay focused. Create a place that is comfortable, has good lighting, and has space for your supplies and books. It is easier to make time to study when you have a place to do it. If you have nowhere at home that is quiet and roomy, then search for a place on campus or in a local library that offers study space. Some people find that studying away from home is better because they are not distracted by the television, phone, or family members.

If you have small children, make a concerted effort to find a quiet spot. If necessary, hire a babysitter or find a classmate who can trade child care with you when you want to study. Many college students who are also parents only have time to study when their children are asleep. Therefore, their best studying takes place late at night or early in the morning at home. Whatever works best for you is what you should do. Just remember that small children may make it difficult to find quiet time.

How to Study Effectively

Setting Study Goals

After you determine when, where, and how much you need to study, it's then time to set study and test-taking goals. Write down the goals you want to achieve when studying or taking a test—to make it happen, you must write it down. The same is true for something as short term as studying for and taking a test. Your goals might be as simple as the following:

- I will use my time wisely so I am able to study all my notes.
- I will ask the instructor questions about any notes I do not understand.
- I will remain calm before, during, and after the exam by practicing breathing techniques and relaxing.

Of course, your goals could also be studying with a group or making a high grade. If you have never established goals for studying or taking tests, start small. Once you achieve your study and test-taking goals, create newer, more challenging ones for each test:

- I will improve my writing skills by practicing the essay questions in a timed environment.
- I will improve my overall retention of the material after the test.

Creating a Study Log

After establishing your study goals, create a study log to help you track your tests and preparation steps. Exhibit 2 is an example of a study log.

Understanding Course Objectives

Another step in studying effectively is to understand the course objectives. You will find the course objectives in the syllabus or other material handed out in class. If a course objective is to identify the processes of cell replication, you can be sure that you will be tested on that topic in some manner. Studying the material referenced in the course objectives helps you focus your time and energy on the right course content.

Using Time Wisely

The type of learner you are influences how much time you spend and how many sessions you schedule. You might start with studying for 45 minutes three times a day over a week to see how well you retain and remember the material. Adjust your schedule as needed. Just remember to be conscious of how effective your study sessions are. If they are not helping you meet your study goals, then change your schedule.

No matter how much time you spend studying, it won't be effective if you are unable to concentrate. Many times you will be distracted by external and internal commotion. Externally, you may have a noisy or messy house, or you may have others who need or want your time and attention. Illness, stress, self-doubt, and fear are examples of internal distractions. Both internal and external distractions make it difficult to study effectively, so you must either eliminate them or tune them out. If not, the time you spend studying will not be productive.

EXHIBIT 2   *Sample study log.*

Class	Chemistry
Date	Tuesday, October 27
Material	Chapters 4–7, extra lecture material
Practice/Previous Tests	In library on reserve; answer key for practice test
Question Types	Multiple-choice, problem-solving
Study Methods	Review notes, work through extra problems, go through practice test, study with group
Time Needed	6 hours
Approved Materials for Test	Paper, pencil, calculator
Number of Points	150, 15% of overall grade

For some students, planning ahead to study effectively is not an option. Because of poor time management or procrastination, these students often try to study in one long session of cramming. Cramming and marathon sessions should be avoided just before an exam because they usually produce more anxiety than learning. If you do find yourself in a situation in which you must cram, try to maximize the effectiveness of the long hours. Organize your time into short periods (no more than one hour) and take many breaks. When you return from your break, review the material you were studying before you begin new material. Try a combination of writing down what you know, drawing pictures to represent the material, reciting key concepts aloud, creating songs with the material, or building a model of a key idea. The more intelligences you use to understand the material, the better your chance of remembering it all for the test.

Critical Thinking

Nadja has little time to study for an exam. She starts cramming the night before and begins to panic because she can't make sense of her notes or the material in the book. What can Nadja do to study effectively in the time she has?

Companion Website

VARK Study Strategies

The VARK study strategies, shown in Exhibits 3 through 6, come from Neil Fleming's website www.vark-learn.com and are used with permission. Study each one and decide which learning style is closest to your own.

Study Tips, Tricks, and Skills

When it is time to sit down to study, you may think that all you have to look forward to is hours of reading, highlighting, and memorizing material—but studying does not have to be so boring. Knowing some clever tips, tricks, and skills to liven up your study sessions will help.

Mnemonic Devices

Mnemonic devices, strategies for remembering, are simple ways to recall what you learn. You may remember using mnemonic devices to help you recall steps in a process or a group of items. Although not recommended for deep concepts, mnemonic devices such as acronyms, rhymes, and acrostic sentences are good for remembering keywords or the order of steps in a process. Mnemonic devices can work in a pinch, but they are no substitute for learning the material well. Use them to start the studying process, but work toward a thorough understanding of the course content.

Visualization Strategies

Sometimes visualization strategies are lumped in with simple mnemonic devices, but they can be more complex and take more effort to create. Roman rooms are one method for storing information and recalling it when needed. This technique is useful when trying to remember a string of seemingly unrelated items or complex material that needs to be pulled together.

EXHIBIT 3   *Visual learning strategies.*

V

If you have a strong preference for **Visual (V)** learning, you should use some or all of the following:

INTAKE
To take in the information

maps
charts
graphs
symbols
diagrams
overviews
underlining
flow charts
highlighters
different colors
colorful brochures
designs, patterns, posters
textbooks with diagrams, models, maps
word pictures (e.g., "marching up the slopes")
different spatial arrangements on the page (like this list)
colorful language (e.g., "*crashing out of space*," "*circling like vultures*")
watch and listen to teachers who use gestures and picturesque language
white space (makes the blank areas around text more significant)

SWOT (Study Without Tears)
To make a learnable package

Convert your notes into a learnable package by reducing them. Make three pages into one page using your diagrams.

Turn tables into graphs.
Draw pictures to show ideas.
Use logos, designs, WordArt®, symbols.
Read the words and convert them into diagrams.
Make complex processes and lists into flowcharts.
Redraw your newly designed pages from memory.
Replace the words with symbols, pictures, or initials.
Look at your pages. Remember their shape and format and color.
Use all the techniques above to make each study page look different.
Reconstruct the images in different ways—try different spatial arrangements on the page.

OUTPUT
To perform well in the examination

Practice turning your visuals back into words.
You still have to practice writing exam answers.
Recall the "pictures" made by your study pages.
Draw things. Use diagrams to answer the questions.
Recall the interesting and different formats of the pages you made.

You like to see the whole picture so you need some overall diagram to make sense of complex material. You like to see where you are up to. You are often swayed by the look of an object. You are interested in color, layout, and design. You are probably going to draw something.

EXHIBIT 4 *Aural learning strategies.*

A

If you have a strong preference for learning by **Aural (A)** and **Oral** methods (hearing and speaking), you should use some or all of the following:

INTAKE
To take in the information

use email and cellphones

explain new ideas to others

explain what happened to others

discuss topics with other students

discuss topics with your teachers

use a tape recorder so you can listen again and again

text a summary of the main points of the class to a friend

attend as many classes and teaching sessions as you can

leave spaces in your class notes for later recall and "filling"

attend discussion groups and other opportunities to share ideas with others

describe the overheads, pictures, and other visuals to somebody who was not there

remember the interesting examples, stories, and jokes that people use to explain things

SWOT (Study Without Tears)
To make a learnable package

Convert your notes into a learnable package by reducing them (three pages down to one page) into memorable ways for you to hear.

Read your summarized notes aloud.

Explain your notes to another "aural" person.

Ask others to "hear" your understanding of a topic.

Talk about your learning to others or to yourself.

Put your summarized notes onto tapes and listen to them.

Your notes may be poor because you prefer to listen rather than take notes. You will need to expand your notes by talking with others and collecting notes from the textbook.

OUTPUT
To perform well in the examination

Practice speaking your answers.

Listen to your voices and write them down.

Tune into your teachers talking about the topics.

Spend time in quiet places recalling the big ideas.

If the system allows it, choose an oral examination for your learning.

You may still have to practice writing answers to old exam questions.

Imagine you are talking with the teacher as you write your answers.

You would prefer to have this entire page explained to you. The written words are not as valuable as those you hear. You will probably go and tell somebody about what you have learned. You want to discuss some issues in it.

EXHIBIT 5 *Read/Write learning strategies.*

R

If you have a strong preference for learning by **Reading (R)** and **Writing,** you should use some or all of the following:

INTAKE
To take in the information

lists
notes
essays
reports
contracts
textbooks
glossaries
definitions
quotations
dictionaries
PowerPoint©
printed handouts
wordy mind maps
readings—library
laboratory manuals
websites and webpages
meanings in headings
taking class notes (verbatim)
computer and other mechanical manuals
listening to teachers who use words well and who have lots of information in sentences and notes

SWOT (Study Without Tears)
To make a learnable package

Convert your class notes into a learnable package by reducing them, three pages down to one page.

Write out the words again and again.
Read your notes (silently) again and again.
Do the "extra" reading requested by the teacher.
Rewrite the ideas and principles into other words.
Organize any diagrams, graphs into statements (e.g., "The trend is . . .").
Use a word processor to arrange your ideas and to "play" with words.
Turn reactions, actions, diagrams, charts, and flow diagrams into words.
Imagine your lists arranged in multiple-choice questions and distinguish each from each.

OUTPUT
To perform well in the examination

Write exam answers.
Re-order your lists into priority order.
Practice with multiple-choice questions.
Refer to publications—citing references.
Use your word processor to prepare answers.
Write your notes into lists (a, b, c, d; 1, 2, 3, 4).
Write paragraphs; their beginnings and endings.
Arrange your words into hierarchies and bullet points.
Search the Internet for new ideas and confirmation of old ones.

You like this page because the emphasis is on words and lists. You believe the meanings are within the words, so talk is OK, but a book is better. You are heading for the library for more books to read or you are going to write somebody about this.

EXHIBIT 6 *Kinesthetic learning strategies.*

K

If you have a strong preference for **Kinesthetic (K)** learning, you should use some or all of the following:

INTAKE
To take in the information:

field trips
case studies
trial and error
applied opportunities
examples of principles
do things to understand them
exhibits, samples, photographs
laboratories and practical sessions
teachers who give real-life examples
hands-on approaches (e.g., computing)
recipes, solutions to problems, previous exam papers
use all your senses—sight, touch, taste, smell, hearing
videos and pictures, especially those showing real things
National Geographic and the History Channel on television
collections of rock types, plants, shells, grasses, bones
listen for the examples—they hold the key to understanding the abstract bits

SWOT (Study Without Tears)
To make a learnable package

Convert your class notes into a learnable package by reducing them—three pages goes down to one page.

Remember the "real" things that happened.
Talk about your notes with another "K" person.
Search for the reality and the applications in any ideas.
Go back to the laboratory or your lab manual or your practical notes.
Use case studies and applications to help with principles and abstract concepts.
Find pictures and photographs that illustrate an abstract idea, theory, or principle.
Your class notes may be poor because the topics were not "concrete" or "relevant."
Recall the experiments, field trips from which you learned the applications and turned them into principles.

OUTPUT
To perform well in the examination

Role-play the exam situation in your own study room.
Put plenty of examples into your notes and your answers.
Write practice answers, paragraphs. You cannot avoid writing.
You want to experience the exam so that you can understand it.
Recall previous examinations, especially those on which you did well.

You like the ideas above because they emphasize examples and real, concrete things. You enjoy learning by doing things and trying things out for yourself. Practicing and experimenting is your way of trying things. You are probably going to try some of the ideas mentioned above to see if they really work.

Common Mnemonic Devices and Examples

Acrostic sentences. By taking the first letters of the items in a series, you can form sentences to help you remember the items and their order. For example, in music, students remember the order of the keys with the sentences "Every Good Boy Does Fine" and "All Cars Eat Gas." When remembering the planets and their order, the following sentence is useful: "My Very Elegant Mother Just Sat Upon Nine Porcupines." To recall the order of the biological groupings used in taxonomy, just remember "Kids Prefer Cheese Over Fried Green Spinach."

Acronyms. If the first letters of the items in a series spell a word, you have an *acronym*—a simple memory device. Here are a few examples of acronyms we use every day: AIDS (Acquired Immune Deficiency Syndrome), SADD (Students Against Drunk Driving), REM (Rapid Eye Movement), and SCUBA (Self-Contained Underwater Breathing Apparatus).

Rhymes. Rhymes are a little more difficult to develop than acronyms and acrostics, but you may have an easier time remembering them. Who cannot remember "Thirty days hath September . . ." and "In 1492, Columbus sailed the ocean blue"?

To create a Roman room, visualize a familiar place, such as a room in your house. If this room is connected to other rooms, then you have more "places" to put ideas. When you visualize your room, pay particular attention to details already in the room such as furniture, peeling paint, or favorite pictures. The more vivid the visualization, the easier it is to remember the items you place there.

Once you have your room memorized, add items you want to remember. For example, if you want to remember the process for writing an essay, your visualization might be something like the following:

Before I even walk into my house, I see the **topic** pasted on the front door. When I open the door, I see people in my living room who will be my **audience.** I hand them the topic, which I have taken from the door, and they tell me my **purpose.** I then go to the fireplace where I light logs that have the word "ideas" on them. The flames and the smoke carry my **specific details** in them and the ashes fall to the floor. I sweep up the ashes, which are my specific details, and carry them to the dining room where I lay them out. Using paper and glue, I attach the pieces of ash to make a visible representation of the paper. The glue helps connect the pieces of ash as **transitions** connect ideas within and between sentences. When I am finished, I show my work to the audience in the living room and they tell me if they understand what I did.

Practice

Create a Roman room for the reading strategy OK5R. Once you visualize your room, draw a picture of it, placing the five reading strategies in the room.

Companion Website

Of course, depending on the complexity of the material you are studying, your room can be much more detailed; the more unusual the details, the easier it is to remember them, which should trigger the connection you made.

"Cheat" Sheets and Index Cards

Creating "cheat" sheets was once considered an activity only for those who intended to cheat; however, many educators acknowledge the benefit of creating such sheets. You may have a professor who says you can bring a 3-by-5 index card to an exam with anything you want written on it. Students who didn't study much beforehand usually jump at the chance to cram as much information as possible in that tiny white space. The result is the students retain more information than they would had they not created the cheat sheet. Many times, the cheat sheets are not needed because the student has, in effect, studied adequately.

Even if you can't bring a cheat sheet—and only do so if given permission—you can still reap the benefits of this technique by closing your books and notes and writing down as much as you can remember about the subject. For example, if you have a test on genetics, take a blank card and write everything you know about DNA on the front and back. Organization is not important unless you will be using it for an exam; what is important, however, is to see how much you have learned already. Once you fill the card, go back through your notes and books to see what you missed.

Previous Exams and Practice Tests

If allowed by the instructor, study copies of old tests. Your instructor will put them on reserve in the library, post them online, or hand them out in class. Previous exams are an excellent source of questions you will be asked. If someone offers you his old tests from the previous semester, ask your instructor first if you can study from them before taking them.

Equally beneficial to understanding how your professor will test you is to take advantage of any practice exams offered. Some instructors provide opportunities for students to take a practice exam during office hours or online.

Having a Good Time

There is no reason that studying cannot include having fun. There are books, magazines, and websites that offer games and fun quizzes to help you study. You don't have to look for games produced by others—you can create your own. Create flashcards to quiz yourself or others if you are in a study group. Or tape record questions and answers; play the question, stop the tape and answer it aloud. Then, play the answer to see how well you did. If you can push yourself to enjoy studying, you will do it more often.

Studying in Groups

One of the most underused and underrated ways to study for a class is to form a study group. A *study group* is two or more people taking the same course who get together to study the course material. The benefits of studying in groups, rather than alone, are many. First, you benefit from others' notes—both to fill in gaps in your own and to cover a class you missed. Sharing notes exposes you to the others' perspective on the subject, and you may find your classmates can explain major concepts better than the professor. Another advantage is a built-in support system. These people may become good friends during the process of studying.

Key to a successful study group is limiting the group to four or five participants. More than five participants makes it harder to remain on track. It is also best to study with people who are not close friends to minimize distractions and off-topic conversations. When choosing group members, find out what each expects from the group. You want members who will contribute and take on specific responsibilities to benefit the whole group.

Once the participants are selected, exchange contact information (cell phone numbers and e-mail addresses) and choose a leader. The leader can change from meeting to meeting, but one person should be responsible for contacting everyone to announce the time and place for the first session. The leader is responsible for keeping everyone on task and assigning roles to the members.

When the group meets, be sure that each person contributes to the study session and "teaches" the assigned part. Take breaks periodically to keep people focused. To make studying comfortable, meet in a quiet location that allows food and drink; this reduces the need for breaks for those who are hungry and thirsty. Consider taking turns bringing snacks or chipping in for pizza. Better yet, go out for a meal *after* studying—everyone then has a goal to look forward to.

Forming study groups at a community college may be hard because many students lead full lives and have little time to schedule extra activities. Their free time may not be consistent because of work or their daily family responsibilities. To make your study group work, be creative with scheduling and organizing time. For example, join a chat room or use e-mail to make assignments or quiz each other about exam material.

Another study group type consists of two people—you and a person who took the class previously. Try to find a partner who is taking a class that you

One key to a successful study group is to limit the group to four or five participants.

Dennis MacDonald/PhotoEdit

have finished. The information exchange helps each person learn the new material. This kind of study group is harder to form because it requires that both participants be taking a similar class schedule or degree program. However, the potential benefits make it worth trying.

GENERAL TIPS FOR STUDY GROUPS

- Start with a small group—three to five people.
- Choose a leader for each meeting.
- Keep a master list of contact information.
- Schedule a time and place that is convenient, comfortable, and conducive to studying.
- Be creative about meeting. Try doing some of the work (e.g., creating sample test questions) online using chat rooms or e-mail.
- Assign each person part of the material to "teach" the group.
- Do your homework before meeting by preparing to "teach" your material.
- Review notes with each other.
- Quiz each other over the material before leaving the meeting.
- Be respectful of others' commitments.
- Take frequent breaks.
- Stay on task.
- Meet often for shorter periods rather than in "marathon" sessions.

Studying Alone

If you can't or don't want to belong to a study group, there are still advantages to studying alone: You don't have to worry about someone slacking off or taking control of the group, scheduling conflicts, and misinformation. Because you are in control of the studying, you will receive all of the glory of doing well on exams.

Test Question Types

Learning how to take tests is just as important as learning the material. Knowing how to answer each possible type of test question makes taking an exam just that much easier; at least, your anxiety will be reduced because you know what to expect.

There are two categories of question types: objective and subjective. *Objective questions* ask you to recall facts and concepts and usually take the multiple-choice, true/false, fill-in-the-blank, and short-answer forms. *Subjective questions* ask for your opinion about the material or ask you to apply the material in a new way. Essay and problem-solving (critical thinking) questions are subjective because there are many ways to answer them correctly. Some students believe that there are no "wrong" answers to subjective questions, and that may be true, but there *are* better ways to answer them. The next sections discuss typical test questions and how to answer them.

A self-described left-brain and read/write learner, you have three different exams on one day and only two days to study. Your algebra test will be the easiest, you think, while your history test will be the hardest. However, you really need to raise your grade in the computer concepts class. If you have two periods of 12 hours to study, how do you best divide your time? What study strategies might work best for you?

Consider how understanding your personality style or learning preference can help you through challenging situations.

*PERSONALITY + LEARNING STYLE = UNDERSTANDING SITUATIONS

Multiple-Choice Questions

Multiple-choice questions test information recall or they assess your ability to apply information or analyze situations. Despite a reputation for being easier, expect more difficult and time-consuming multiple-choice questions on college exams and don't be alarmed if the answers are not obvious.

To answer multiple-choice questions, first, read the question or statement carefully. Then, mark any special words in the question or statement such as *not*, *always*, and *only*. Before looking at the choices, try to answer the question. For example, consider the following question:

1. **What should you NOT do to alleviate anxiety when taking a test?** [Notice the word NOT and think in terms of what is not an acceptable answer.]

   a. **Arrive early for the exam.** [This is something you SHOULD do, so it is not the correct answer.]

   b. **Skip over the directions.** [This is something you should NOT do, so it may be the right answer. Lightly mark this one, but keep reading the rest of the choices.]

   c. **Pay attention to the time limit.** [This is something you SHOULD do, so it is not the correct answer.]

   d. **Read all of the questions before answering.** [Again, this is something you SHOULD do, so it is not the correct answer.]

After reading through all of the choices, it is apparent that B is the only correct answer.

Consider another multiple-choice question:

2. **When answering an essay question on a test, be sure to**

   a. **Answer each part of the question thoroughly.** [This is something you should do. Keep reading the rest of the choices.]

   b. **Organize your essay before writing it by sketching out a quick outline.** [This is something you should do. Keep reading the rest of the choices.]

   c. **Read the directions carefully.** [Again, this is something you should do. Keep reading the rest of the choices.]

   d. **All of the above.** [This seems the best choice because all of the other choices are correct.]

After reading all of the choices, D is the correct answer because A through C are correct statements.

Read each choice carefully and eliminate any that are obviously wrong. If you have to guess, eliminate any answer that has a misspelled word (usually a sign that the instructor hurriedly added false answers) or any answer that is shorter than the others. Also, pay attention to any "All of the above" and "None of the above" choices. If you determine that at least two of the choices are correct, then "All of the above" is probably the correct answer. Likewise, if at least two of the choices are not correct, then "None of the above" is probably the correct answer.

Examples of multiple-choice questions. Circle the correct choice for each question.

1. The reading strategy OK5R includes the following steps:

   a. Overview, key ideas, read, record, review, remember, and recite.

   b. Overview, key ideas, read, record, recite, review, and reflect.

   c. Overview, key concerns, read, record, review, remember, and reflect.

   d. None of the above.

2. SQ3R stands for survey, question, read, recite, and:

   a. Record

   b. Reflect

   c. Review

   d. Remember

3. The step in the OK5R process where you look back over your notes to see if you can fit all the jigsaw pieces together is called:

   a. Review

   b. Reflect

   c. Recite

   d. Remember

4. Which of the following activities describes the "Reflect" step of the OK5R reading strategy?

   a. For each paragraph or page, write a one- or two-word summary of the key ideas.

   b. Take some time after reading to think about how the ideas fit into your life.

    c. Look over your notes soon after reading.

    d. Go through the assignment and look at chapter titles, headings and subheadings.

5. Which of the following statements is the MOST accurate assessment of the SQ3R and OK5R reading strategies?

    a. Both strategies have the same number of steps.

    b. OK5R includes taking time to think about how the reading material fits into your life, while SQ3R does not.

    c. SQ3R includes questioning the text, while OK5R does not.

    d. SQ3R includes a step for getting a broad idea of what the reading will be about, while OK5R does not.

Matching Questions

A matching section presents you with two columns: a list of words or phrases that are to be matched with a list of descriptors. Matching sections usually require a basic recall of information, but read the directions *carefully*: There may be more than one match for an item or there may be extra descriptors.

    To answer matching questions, read through both lists completely. Then, answer the easiest ones first, progressing to the more difficult. Be sure you write the correct letter in the appropriate blank—check your work after you finish.

Examples of Matching Questions. Match the interests and strengths descriptions with the appropriate multiple intelligence. The multiple intelligences may be used more than once; some may not be used at all.

_____ 1. Enjoy outdoor activities	A. Verbal/linguistic
_____ 2. Know how and why they act	B. Logical/mathematical
_____ 3. Good at design, architecture	C. Visual/spatial
_____ 4. Choose careers in science, computer technology, engineering	D. Bodily/kinesthetic
_____ 5. Use voice or instruments to express themselves	E. Musical/rhythmic
_____ 6. Enjoy reading and writing	F. Interpersonal
_____ 7. Can read others' feelings well	G. Intrapersonal
_____ 8. Fascinated with pictures	H. Naturalistic

True/False Questions

True/false questions can be tough even though there are only two possible answers. Guess or randomly answer true/false questions only as a last resort. Read the statements carefully, noting keywords that could point to the correct answer—*frequently, sometimes,* and *a few.* These words usually indicate a true statement. Words such as *never, only,* and *always* usually indicate a false statement. If you have trouble answering a true/false question, don't confuse yourself worrying about how the statement is worded—go with your gut instinct. If you are not entirely sure what the statement is expressing, write down a justification for your answer on the test. Some professors give partial credit if the wrong answer is clearly justified.

Examples of true/false questions. Determine if the statements are true or false. Circle the appropriate choice.

1. Howard Gardner's theory of multiple intelligences includes the category Nutritional/Health.

    a. True

    b. False

2. OK5R is a test-taking strategy.

    a. True

    b. False

3. Priorities are beliefs shaped by experience and are not the same for everyone.

    a. True

    b. False

4. A mission statement is important because it declares your beliefs and your goals.

    a. True

    b. False

5. A priority is something that keeps you from achieving your goals.

    a. True

    b. False

Fill-in-the-Blank/Short-Answer Questions

Fill-in-the-blank and short-answer questions require you to recall definitions of key terms or items in a series. To complete these questions, read the sentence or question carefully. Often, points are lost if you don't provide an exact answer or you misspell the correct term.

Examples of fill-in-the-blank/short-answer questions.

1. The T System for taking notes is also known as the _____.

2. Abbreviating words and phrases is called _____.

3. An instructor who is difficult to understand is an example of a listening _____.

4. _____ listening includes making a decision to concentrate on what is being said.

5. _____ is a method of note taking that involves numbering items and organizing them.

Problem-Solving Questions

Problem-solving, or critical thinking, questions usually require students to demonstrate or apply the concepts or ideas they learned. To answer problem-solving questions, read the question carefully, marking any multiple steps or parts in the directions. Next, determine what information you need to solve the problem. Then, break the problem into parts and write down the process or operation you need to perform. Work through the problem, and once you arrive at an answer, check the question again to make sure your answer is adequate.

The following is an example of a problem-solving question:

> *Beatrice has a scholarship that requires her to maintain a 3.2 GPA while in college. During her first semester, she took four 3–credit hour courses and made two As and two Bs. Now, she is taking 1 four-hour course and 4 three-hour courses. Can she make an A in her four-hour course and Bs in her three-hour courses and still keep her scholarship?*

To answer this question correctly, you have to know how to calculate a GPA. Breaking the steps down further, you have to know the definitions of grade points and quality points, and how a GPA is calculated for more than one semester. Finally, you have to know how to multiply, add, and divide. These sound like commonsense steps, but writing down every necessary operation enables you to answer the question correctly and helps you check your work.

Practice

Answer the question about Beatrice's GPA. Will she be able to keep her scholarship? Show the steps you used to answer the question.

Companion Website

Examples of problem-solving questions.

1. Lenise's history class grade is determined by her scores on four exams. So far, she has a 65 and a 74. What are the lowest grades she can get to earn a C in the course? Is it possible for her to earn a B?

2. In Carlos' biology class, the final grade is comprised of the following: homework (20 percent), mid-term exam (30 percent), and final exam (50 percent). If Carlos gets an 85 on his final, a 71 on his mid-term, and a 68 for his homework, what is his final average?

3. Lester needs a 3.63 GPA to be inducted into the Phi Theta Kappa honor society. This semester, he earned two Cs, an A, and two Bs. Will he be inducted? Show your work.

Essay Questions

Instructors use essay questions to measure the students' ability to analyze, synthesize, and evaluate the concepts they learned; this question type gauges more than the students' recall of facts or terms. You will encounter more essay questions in college because they allow students to demonstrate a deeper understanding of the material.

Although you won't have a great amount of time to complete an essay (typically, 15–20 minutes), your professor still expects your answer to be thorough and clear. Always read the directions carefully. If the question has more than one part, be sure to mark each part in the body of the essay. If the

directions specify a length, be sure to meet it. Before you begin writing, create a brief outline of what you want to cover. Make a short list of transitions and details you can refer to if you get stuck during the exam.

Finally, because your professor will be reading and grading many essays, a clearly organized essay stands out and makes it easy for her to tell whether you discussed the key points. Give yourself plenty of time to write the essay and use any remaining time to proofread and edit your work.

Examples of essay questions.

1. Do you think colleges should strive, at whatever cost, to ensure that their campuses are diverse?

2. Should colleges prohibit personal and/or intimate relationships between professors and students? Support your position and refer to the college's policy regarding student–professor relationships in your essay.

3. How have your relationships at home and work changed since entering college?

Practice

EXERCISE 6

Create two sample test questions for each type described. Base your questions on material in this chapter.

Companion Website

Test Types

 ust as important as the types of questions is the type of test you can expect in different classes; for example, a math test looks quite different from a music test. The strategies for studying for them and taking them are different. The next sections discuss only a few of the various tests you may encounter in college, but you can apply the same tips to exams in other disciplines.

Math and Science Tests

For math and science tests, it is best to first work through the problems you know. Then, tackle the problems you do not know as well. If you finish the test early, consider reworking the questions again on another sheet of paper and comparing the answers. If you discover two different answers for the same problem, determine which answer contains the error. Always show your work and complete as many parts of a multiple-part problem as possible. You may receive partial credit for doing the process correctly even if you do not arrive at the right answer.

When answering science test questions that involve processes or major concepts, draw a picture to create a visual of the process to help you answer questions about the steps. Regardless of the question types, you will be required to recall terms and definitions.

Fine Arts and Literature Tests

When taking exams for fine arts and literature classes, it is as important to explain the significance of a selected work as it is to identify key passages, authors, terms, and eras. Work through the easier questions first and save plenty of time for the written portions. Think about the major themes and the historical importance of the works and look for those themes to be part of the test questions. Although recalling facts about eras, dates, and creators is tested, there should be more emphasis on synthesizing the material.

Open-Book and Take-Home Tests

On occasion, you may be given an open-book or take-home test. Although they sound easy, professors who give open-book tests make sure you work hard to answer the questions. They may be harder than in-class, closed-book exams. Even if you know ahead of time that the test will be open-book, you still have to study for it so you don't waste time looking through your book and notes for the answers. Take-home exams are also often more difficult and time-consuming than a regular test. Your instructor expects more when he allows you to take the test home. Because the expectations are higher, give yourself plenty of time to formulate your answers and check your work. Even though the exam is unsupervised and you may be expected to use a variety of resources, you must still maintain integrity. Unless you receive permission from your instructor, do not accept or give help.

Online Tests

Whether you take an online class or not, you may be required to take a quiz or test through an online learning system or through a website, such as a publisher's site that supports your textbook. Online tests are usually timed, which means you must be aware of how much time is left after you answer each question. Instructors often place a time limit on online exams to discourage students from reviewing notes, using the text, or surfing the Internet for answers. If your professor provides a practice test, consider taking it so you get a feel for how much time it takes and what types of questions are included. Additional considerations include reviewing the questions, if possible, to ensure you have not chosen the wrong answer for a multiple-choice question; saving your answers before submitting your exam; and not sharing exam information with other students who have not taken it yet.

Collaboration

Working in a group, brainstorm a list of tips to help students study and effectively take tests. Divide your tips into visual, aural, read/write, and kinesthetic categories.

Companion Website

General Test-Taking Strategies

Preparing for the Exam

Before you can begin to think about a test and how you should study, you must make sure you are taking care of yourself. Eating and sleeping are fundamental to doing well on tests. If you are not healthy, you cannot perform at your highest level. Just as athletes prepare in advance by eating carbohydrates and resting, you should focus on getting regular sleep

and eating well days before the exam. At the least, get a good night's rest the night before and avoid refined sugar (e.g., candy, cakes, and cookies) and caffeine.

Maintaining a good attitude as you prepare for the exam is an effective strategy. Monitor and eliminate any negative self-talk about your ability to do well. Instead, visualize yourself taking the test successfully and earning a good grade.

Reflection

EXERCISE 8

What common health mistakes do students sometimes make before tests?

Companion Website

Taking the Exam

If you properly prepare for the exam, both physically and mentally, you should be ready to take it. Before leaving for class, be sure you have the appropriate supplies: Do you need a watch, paper, pen, pencil, a calculator, or a dictionary and thesaurus? Are there any approved test-taking aids you should bring as well? Can you use your textbook or a cheat sheet with formulas on it? Once you arrive in class, sit away from distractions where you feel comfortable. If you are not wearing a watch, sit somewhere you can see a clock. When taking tests that use a Scantron or bubble form in which you mark your answers by filling in circles, be sure to bring at least two sharpened pencils.

When you first get the exam, read through all of the questions, noting which will take longer to answer. Taking the time to read all of the questions is actually a time-saver because you then know what to expect and can pace yourself. Turn the paper over and check the back—it may be a two-sided test.

Read the directions for each section carefully and mark any special instructions. For example, in a matching section, there may be more than one match for an item; in an essay section, there may be a choice of topics. Also, be aware of how many points each section is worth. If one section is worth half of the points for the entire exam, spend half of your time on that part.

Pacing yourself during the exam is very important. Before beginning the test, determine how much time you should spend on each section based on the question types, your comfort level with the questions, and the amount of points it is worth. As a general rule, spend less than a minute on each multiple-choice and true/false question and 15 minutes or more on each essay question. For the other types, spend somewhere between one and five minutes. If you get off track and spend too much time on one section, don't panic—just work quickly and carefully on the rest of the exam.

Work the easiest questions first and mark those questions you don't know or find confusing. Don't come back to them until you finish all of the questions you can easily answer. If you are unsure of an answer, mark the question and review it before turning in your exam. If the question or problem has multiple parts, work through as many of the parts as possible. Do not leave questions unanswered. Partial answers may receive partial credit.

Finally, leave yourself 5 to 10 minutes to check your work. If you finish an exam early, always go back through to ensure that all questions are answered and all parts are completed. If there is an essay, read through your response, checking for grammatical, spelling, and punctuation errors. Initial and number each page of your essay, if appropriate. Turn in your exam with any paper you used to work problems or draft an essay.

Maintaining Integrity

You may have read about the new ways students try in order to cheat on exams or plagiarize. Advances in technology make cheating easier and make it seem widespread. Although there is no clear evidence that more students are cheating now than they did 30 years ago, there does seem to be more confusion about what constitutes cheating. For example, some professors require group presentations and project collaboration; however, very few offer guidelines on who should do what and how to doc-

Gary Conner/PhotoEdit

Before beginning the test, determine approximately how much time you will need to spend on each section.

ument the part each student does. In addition, collaboration on homework assignments, which was encouraged in high school, may now be prohibited in college. When in doubt about how you should complete homework or group projects, ask your instructor for specific guidelines.

The integrity rules are a little clearer when taking a test. Unless otherwise stated, do not use notes, books, or classmates as references for the exam. Most instructors ask you to clear your desk of any material except paper and a pen or may ask that you move away from the nearest person. All of these requirements ensure there are no questions about the originality of your work. Other instructors are more trusting and may leave the classroom or give the class a take-home test. An instructor who allows such freedom is sending you a message about integrity: He trusts his students to act maturely, responsibly, and honestly. Violating that trust can have grave consequences because not only did the cheating student create problems for herself, but she also damaged the trust relationship for the entire class.

Act with integrity when taking an exam, whether supervised or not—do your own work and keep your work surface clear of books, papers, folders,

INTEGRITY MATTERS

According to Dr. Donald McCabe at the Center for Academic Integrity, 75 percent of college students admit to some cheating. Almost 25 percent admitted to serious cheating, while nearly 50 percent admitted to cheating in one or more instances.

Source: "CAI Research." Retrieved August 2, 2005, from www.academicintegrity.org/cai_research.asp.

cell phones, pagers, and even drink bottles. If possible, distance yourself from other students so they are less likely to cheat off you. If you are ever in doubt, however, about your actions or the exam requirements, ask your professor.

Beating Test Anxiety

All of the information in this chapter is difficult to put into practice if you have an overwhelming anxiety about taking tests. It is not unusual to experience nervousness, anxiety, and fear before or during an exam, but extreme anxiety accompanied by excessive sweating, nausea, or crying is not normal. If you experience such reactions, see a college counselor or other professional. However, if you occasionally experience mild anxiety, there are some techniques to help minimize it. Remember that some degree of nervousness is normal.

To cope with mild anxiety, use basic relaxation techniques such as deep breathing and visualizations to take the edge off. Take the time to breathe deeply whenever you feel overwhelmed. Also, visualize yourself relaxing or succeeding on a test to help you get beyond self-defeating doubt and stress.

Critical Thinking   EXERCISE 9

Do you procrastinate when studying? Brainstorm a list of reasons why you procrastinate, then brainstorm a list of goals you can achieve by studying.

Companion
Website

Learning Styles Application

This chart lists the four learning styles and tips based on the chapter's main ideas. Locate your learning style and read the corresponding tips to maximize your success in college.

VISUAL

As a visual learner, work through test-taking anxiety by visualizing yourself going through the exam questions and answering them successfully. You may want to use images of success to decrease test anxiety.

AURAL

Learners who learn best by hearing may be able to talk through test anxiety with a close friend or family member. Listening to soothing music is another way you can ease the stress of anticipating a difficult exam.

READ/WRITE

Read/write learners who are experiencing test anxiety can alleviate symptoms by journaling or reading something for fun rather than for studying. You may also create a studying blog that will help you channel your frustrations.

KINESTHETIC

Getting out and moving is a good way for kinesthetic learners to relieve tension from test anxiety. Deep breathing exercises and stretching will relax you as well.

Path of Discovery

How do you study best for tests? How did you develop these study habits? What do you want to change, if anything, about how you prepare for an exam?

FROM COLLEGE TO UNIVERSITY

How studying and testing may differ after transfer

One of the biggest differences that community college students notice when they transfer to a four-year university is the amount of material they must read and study. The number of exams and papers seems to get fewer, but their importance to the overall course is greater. Some classes may require only one exam or paper, which means you will not know how well you did until the class is over. Your reading load will increase and the subject matter will get more technical. You may also find yourself reading a variety of material: textbooks, journal articles, lab manuals, dissertations, novels, surveys, charts, graphs, and statistics.

When you take upper-level courses, you are expected to move beyond summarizing, or retelling, the material presented in class to formulating your own opinions and ideas about the material or applying the material to new situations. Your critical thinking skills are essential to making it through these courses. Your professors expect you to have strong study skills and solid test-taking strategies.

This is not to say that university professors are cold and uncaring about your learning; instead, they are more concerned with pushing your abilities in terms of thinking and learning. If you have a solid foundation of skills and strategies, then you will be successful—just monitor your progress and make adjustments as necessary. For instance, if you have not studied with a group before, at the university, you may find that study groups are essential to cover the massive amounts of material. Your goal should be finding what works best for you and what continues to help you succeed.

FROM COLLEGE TO CAREER

Preparation counts

Just as you prepare for exams and presentations in college, you will use the same skills at work. Time management, attention to detail, and careful preparation are necessary to be successful in your career. Depending on your career choice, you may have to pass proficiency tests or certification exams at least once or even once a year. Although failing an exam in college does not mean the end of your academic career, failing a licensing exam or a certification test could very well be the end of your job. Thus, the stakes—and the stress—are much higher.

The pressure to pass is greater, but because you attended college, and passed many tests, your test-taking skills will get you through exams at work. In addition to reviewing the test-taking strategies outlined in this chapter, take advantage of any test preparation seminars your employer offers. Also, now is the time to demonstrate your ability to study with others. There is no better study group than your coworkers because they all have the same interest as you: They want to pass the exam in order to keep their jobs or advance to a higher position.

Chapter in Review

1. List the different study strategies for visual, aural, read/write, and kinesthetic learners.
2. How would a kinesthetic learner best study for an exam in music and an exam in biology?
3. What are the drawbacks to using mnemonic devices to remember key concepts?
4. Compare and contrast studying in a group with studying alone. What are the benefits of both? What are the drawbacks to both?
5. What is the purpose of tests? Can they truly measure a student's understanding of course material?

Case Scenarios

Read the following case scenarios and determine what each person should do. Refer to the information in this chapter as you write a description and plan of action for each student.

1. Sylvia's accounting professor announced to the class that he allows students to study from old tests. In fact, he keeps a folder of previous exams in the library for students to access. One of Sylvia's classmates asks her if she wants to study for the test, and she agrees. When they meet, her classmate pulls out a copy of a test with the current semester's date on it. Sylvia questions her classmate, who says that the professor gave her a rough draft of a test that he decided not to use. When Sylvia gets to class, she recognizes every question because it is the same test her classmate had. What should Sylvia do?

2. Ryan does not think he knows how to study well. He glided through high school without opening a book. Now, he is in college and taking five classes: Intermediate Algebra, Reading Improvement, Introduction to Sociology, Speech Communication, and Concepts of Health and Wellness. He is struggling with his health and math classes. What can you tell him about studying for those subjects to help him get back on track?

3. Betty gets sweaty palms and wants to throw up each time she takes a test. She failed classes before because she couldn't calm herself enough to take a major test. This semester, though, Betty wants to do better because she cannot keep dropping or failing her classes. What advice can you give Betty to help ease her fears? What can she do so she can be successful?

Research It Further

1. Investigate methods of cheating that occur with "high-stakes" testing such as licensure and college-entrance exams. Write a report about these methods and the effects they had on how organizations test.

2. What are the most popular ways that students study at your college? Create a questionnaire that asks students how, when, and where they study. Once you tally the results, determine whether the students need a one-page reminder of how to study effectively. If you think they do, create one based on the shortcomings of their study methods.

3. Using the material in this chapter, create two or three games that can help students remember and understand course material.

Writing and Speaking Effectively

7

Writing and Speaking Effectively

egardless of your major or final career destination, you will be asked to write and speak in college and at work. As Jill explains, writing well is an important skill, and just as important is learning to speak effectively.

Although a discussion of all aspects of speaking and writing is beyond the scope of this chapter, it does give you an overview of both writing and speaking well. It will also serve as a good reference after completing your composition and speech classes to refresh your memory of what effective writing and speaking are.

Specifically, this chapter answers the following questions:

- ❂ Why is writing well a necessary skill for success?

- What kinds of writing will I have to do in college?

- What will professors expect from my writing?

- What steps do I follow to give a good speech?

- How do I improve my speaking skills?

C O M M U N I T Y · C O L L E G E ·

Student Profile

NAME: *Jill Lampe*   AGE: *19*

MAJOR: *Public Relations*

1. **What writing have you done so far in college?**

   I have taken Composition I and Composition II as well as a creative writing class. I have written essays, research papers, stories, and poems.

2. **What do you think students should know about writing in college?**

   They shouldn't hold back what they feel. They also have to prepare—you can't procrastinate when writing a paper. Procrastination wears you out and the paper won't be very good.

3. **How have you improved your writing?**

   I learned how to follow the MLA format. I learned how to tie all my ideas together, organize the papers so the ideas flow together.

4. **What is your VARK?**

   Aural.

Writing in College

riting well is important to your success. Although your composition class is the place to learn how to write, this chapter gives you an overview of the basics.

In a society that craves "quick and easy," there is nothing quick and easy about writing effectively. Whether you are just learning grammar and spelling basics or you are comfortable with preparing 20-page research papers, writing is hard work. Students often ask, "What can I do to be a better writer?" Writers and professors always have the same response: Read and write every day. To become a better writer, you must be a good reader and you must practice writing regularly just as a concert pianist or a star athlete practices frequently. Regular reading and writing help you recognize the grammatical construction of sentences, build your vocabulary, and improve your spelling. You don't have to read a book and write a paper each day to keep your skills in good shape. No matter what you read and write, nor how often, you will improve your skills just as any amount of exercise a day is better than none.

Another tip for writing well in college is to buy a good dictionary and thesaurus—and carry them everywhere. Although the spell checking function and www.websters.com are fine sources for writing papers on the computer, they don't beat the convenience and portability of paperback reference books. Be sure, though, that both books are appropriate for college students. Some reference books do not have words commonly used in college texts, so the *American Heritage Dictionary* and *Roget's Thesaurus* are excellent choices for college students. Surprisingly, some dictionaries with the word "college" in the title often are not comprehensive enough for college classes. Be sure to use the dictionary any time you encounter an unfamiliar word. The best ways to learn new words are to write them down, look them up, practice saying them aloud, and use them in your writing.

Reflection

EXERCISE 1

Do you write regularly? If so, for what purposes? How is writing an integral part of living?

Companion Website

Top Eight Writing Skills for College

The demands of college writing are more than they were in high school. Although the standards may be higher, they are achievable. At the very least, your writing during the first two years of college should be clear and to the point, yet adhering to the assignment. The following eight skills are required for effective college writing.

1. **Fulfillment of the assignment.** To receive full credit for writing assignments, read the directions carefully to ensure you fulfill all requirements. Omitting one element—such as a reference page—could lower your grade significantly.

© Tom Stewart/Corbis

All good writing must have a clear point, a main idea.

2. Main idea or point. All good writing must have a point or a main idea. Make sure your main idea is clear throughout the assignment. One question to ask yourself as you read the sentences and paragraphs is "How does this relate to my topic?"

3. Clear organization. Even if your ideas are insightful and enlightening, without clearly organized details, those ideas will not be communicated effectively. It is a good idea to start with an outline before you begin writing.

4. Focused paragraphs. Paragraphs that handle one minor idea at a time are considered focused. Each minor idea must support your overall point for the writing assignment. Paragraphs that cover too many different things are unfocused.

5. Concrete, specific details. Concrete details are the specific examples used to support your main idea. For example, if you are writing a review of a restaurant, provide concrete, specific details to re-create the experience. Writing merely "The main course was delicious" does not allow your readers to visualize or experience the meal—the detail is not specific or concrete. Instead, revise the sentence to: "The main course of chicken parmesan in the tangy tomato sauce that generously covered a bed of pasta was irresistible. Although the breading was crunchy, it was not overwhelming, and the melted mozzarella cheese created a perfect complement to the juicy chicken." Besides appealing to the readers' senses, providing specific details shows your professor you thought about the assignment and took the time to respond thoughtfully.

6. **Neat presentation.** Although the paper's presentation is not as important as clearly expressing the main idea, make sure it is neatly printed on quality paper. Your professor may have more specific guidelines to follow. If your paper looks messy or does not follow the format requirements, the first impression is that you hurried through the assignment.

7. **Grammatical sentences.** Good grammar is essential to effective writing. Some instructors demand near perfect grammar, while others allow for a few errors in an otherwise well-written paper. If you know that you make the same grammatical mistakes in each writing assignment, get help from the professor, the writing or tutoring center, or the resources in your library. There are many websites, as well, that offer grammar help. Do not rely, however, on the grammar checking function in your word processor. Most of the time, the grammar suggestions are incorrect.

8. **Correct spelling.** With the advent of the spell checking function in word-processing programs, most students do not correct spelling errors by using a dictionary. Although spell checkers are more accurate than grammar checkers, they cannot correct every misspelled word. For example, if you use "there" when you mean "their," your computer software considers the word spelled correctly. Correct spelling does not necessarily indicate a good paper, but it does show your readers that you pay attention to details. There are students who have difficulty spelling because of a learning disability such as dyslexia. These students have to take more time to check spelling, but they shouldn't let spelling overwhelm them. Instead, they should talk to their instructor about their spelling difficulties.

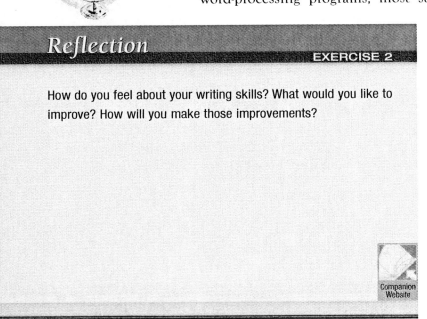

Reflection

EXERCISE 2

How do you feel about your writing skills? What would you like to improve? How will you make those improvements?

Companion Website

Different Types of Writing Assignments

Many students underestimate the importance of reading and understanding the writing assignment before they begin writing. Carefully reading and noting what you are asked to do saves you time—and points—in the long run. One of the benefits of writing well is that you can easily move from one assignment type to another. The key to fulfilling an assignment is to know what the professor wants you to do. The following is a discussion of the common writing assignment types.

Summarize. A summary is a brief retelling of a subject. A summary covers the main points of an event or text, but does not contain your opinion on the subject.

EXAMPLE

Summarize Freud's contributions to psychology.

Evaluate, review, assess, state your opinion, critique. An evaluation assignment asks for your opinion. You should consider the subject's strengths and weaknesses, and provide specific examples to support your ideas.

EXAMPLES

Evaluate a website's use of graphics.

Assess the effectiveness of the information you received from the financial aid office.

Synthesize. A synthesis assignment sounds more complicated than it is. If you have ever written a research paper using two or more sources, then you wrote a synthesis. When your professor asks you to synthesize two articles' approaches to understanding the impact of immigration, read those two sources, form an opinion about them, and use information from the two sources to support your opinions.

EXAMPLE

Read two articles on the importance of higher education and write a synthesis paper contrasting the points made in each article.

Describe, define, discuss, explain. Any time you are asked to describe or explain a subject, you must know the topic well. Discussion questions are usually intended to assess how well you know a topic. The more specific details you provide, the more likely you have described or defined the subject adequately.

EXAMPLES

Explain the major events that led up to the Civil War.

Define the terms "values," "goals," and "mission statement."

Analyze. To analyze a subject is to break it apart and look at its components carefully. Once you have investigated the parts, you must put the subject back together again. When you analyze a poem, you might break it apart into "rhyme scheme," "language," "images," and "speaker." To examine each of these parts is to analyze the poem. Once you have completed your examination, bring the parts back together again with commentary on how the parts all work together. For those more mechanically minded, analysis can be used to figure out why your computer won't connect to the Internet—you analyze different components of the computer to discover the problem. "Putting it all back together" is your final diagnosis of the computer's problem.

EXAMPLE

Analyze the character of Willy Loman in Death of a Salesman.

Compare and contrast. The purpose of a compare/contrast essay is to examine two subjects more carefully. When you are asked to compare and contrast two subjects, first make a list of the similarities and then list the differences. After discussing the similarities and differences, make a point about them. For example, if you are asked to compare and contrast apples and oranges, first describe their size, color, texture, and taste. Then you have to make a significant point about those details. Is one more nutritious than the other? Is one more popular than the other? Expressing the significance of the similarities and differences satisfies the purpose of your compare and contrast.

EXAMPLES

Compare and contrast two types of welding techniques.

Compare and contrast two kinds of bacteria.

Persuade, argue. Persuading an audience and arguing a point demand that you take a stand about a topic. Whether or not you are passionate about the assigned topic, you must argue passionately about it. An argument is most effective when specific, accurate details are presented. Effective persuasion requires that you treat your readers with respect and present your argument fairly. Exaggeration and misrepresentation are not characteristics of a successful argument.

EXAMPLES

In an essay, persuade the college administration that students should have a study day before finals.

Write an essay in which you argue that the American legal system should be reformed.

Reflect. When you are asked to reflect on a topic, you are being asked for your thoughts about it. Reflections are usually used in an informal setting and are a way for the professor to get to know more about you. If you are asked to reflect on your progress during the semester or how you felt about writing a research paper, be sure to provide plenty of details that explain your ideas. Some students hurriedly answer reflections because they do not understand their importance or they think the professor is not really interested in their answers. Saying "I have done well" or "I can't wait to get the paper written" is not what your instructor is looking for. Elaborate on your answer to such a question; the more details you provide, the more thoughtful and helpful your response is.

EXAMPLES

What have you learned about the writing process so far this semester?

How did you feel about your performance on the last exam?

Audience, Purpose, and Length

Audience, purpose, and length are other key factors to understanding writing assignments. For many assignments, you will be assigned a *length* such as a two-page paper or a 1,500-word essay. Professors assign a length to help you gauge the development necessary to fulfill the assignment adequately. For instance, if your instructor assigned you a one-page review of a website, don't turn in a 10-page paper. Conversely, if you have a 2,500-word research paper to write, don't turn in a 750-word paper. Obviously, a paper that is shorter than the required length does not contain enough information and reflection to fulfill the assignment. If you are worried that you cannot meet an assignment's length requirement, talk to your instructor as soon as possible. She can help you narrow or expand your topic so you have enough material to work with.

The *audience* for your assignment is both the immediate readers and the potential readers of your paper. When creating a writing assignment, many professors assume that the audience is your classmates or people interested in your subject—many students, however, assume that the only audience is the professor. If an audience is not specified for your assignment, imagine you are writing for college students who are studying the same subject—such as your classmates. How you present your ideas and the words you use should be appropriate for other college students.

There may be, however, times when you are assigned a particular audience as part of the requirements for a writing project. The reason professors assign a particular audience is to help you focus your ideas, language, and argument. Consider, for example, an assignment that may be part of a health class:

WRITING ASSIGNMENT

In a three-page paper, discuss the latest information about sexually transmitted diseases.

This is a straightforward assignment that can be completed by anyone who has access to the current information. However, how might the assignment change if your audience is 12-year-old public school students? What information would you add or eliminate? What kind of language would you use? Would you include diagrams and definitions or cartoons? How much detail would you provide? These are all new considerations because your audience has certain limitations. Unfamiliar vocabulary, technical terms, detailed information, and photographs may be inappropriate for these students. Simple terms, diagrams, and personal stories about kids their own age may be a better way to convey the more complicated information.

Now, consider the same topic with a different audience: 70- to 80-year-old men and women who live in a nursing home. Again, you have the same questions: What information would you add or eliminate? What kind of language would you use? Would you have to include diagrams and definitions or cartoons? How much detail would you provide? Obviously, this audience has different needs than the young students. Because your audience is much older and experienced, you have to think about how to approach a topic that they have definite ideas about. Some may be resistant to hearing about the topic because they believe it is not appropriate to discuss it in an open setting; others may feel they know enough to make their own decisions about their bodies. Still others will not see the relevance for them. These challenges are unique to your audience and, as you have seen, changing *who* you are writing for changes *how* you approach the presentation of information.

A final consideration for your assignment is your *purpose.* Your purpose for writing is usually closely connected to your assignment, but there

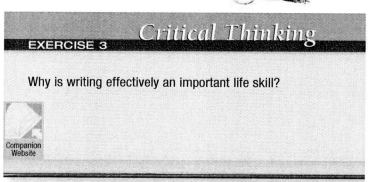

EXERCISE 3   *Critical Thinking*

Why is writing effectively an important life skill?

Companion
Website

are other purposes for writing. For example, in addition to evaluating a website, another purpose could be to make your audience laugh. When you compare two popular diet plans, your purpose could be to persuade readers that one plan is a healthier choice. The purposes for writing are endless, but it is important to ask yourself why you are writing and what you want to accomplish. The answers to those questions are your purpose for writing, and knowing that purpose will help you complete your assignment effectively.

Prewriting Techniques

Once you have read and understood the writing assignment, it is time to use one or more prewriting techniques to get your ideas down on paper. You may have your own way of writing, but it is worth investigating some of these proven methods for generating ideas. Most student writing suffers from a lack of appropriate, specific details, in part because they skip this first step in favor of saving time. In reality, using a prewriting technique before you begin to write saves you time in the long run because you have plenty of ideas to work with.

There are three common prewriting techniques you can use to generate details for your paper. *Freewriting* is an easy way to get ideas down on paper. The only rules to freewriting are to start with an idea and stop only after you have filled a page or after a certain amount of time has passed. When freewriting, allow your mind to wander off the subject; you must, however, write down everything that comes to mind. Later, when you start organizing your details, you can eliminate anything that does not pertain to your subject. If you are a good typist, you can freewrite by typing. Don't worry about spelling, grammar, or punctuation when you freewrite—the purpose is to free your mind of that little voice that censors everything you think.

FREEWRITING ON THE TOPIC "FINANCIAL AID"

Financial aid is a great way to help students go to college, but it is so hard to fill out all those forms and get all the information that I need. I can't think of anything harder to do than fill out a financial aid form correctly. when I applied I forgot to put my social security number and I can't believe I did that. They called me to tell me that my application had been delayed because of the oversight. I could have died because I needed to buy my books and get an apartment. I don't think they understood that I didn't have time to waste; I had bills to pay and I needed my financial aid to get into my classes and start school. Now that I got everything straightened out I am glad I went through the process. I know how to do it and know what to watch for and overall it hasn't been that bad but I was really stressed those first few weeks. Maybe the school needs to have workshops for new students that show them how to fill out forms and that stress the importance of filling them out correctly. That would be a good idea.

Note that the student didn't worry too much about punctuation or even where she was going in the freewrite. Instead, she listed all of her thoughts about financial aid—she recently experienced what it was like to be stressed because her financial aid was delayed.

Clustering is another method of prewriting that works well for those who are strong visual learners. Clusters, or think links, are visual representations of ideas and their relationship to each other. The key to clustering is to start in the middle of your paper—leave yourself plenty of room—by writing down

EXHIBIT 1 *Clustering for the topic "Sexually Transmitted Diseases."*

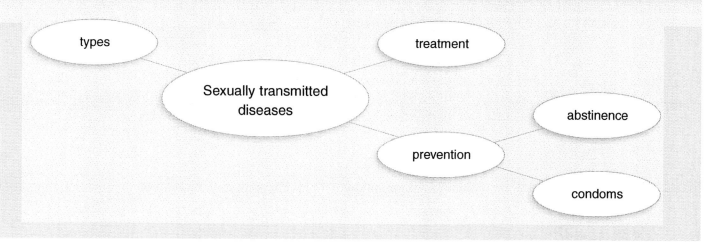

your topic and circling it. Draw a line from your subject and write down a related topic. For instance, "types," "prevention," and "treatment" are all parts of the topic "sexually transmitted diseases" (see Exhibit 1). Then, there are subtopics that branch off "prevention"—"abstinence" and "condoms." The words and phrases that surround a topic or subtopic must be connected to it, both logically and literally by drawing a line.

Practice

EXERCISE 4

Fill in the cluster bubbles below.

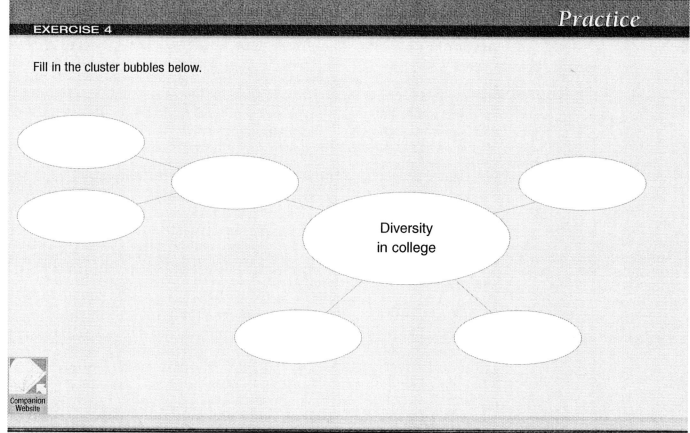

Companion
Website

Another effective method of generating ideas is *brainstorming*, which involves writing down ideas as they come to you. The goal in brainstorming is to get as many ideas down on paper as you can, no matter how ridiculous or off-topic they are. The more details you generate, the more you have to work with as you begin organizing your paper. To brainstorm, write your topic at the top of a sheet of paper, and then start listing any and all ideas that come to mind. Using the same subject, "financial aid," the following is a brainstorming list.

BRAINSTORMING LIST ON THE TOPIC "FINANCIAL AID"

Forms

Information

Financial Aid Officer

Trouble getting the information filled out properly

Fear that I won't get enough money to pay my college bills

Worried that I won't be able to pay it back

Feel good about how helpful the people at school are

Need to know more about when I start paying it back

Need to find out what I need to do to renew it each year

Wish there was a handbook for students that is easy to read and reassuring

As you can see, the first details are just a few words, but further down the list, the details get more specific and yield more ideas to work with.

Organizing Details

Once you have a list of details you want to use, give some thought to how they should be organized. There are a variety of ways to organize a paper effectively. You can arrange the details from most to least important or least to most important. Details can also be arranged chronologically, especially if you are writing about an event that follows a specific time line. Moreover, details can be arranged from general ideas to specific details or vice versa. It is important to organize the details logically, and this depends on your purpose and audience.

For example, you are writing a paper on the greatest challenges to diversity on your campus, and your details include the lack of cultural appreciation activities, a recent racially motivated incident, few minorities in administrative roles, and the lack of African American literature classes. The current order of the details provides no logical connections between them, and your audience will have a difficult time understanding the magnitude of the problem. Instead, order them according to importance.

Which of the details do you think is the most important indication of the challenges to diversity on your campus? Certainly, the most striking is the racially motivated incident. You might use it as the first, most important detail to grab your readers' attention and keep them interested in and sympathetic to your thesis. On the other hand, you might start with the least important detail and use the incident detail as your last, most important point. How you arrange your details, as long as each detail builds on the others and supports your thesis, depends on your purpose for writing.

Writing Paragraphs

A *paragraph*, a group of sentences considered one complete unit, is the building block of an essay. Paragraphs begin with an indentation, known as a tab, on the left-hand side of the page. Well-developed paragraphs, the mark of a thoughtful writer, can be any length; however, if a paragraph is too short, the reader may think something is missing. If they are too long, your reader may get lost in what you are trying to say. The keys to writing a good paragraph—and you will write many in your college career—are to stay focused on one topic at a time and to let your reader know what that main idea is by using a *topic sentence*. A topic sentence can appear at the beginning of the paragraph, in the middle, or at the end. As long as your reader knows what the whole paragraph is about, then the topic sentence has done its job.

After you determine what the paragraph will focus on, start putting the details in place. Just as you consider the overall arrangement of the details in your paper, give some thought to arranging the details *within* the paragraphs. The same detail organization for an entire paper works for paragraphs as well: general to specific, specific to general, order of importance, or chronological. You can use a different method for each paragraph as long as all of the paragraphs support your thesis. Here is an example of a chronologically ordered paragraph on the racially motivated incident that demonstrates your campus has challenges to diversity:

> One of the most important reasons I believe our campus needs to overcome its diversity problems is the recent racially motivated incident that occurred after the football game [topic sentence]. The incident started when a group of black and white students from our school started yelling insults at the predominantly white team members [first detail in chronological order]. Then, the taunting turned into throwing bottles at the white team members [second detail in chronological order]. While some of the team took cover, others fought back with rocks [third detail in chronological order]. The incident ended with three people in the emergency room, being treated for cuts, scrapes, and a broken bone [last detail in chronological order]. If our campus did more to promote cultural sensitivity and racial diversity, then outrageous behavior such as this would be a part of history rather than the present [conclusive statement that restates the point of the paragraph].

Transitions

To make your sentences flow smoothly and your paragraphs relate clearly to one another, use transitions. *Transitions* are words or phrases that signal to the reader that you are moving from one thought to the next. Imagine describing over the phone how to get from the college to your house. If you didn't use transitions, your listener may be confused as to how to get there. Words such as *first, next, then,* and *after* are transitional words that help your reader see how each sentence relates to another.

When you move from paragraph to paragraph in your paper, you definitely need a strong transitional phrase or sentence to indicate that a new idea or point is forthcoming. Phrases such as "In addition to . . ." and "Even though . . ." and "Contrary to the point above . . ." are strong enough to slow the reader so he pays attention to your next major point. The following paragraph contains bolded transitions so you can see how each word or phrase is used:

> **The first step** to effective listening is to prepare to listen before you get to class. You should read the assigned pages or chapters before class so you know what the lecture or discussion topic will be. **If you read the chapters ahead of time,** you will be familiar with new words and concepts. Preparing to listen **also** includes reviewing your assigned readings before you get to the classroom. **If you have a few minutes between classes or on the bus,** pull out your book and skim the major headings, bolded terms, and textboxes.

The bolded words and phrases indicate the beginning of an idea and how each idea connects to the others. The words "The first step," tell you something important: This idea is the first in a series of steps that will follow. The transition "also" tells you that another point is being made in addition to the one at the beginning of the paragraph. Finally, the phrases that begin with the word "If" in two different sentences tie the ideas from the previous sentences to the ones in the next sentence. They serve as a bridge to connect the ideas together.

In addition to connecting ideas, transitions also improve the paper's readability. If you read your work out loud and it sounds "choppy" or repetitive in rhythm, you may have to add transitions. Adding transitions effectively takes practice. The list below gives examples of transitions of various types. If you need help, see your instructor or someone in the writing center at your college. With a little work, the flow of your writing will improve.

COMMON TRANSITIONAL WORDS AND PHRASES

- *Transitions of addition:* also, and, in addition, moreover, furthermore, again, first, second, last, finally, next, another point.
- *Transitions of compare and contrast:* likewise, on the other hand, in contrast, in comparison, however, nonetheless, nevertheless, but, on the contrary.
- *Transitions of conclusion:* in conclusion, as a final note, in sum, therefore, thus, in summary, on the whole.
- *Transitions of example:* for example, for instance, to illustrate, in this case.
- *Transitions of time:* first, second, next, after, before, then, finally, a few hours later, immediately.

Essays

The word *essay* has its origins in French and means "an attempt" or "a trial." For college students, writing essays is an attempt, or a trial, in some sense, to complete the assignment without going crazy! In the context of college, an essay is a composition on a particular subject that offers the author's view. If, for example, you are asked to write an essay on the death penalty or obesity in children, then present your view on the subject. Essays do not usually contain research; instead, they are based on your observations, details, and opinions. They are, in essence, an attempt by you to convey your view on a subject.

When assigned an essay for a class, you should include some basic components. Without all of them, your essay is just a piece of writing—just as a few bones do not make up an entire skeleton. At a minimum, the essay should contain the following five parts:

Title. All essays must be titled, preferably something original and a reflection of the essay's topic.

Introduction. This is a paragraph that introduces the topic and explains to the audience why you are writing the essay. It can also function as an attention-grabber that lures the reader into the essay.

Thesis. The thesis is a sentence or two that tells the reader what you will be discussing, or proving, in the essay. For example, your thesis could be: "The worst summer I ever had was in 2000." Your reader, then, will expect you to prove to her why the summer of 2000 was the worst.

Body paragraphs. Without body paragraphs (three or more, depending on the assignment), you don't have an essay. A general rule, for a short essay, is to have three body paragraphs, each making its own point. Continuing the earlier example of the summer of 2000, one paragraph might discuss breaking up with your girlfriend. The second paragraph deals with losing your job, and the third paragraph might talk about breaking your leg in a water-skiing accident.

Conclusion. The final paragraph of your essay should convey your concluding ideas about the subject. You might conclude your essay on the worst summer of your life with reflections on what you learned from all of the disasters. The reader should understand how all of the points come together to support your thesis.

Portfolios

A *writing portfolio* is a collection of your writing throughout the semester. Portfolios are popular with composition instructors because they allow students to work on their writing all semester. Instead of getting a grade on the first draft, students can revise their papers until they meet the minimum standards for the course. The benefit of the portfolio method is that students can focus on the process of writing instead of a final product. Some students, however, find it difficult to do because they are not used to the way portfolios are evaluated. Some students want to get a grade, no matter what it is, and move on to a new project; the thought of rewriting and rewriting until the paper is "perfect" is not appealing to them at all. On the other hand, some students like the idea that they can improve their grade on a paper by reworking it.

The best way to handle a writing portfolio is to review its requirements, including due dates and policies on completing final drafts. If you have questions about the expectations, especially if you have not done a portfolio before, ask your professor and schedule periodic meetings to ensure you complete the components successfully. Take advantage of the opportunity to submit multiple drafts and receive feedback on them. Although revising essays for a portfolio is time-consuming, you receive extensive feedback and help with improving your writing.

INTEGRITY MATTERS

HOW TO AVOID PLAGIARISM

- Do not buy or download a paper from the Web and turn it in as your own.
- Do not cut and paste any amount of material from a website without telling the reader who the original author is and without placing the material within quotation marks.
- Do not borrow a paper from someone else to turn in as your own.
- Do not ask someone else to write a paper for you.

Avoiding Plagiarism

No word strikes fear and confusion in students more than plagiarism. Simply defined, *plagiarism* is the use of another's words or ideas without proper acknowledgment. If the information or the expression of the information came from another source, not your own brain, you must let the reader know what that source is.

Critical Thinking   EXERCISE 5

A friend is taking a course you took last semester and asks to borrow the paper you wrote for the research requirement. You worked hard on the paper and made a good grade, but you fear that your friend wants to copy part or all of the assignment. What can you do to help your friend without compromising your integrity?

Companion
Website

How College Professors Evaluate Student Writing

College professors vary in the methods they use to evaluate student writing. Some look for and reward keywords and concepts, while others mark and take off for grammatical, mechanical, and organizational problems even if the key concepts are easily identified. You will soon learn, if you have not already, that each instructor has his own criteria for grading written assignments, and the sooner you learn what the criteria are, the better your writing will be. Remember, instructors expect you to write at a college level. Your instructors' job is to make you a better thinker and writer, no matter the subject, and they will correct errors and make suggestions for improvement. Sometimes, students are shocked when they receive extensive feedback on their writing from instructors in disciplines other than composition. Your job, therefore, is to consider feedback from all of your instructors and make the improvements they suggest.

Knowing When to Get Help

There may be times when a writing assignment is confusing or overwhelming. If at any time you don't understand what you are supposed to do, contact your instructor as soon as you can. Professors know you

have other responsibilities and classes and are often willing to work with you if you plan ahead and ask for help early.

If your college has a writing center, make an appointment with a tutor as soon as you realize you need some help. Because writing center tutors are employed by the college, their job is to help you with the kinds of assignments instructors give. Writing center tutors may also be able to explain what you should do to complete the assignment.

Other students in the class and friends who are not in the class can be other sources for getting help, but be careful. Your classmates may not know much more about the expectations than you. Moreover, your instructor may prohibit any kind of collaboration—even if it is only to better understand the assignment. Getting help from people who are not in the class or not taking college courses should be your last resort because they don't know your instructor's expectations. The most they may be able to help you with is the grammar and mechanics.

Collaboration

EXERCISE 6

Working in a group, write down three career paths. Then, brainstorm a list of writing activities that you might do in each job. Also, consider what skills will be most important in those writing activities—accuracy, clarity, grammatical correctness, brevity. Present your information to your classmates.

Companion Website

When You Have Received Too Much Help

How do you know when you have received too much help on a writing assignment? If someone else writes whole sentences, paragraphs, and pages for you or supplies you with many main ideas and examples that you use in your paper, then you have probably received too much assistance on your writing assignment. Some professors disapprove of editing and proofreading services as well. When in doubt, check with your professor and explain what kind of help you are getting.

Common Writing Mistakes Students Make

* Not following directions, including format requirements (e.g., cover page, works cited page, copies of sources).
* Not asking questions about how to complete the assignment.
* Not managing their time properly (e.g., trying to write a paper the night before).
* Not believing that writing rough drafts is a good use of time.
* Not writing the paper themselves (e.g., allowing someone else to help too much).
* Not writing formally for college (e.g., using slang or informal language to discuss academic issues).

Speaking in College

Speaking effectively is a skill that will benefit you not only in your career, but also in life. For example, you may have to speak on behalf of the parents at your children's school as president of the Parents and Teachers Association, or you may be asked to make weekly announcements at your church. In your college classes, you usually get a specific assignment (a five-minute persuasive speech on a current event) or a specific topic (cloning). However, not all speaking experiences begin with detailed directions. You may be asked to introduce someone or to "talk for 10 minutes about whatever you think will interest the audience." Regardless of how you are assigned a speech, the process is the same: You have to plan, prepare, deliver, and assess.

Planning

Choosing a topic is the first step in preparing to speak. Sometimes you will be given a topic, but in some of your classes—or for some occasions—you will be allowed to choose your own. Speech topics can come from your personal experience, current events, or from in-depth research. If you are not sure which topic you want to explore, use brainstorming or another method of generating ideas to determine which topic interests you the most.

Deciding on your purpose is the next step. You may have to inform, persuade, or entertain your audience. If informing them on your topic, use

Not all speaking is formal speaking—your assignments or job may involve many types of presentations.

Stockbyte

Types of Speeches

* **Impromptu.** A speech delivered on the spur of the moment with no time for preparation. Impromptu speeches sometimes occur at award ceremonies when a person is asked to "say a few words."

* **Extemporaneous.** A speech where the speaker is given a topic, allowed time for research, and then delivers the speech from notes. Extemporaneous speeches are often assigned to help students develop time management, research, and organization skills.

* **Memorized/Manuscript.** Both the memorized and manuscript speeches are written in advance. The memorized speech is delivered without notes. The manuscript speech is read either using pages at a podium or a TelePrompTer. Memorized and manuscript speeches are often used by politicians or those delivering a speech that is broadcast on television.

certain details and language to present the information in an unbiased manner. If persuading your audience, use examples and language to change their attitudes or beliefs. Entertaining your audience requires you to use information, details, and language to amuse. Your speech may have more than one purpose—and sometimes all three—but one will be emphasized the most.

Just as writers must decide who their audience is before they begin writing, speakers must also consider who they will be addressing. Audience analysis is the process by which speakers determine who will be the receivers of the message.

Here are examples of audience analysis questions:

How many people will be in the audience?

You may need to modify your delivery style if you have 200 as opposed to 20 people. Fewer people often means more opportunities for interaction, while more people means fewer opportunities.

What are the characteristics of the audience (e.g., gender, ages, race, culture, educational background, learning style)?

Depending on the audience's makeup, your language, tone, and use of examples will change. You will speak very differently to a group of Japanese businesswomen than to a group of retired military men—even if it is the same topic and thesis.

What are their attitudes toward your topic? What do they know about the topic?

Your audience may be very knowledgeable about your subject, but they are looking for new ways to think about it, or they may have preconceived notions about the issue and be more difficult to persuade.

Are there any other aspects of the audience's makeup that you should consider?

Did the group just experience something exciting and energizing, or did they just suffer a tremendous physical or emotional blow? What you know about their recent collective experience colors how you speak, what words and examples you choose, and how you carry yourself.

Here are examples of occasion analysis questions:

When are you speaking? Will you be speaking first thing in the morning, before or after lunch, or in the early evening?

Typically, an audience's energy level in the morning is a little higher than right after lunch. It may be easier to speak about important, serious issues early in the day, while taking a lighter, more humorous approach in the early afternoon. You may not always get to change your presentation to match the audience's energy level, but keep in mind how you might alter your delivery depending on what the time of day is.

How long do you have to speak?

An important part of planning is knowing how much time you have to speak and then preparing a speech that is appropriate in length and scope. Unlike writing a paper, how much time it takes to deliver the speech can mean the difference between success and misery. Remember, your audience expects you to manage your time; if you don't, even a brilliant message may get lost in the process.

What is the space like?

Is it outside or inside? What is its size and shape? Are there architectural elements, such as columns, that might prevent people from hearing or seeing? These are questions to ask so you can determine what body movements you can make and how you should use your voice.

What kind of equipment will be present? Will you be videotaped? Will you have access to audiovisual equipment?

Again, the kind of equipment available, whether it is a computer with a data projection device or an overhead projector, determines how you make your points during the presentation. If you are being videotaped, your movement may be limited and you have to be conscious of speaking loud so the microphone can pick up your voice.

What else will you need? Visual aids, handouts, or time for questions or discussion?

All of these miscellaneous questions help you decide how to prepare and what to bring.

Preparation

Once you determine your topic, purpose, and audience, it is time to generate ideas, research if necessary, organize the details, create an outline, draft

You have right-brain and visual learning preferences and were asked to speak in front of the college's Board of Trustees (most of whom have left-brain and read/write learning preferences) about creating a fine arts program at your institution. You feel strongly that theatre, music, and art classes will enhance the learning environment at the college, but you know that two of the board members are against adding any liberal arts classes because they feel these classes take away from the college's emphasis on technical and industrial career preparation. With this information in mind, how do you plan your persuasive speech?

Consider how understanding your personality style or learning preference can help you through challenging situations.

*PERSONALITY + LEARNING STYLE = UNDERSTANDING SITUATIONS

the speech (citing sources if necessary), provide transitions between main ideas, revise, and practice. This may sound like plenty of work, but if you break the steps down and focus on one at a time, then the process is easier to complete.

To generate ideas, try freewriting or brainstorming. If you need to do research to gather details, follow your instructor's directions on citing sources and write down the material's source. You may organize your speech chronologically (this happened first, this second), from most important to least important, or general idea to specific idea. Choosing the right organization for your speech depends on your topic, purpose, and audience.

Organizing your details and writing an outline are usually completed at the same time. An outline, though, can be a formal written assignment that you must turn in before or after you make your speech. For example, the following is an outline on public speaking anxiety:

I. Causes of public speaking anxiety
   A. Fear of the unknown
   B. Fear of negative feedback

II. Effects of public speaking anxiety
   A. Physical effects
   B. Psychological effects

III. Methods of reducing public speaking anxiety
   A. Mental exercises
   B. Physical exercises

(Remember that when you break a main point or subpoint down, it must have at least two parts to it.) Once you have an outline ready, start drafting the speech. A benefit to writing out the speech, even if you do not have to turn in a final draft, is that it helps you determine how to elaborate on each point. You may even want to note stories or elaborate points to ensure you include all necessary details. As you draft your speech or create a more developed outline, remember to credit any source you used to prepare your speech. In addition to citing sources in the outline or speech manuscript, verbally cite the source before providing the audience with the information. Cite the information on any visual aids such as handouts and slides as well.

As you draft and shape your speech, consider the different elements that make a speech fit together and flow well. An introduction, or opening, sets the stage for the topic and provides the audience with your thesis. Give some thought to what you will use as an attention getter. Your audience is listening to instead of reading your introduction, so you may pose a question, relate a story, or even sing a verse or recite a poem.

As you move to the body of your speech, pay attention to the use of transitions. Unlike readers, listeners cannot go back to your earlier statements and review; thus, your audience needs clear signals that you are moving from one idea to another; for example, "**Even though I experienced anxiety for five years,** I learned to cope by using visualization techniques." The bolded part of the sentence reminds the listener the speaker has moved from telling us about her suffering to a method she used to manage her fear. You may also reference visual aids, such as slides or handouts, to indicate a change in point or idea.

Saying "That's all folks!" or "That is the end of my speech" are not effective ways to conclude a presentation. There are many more effective ways to provide closure and underscore your main point. Leave the audience with a question, quote, or visual element such as a cartoon, or tell a funny story to make your point and leave an impression.

Practice

EXERCISE 8

Using the topic "first day of the semester," make a list of details that you could use in an extemporaneous speech. Then, put the details in an order that you think would be most effective for new students.

Companion
Website

Delivery

Vocal. What if you crafted a fantastic speech and no one ever heard it because they couldn't understand what you were saying? Sound impossible? It has, unfortunately, happened before: a great speech is lost because the speaker didn't project his voice or mumbled through the words. For vocal delivery, then, the most important aspect is getting the words out successfully. Consider the following suggestions when practicing and delivering a speech:

- Pay attention to the tone and pitch, or vocal quality, of your voice. Is it soft or harsh? Do you sound angry or giddy? Audience members prefer voices that are easy to listen to.

- Speak slowly and deliberately, making sure that you are properly pronouncing words (check the dictionary) and using correct grammar (consult a writing handbook). Open your mouth and move your lips to ensure you are enunciating. Speaker credibility is lost when words are not used properly or are poorly pronounced.

- Use variety when speaking. Vary volume, pitch, and speed to create interest. Pause between points for effect. Do you remember the mono-tone teacher in the movie *Ferris Bueller's Day Off*? He didn't vary his volume, pitch, or speed, and his students were either asleep or not paying attention.

Speak slowly and deliberately, enunciating clearly, to gain credibility as a speaker.

Physical. Appropriate nonverbal communication while speaking can mean the difference between an effective and an ineffective speech. Paying attention to and practicing your body movements will help you develop good physical habits when speaking. Here are just a few to consider:

- Dress appropriately. If you look professional, you appear more credible. Unless you are making a point by dressing down or in a chicken outfit, dress up. A neat and clean appearance also suggests attention to detail and importance.

- Smile at the audience. It demonstrates a positive attitude and puts the audience at ease.

- Plant your feet firmly on the floor and stand up straight. Slouching or slumping lessens your effectiveness.

* Act naturally. The more you practice, the more comfortable you will be with your body movements and the less likely to use unnatural, mechanical hand gestures and head movements.

* Move from the waist up only. Shuffling and pacing are distracting.

* Step out in front of the podium when speaking to groups of 30 or fewer. With larger audiences, using a podium works well and focuses the audience's attention to you. In smaller settings, moving from behind the pectern creates intimacy and connection.

* Use hand gestures appropriately. Keep your arms and hands close to your body. Avoid pointing your finger to emphasize an idea; instead, use a closed fist with thumb slightly up. Open hands work well, but avoid banging on the lectern or table.

* Remember to maintain eye contact with your audience.

Assessment

After you deliver your speech, you have one more step left: assessment. Assessing both the audience and yourself helps you determine what you did well and what you need to work on the next time. Although it may sound challenging to evaluate yourself and those who listened to you, there are some techniques you can use to determine how successful you were.

The questions below are just a few to start you thinking about self-evaluation and improvement. As you become more experienced speaking in public, you will become better at gauging your effectiveness and the audience's reaction. You will also be more open to asking for feedback from your audience.

Self-Assessment

PREPARATION ASSESSMENT

* Did I prepare adequately for the speech?

* Did I anticipate what I should do to deliver an effective presentation?

DELIVERY ASSESSMENT:

* Did I use nonverbal communication effectively? Did I smile, move my body, and keep eye contact?

* Did I clearly state my topic and thesis? Did I provide adequate transitions and use repetition to keep my message focused?

* Did I provide a clear conclusion that effectively ended my speech?

* Did I enunciate and project my voice so I could be heard?

* Was I generally successful?

Audience Assessment

NONVERBAL AND BEHAVIORAL ASSESSMENT:

- Did they seem interested?
- Did they react appropriately to what I said or showed them?
- Did they leave quickly after the speech?

VERBAL AND WRITTEN ASSESSMENT:

- Did some of the audience members stay after my presentation to give me verbal feedback?
- If I provided a survey, what did the results show?

Tips for Effective Speaking

s with learning to write effectively, there are tips for successful speeches. Just a few of them appear below.

Repetition. "Tell them what you are going to tell them, tell them, and then tell them what you told them" is often-heard advice about speaking in public. It merely means that you should repeat your main idea at least three times during your presentation: in your introduction as your thesis, in the body of your speech, and in your conclusion as a summary of your main idea. The repetition of words, phrases, and images is also very effective. One example is Martin Luther King Jr.'s "I Have a Dream" speech, in which he repeats the word "dream" to make the point that the dream has not died for him and for African Americans.

Eye contact. Avoid reading your speech or looking anywhere except at your audience. People want to connect with you, and looking at them improves that connection. Maintaining eye contact also demonstrates confidence and improves credibility.

Time. A speaker who uses her time wisely is considered effective. When you speak, be conscious of the time remaining and what you have left to cover. Practice repeatedly to make sure you are delivering your speech in the allotted time.

Humor. Starting the speech off with a joke or a short funny story that relates to your topic is a great way to put an audience at ease and make them lean forward to hear what you have to say next. It also demonstrates that you are a confident speaker.

Dealing with Anxiety

Preparation and practice will make you less anxious when you give your speech, but there may be times when you feel nervous no matter what you do. Be assured, though, that we all get nervous at some time. Try some of these tips to relax:

* *Breathe deeply.* Slow, deep breathing calms your nerves and gets oxygen to much-needed parts. You will think more clearly and respond appropriately.

* *Get into the mind-set.* Focus your thoughts on the task at hand and relax. Imagine yourself walking through the door, walking to the podium, and delivering your speech. Then, imagine yourself concluding, waiting for applause, and exiting the room. Mentally rehearsing the actions you will perform eases your uncertainty and helps you relax.

* *Practice, practice, and practice your speech.* The more you know the speech and what you are going to say, the more likely you can recover from a stumble along the way.

* *Think positively.* Imagine that the audience is enjoying what they are hearing from you. Visualize smiling faces and nodding heads.

* *Consider that what you have to say is important and may change someone's life for the better.* If you think you have an opportunity to make a difference in the world, then your message becomes more important than your nervousness.

* *Recruit loyal friends and family to attend if possible.* Ask them to sit within view so they can provide nonverbal support. Experienced speakers look to others who can provide some sort of positive feedback.

* *Keep water within reach to moisten your mouth if it gets dry.* A little pause to take a drink may be the moment you need to gather your thoughts and move to the next point.

* *Remember that everyone, even experienced speakers, gets nervous in front of others, especially their peers.* If you feel the same sometimes, it is perfectly natural. Remember, you will feel more nervous than you look.

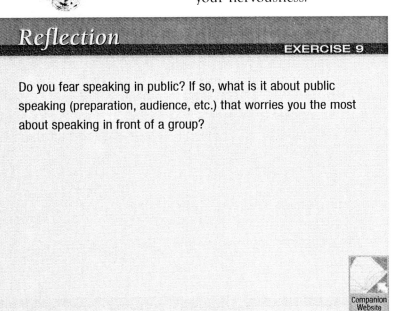

Reflection

EXERCISE 9

Do you fear speaking in public? If so, what is it about public speaking (preparation, audience, etc.) that worries you the most about speaking in front of a group?

Companion Website

Troubleshooting

As you get more comfortable with speaking in public, you will feel more confident in handling everything when it all goes right. But what happens if something goes wrong? First, be assured that well-prepared speakers rarely run into problems, but there may be a time that you are confronted with something that throws you off and turns a good speech into a bad one.

If you do experience a problem, remember that most audience members are generally sympathetic toward you. Many realize how much work it takes to prepare and deliver an effective speech. They also may help you because they want you to succeed. At the very least, they will feel more at ease if you handle the situation professionally and with a sense of humor. Acting angry, speaking negatively, breaking down in tears, and walking out are not options for effective speakers. You will win your audience over more readily if you take unexpected obstacles in stride and continue as best you can with what you have.

In some cases, there are specific actions you can take to minimize the damage from a bad situation. What do you do when:

* *You arrive or start late?* If you arrive late, apologize and explain why you were delayed if appropriate. Make a joke if you can think of something quickly. Then, get going with your speech and be sure to end on time. If there is important information you must leave out, provide contact information for those who may be interested in hearing or reading the omitted points.

* *Your audience is bored or hostile?* Again, humor may defuse a sticky situation in which your audience is not receptive to what you have to say. Another tip is to talk about nonverbal feedback you are receiving; then, highlight why what you have to say is important and why you are enthusiastic about it. Acknowledging their lack of receptivity may be all it takes to change their attitudes. If not, providing time for questions and comments usually defuses tense situations. At least remain calm, especially if someone in the audience is argumentative, and treat the audience with respect.

* *You forget a piece of equipment or visual aid, or something does not work properly?* If you have time, replace the item. You may have to start your presentation and wait until someone can bring a replacement. Any audience that has dealt with technology will usually be sympathetic to someone who has a few technical difficulties. You might modify your presentation and keep going.

* *You trip, spill, tear, or break something?* Accidents happen. Unless it is too obvious, be discreet about the accident and keep on going. Allow people to laugh if it is rather ridiculous, and join in with them. Otherwise, don't mention it and stay focused.

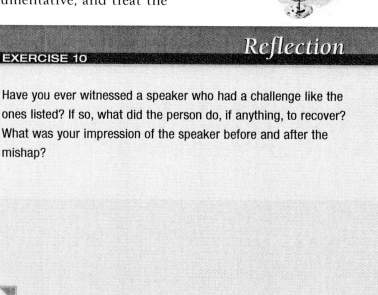

EXERCISE 10

Reflection

Have you ever witnessed a speaker who had a challenge like the ones listed? If so, what did the person do, if anything, to recover? What was your impression of the speaker before and after the mishap?

Companion
Website

* *You draw a blank or lose your place?* First, breathe. Second, if you are using an outline or a written text, glance down to find your place. If you don't remember what you need to say about a particular point, move to the next point. You may be able to go back to the previous point if you remember it later. If you are not using any aids, ask for questions from the audience. A pause in your speech can add drama and may not seem as terrible to the audience as it seems to you.

Learning Styles Application

This chart lists the four learning styles and tips based on the chapter's main ideas. Locate your learning style and read the corresponding tips to maximize your success in college.

VISUAL

Those who learn best with visual stimulation find learning to write easier when they can "see" how an essay is supposed to look. It may be helpful for you to draw the organization for your papers. You enjoy using visual aids when making a presentation because they add interest and are helpful when making strong points.

AURAL

Aural learners may benefit from reading their essays aloud to determine if the paragraphs flow smoothly and fit together. You also enjoy speaking and usually are adept at using your voice to highlight major points and mark transitions in your presentations.

READ/WRITE

Those who learn best by reading and writing are more comfortable writing ideas down on paper and organizing them into a cohesive whole. You enjoy brainstorming and outlining your speeches, but you may have a little difficulty writing speeches for the ear rather than the eye.

KINESTHETIC

Kinesthetic learners enjoy the physical aspects of writing—moving the pen on the page or typing at the keyboard. To help organize your writing, you can try cutting up your essays or outlines and rearranging them until each point flows logically. You also enjoy using your body to make points more clearly when you speak.

Path of Discovery

Journal Entry

How have the writing and speaking expectations changed for you since high school? What do you expect the writing and speaking expectations to be like on the job?

FROM COLLEGE TO UNIVERSITY

How writing assignments and expectations may change

When you take upper-level courses at a university, you will write more and the expectations will be higher. Your professors will definitely assume that any writing challenges you had during your first two years of college have been overcome. Your professors are more concerned with the strength and originality of your argument and with the depth and breadth of your research than with grammar, punctuation, and spelling. Likewise, they expect that lower-level issues such as grammar and mechanics are mastered.

You will be writing more to discover what you think about a particular topic. You will also find writing and research more enjoyable as you settle into a major course of study. Most students who transfer learn that they enjoy writing about subjects that will help them in their careers. This kind of satisfaction takes time, and although you may not enjoy every writing assignment in community college, realize that with each writing assignment, you become a better writer and thinker, which will help make your transition to a four-year university that much easier.

FROM COLLEGE TO CAREER

Why strong speaking skills set you apart at work

Don't think of your speech communication class as the last time you will speak in front of peers and superiors. No matter what career path you take, you will have to use those communication skills to work in groups, relate to your boss, and instruct or present information to your coworkers. You may have to make a presentation to a client, summarize the company's goals and projects for new employees, or present to management a new idea for efficiency. Just as good writing skills are essential to on-the-job success, solid public speaking skills will set you apart from your coworkers as someone who can communicate even the most complicated or mundane aspects of the company. That kind of ability will garner respect and admiration from those who work with you.

Chapter in Review

1. What are the different elements of writing effectively?
2. What should you consider after being assigned a speech?
3. How are speaking and writing different?
4. How do you evaluate a speech or piece of writing? Create your own criteria for what you think makes a speech or text successful.

Case Scenarios

Read the following case scenarios and determine what each person should do. Refer to the information in this chapter as you write a description and plan of action for each student.

1. Renée is barely passing her literature class. She did not do well on the tests or the writing assignments, so she asked someone to help her write her final literary analysis paper. A friend of her mother's, Joan, offered to help her. When Joan meets with Renée, she offers to write down all of Renée's ideas, organize them, and reword her sentences. The result is that Renée's paper earns an A, something that she has not achieved all semester. What do you think of the help Renée received? Is there some other way that she can improve her writing without that kind of help?

2. Paul is having a hard time understanding the research assignment his government professor handed out to the class. He had two months to work on the paper, but he hasn't done anything yet, and now he has only two weeks. Where should he start and what should he do?

3. Jennifer's professor writes very few comments on her papers, so she is not sure how he arrives at her grades. She wants to improve her writing, but she doesn't know where to start. What should she do?

4. Pietra is afraid of public speaking and postponed taking her speech class until her last semester in college. The professor lectured about overcoming speaking anxiety, and she read the material in her textbook, but she doesn't think she can pass the class. What can she do to overcome her intense fear and pass the class?

Research It Further

1. Search the Internet and create a "hot list" of sites that are beneficial to college students. You can focus on a particular aspect of writing such as grammar, or create a list of several topics that concern college writers.

2. Interview two people whose careers are in fields other than writing and ask them how important writing is to their jobs.

3. Interview two people whose careers are in fields other than professional speaking and ask them how speaking effectively is important to their jobs.

4. Create a survey of students' attitudes toward and concerns about public speaking. Poll your class and other students and compile your results. Present your findings to your class.

Thinking Creatively, Analytically, and Critically

8

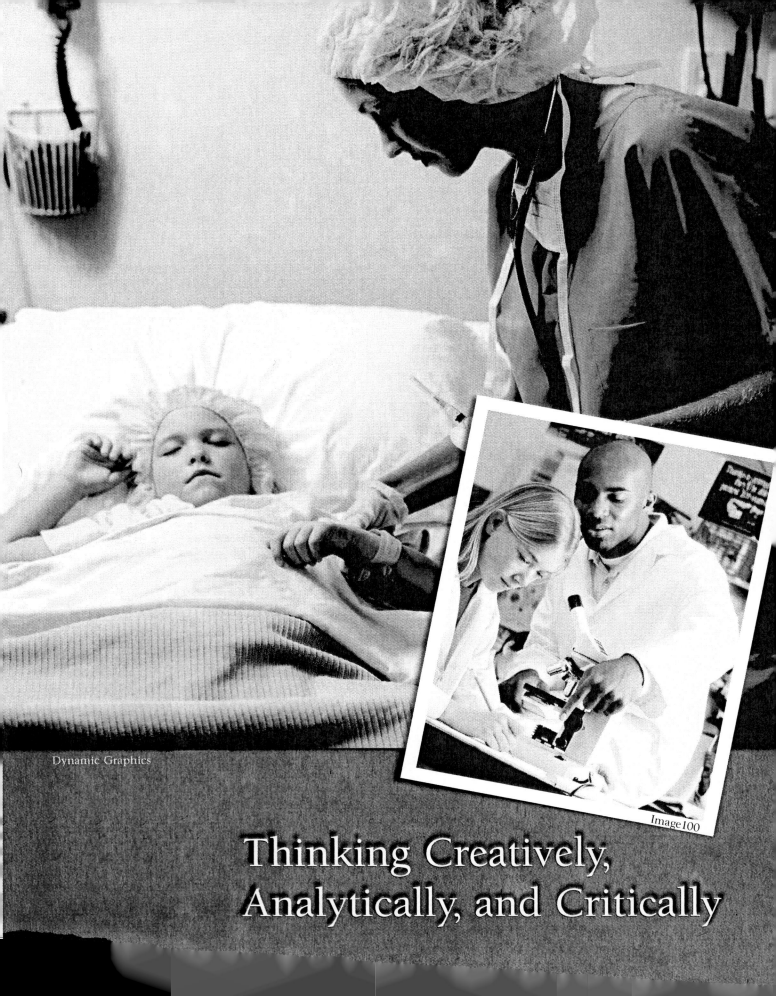

Dynamic Graphics

Image100

Thinking Creatively, Analytically, and Critically

Amanda uses a variety of methods to think creatively and critically in her classes, whether it is generating ideas for writing or evaluating other students' work. This chapter first teaches you how to think creatively, analytically, and critically in your classes and beyond. Then, the last part of the chapter focuses on using critical thinking to solve problems. Although Amanda may not be experiencing any problems so far in college, she can use the skills she learns in class to troubleshoot issues that arise as she completes her degree and enters the workforce. Cultivating strong critical thinking and problem-solving skills makes future choices easier as you complete a certificate or degree.

In this chapter, you will find answers to these questions:

- **What is creative thinking and why is it important?**
- How can I become more creative?
- What is analytical thinking and how will I use it in college?
- What is critical thinking and how is it connected to problem solving?

NAME: *Amanda Ward*   AGE: *19*

MAJOR: *Journalism*

1. **How do you use creative thinking in college?**

   I have to come up with ideas for short stories and poems in my creative writing class, so I use different methods to create new ideas. I usually brainstorm or talk with my friends about ideas.

2. **How do you use critical thinking in your college classes?**

   Working with a variety of people in my creative writing class requires that I think critically. I have to evaluate and assess poems and short stories and explain how one piece of writing may be better than another.

3. **What is your VARK?**

   Kinesthetic.

Think About It

*T**hink about it.** You've heard those three simple words before, but have you ever thought about *how* you are thinking? The term for thinking about thinking is *metacognition*, or being aware of your own thought processes. Thus far, you have thought about what you value, how you learn, what college culture is, and how you relate to others. You were asked to think about what you read and learn, whether it is through the reflection and critical thinking exercises or the end-of-chapter questions and ideas for further research.

The activities that brought you to this point are the same ones you currently practice in your classes. You are moving beyond taking information in only to send it back out in the same form for a test or paper. Instead, you are building creative, analytical, and critical thinking skills with each course. Strong critical thinking skills set you apart in the classroom and the workplace: You are better informed because you know to seek the information you need; you make better choices because you think through all the possibilities; and you continue to improve on your chosen solutions because you understand that evaluating your solution is key to making better future choices.

Bloom's Taxonomy

*I*n 1956, Benjamin Bloom and his colleagues (Soto, 2005) described six levels of learning behavior that they considered part of the cognitive domain. These six levels are known as Bloom's Taxonomy. The first three levels are considered "lower-order" thinking skills because they require little more than recalling or using information in the same manner in which it was presented. Since the publication of Bloom's levels of thinking, instructors have used his theory to create course material and assignments that incorporate the higher levels: analysis, synthesis, and evaluation. These "higher-order" thinking skills are part of critical thinking because they involve breaking information apart, creating something new from the information, and assessing the information for reliability or usefulness. A majority of your classes in college focus on the last three levels.

Exhibit 1 contains each level of Bloom's Taxonomy as well as a list of actions connected to each level. You may recognize some of the verbs in your assignments or on your exams. Consider how you encounter the different actions in your course work. Do you have some classes that require more assignments at the knowledge and comprehension levels? Do you

Reflection   EXERCISE 1

What levels of Bloom's Taxonomy do you find in most college assignments? Provide two examples of assignments you had at the three higher levels.

Companion
Website

EXHIBIT 1 *Bloom's taxonomy.*

LEVELS	ACTIONS
Knowledge	Describe, list, tell, locate, find, state, name, relate, identify
Comprehension	Explain, interpret, restate, compare, discuss, predict
Application	Solve, show, use, construct, complete, examine, classify, apply, compute, produce, solve
Analysis	Analyze, distinguish, examine, compare, contrast, separate, break down, diagram
Synthesis	Create, compose, plan, design, imagine, propose, rewrite, modify
Evaluation	Judge, select, choose, decide, justify, debate, argue, assess, rate, appraise, conclude

have some classes that require you to synthesize and evaluate in most assignments? Just as knowing your learning style helps you make better decisions when you read, take notes, and study in college, understanding the different levels of Bloom's Taxonomy helps you see the purpose for the kinds of test questions and assignments you encounter. This awareness, like an appreciation for learning styles, helps you understand what kinds of thinking skills are necessary to be successful in college.

Critical Thinking

Read the review questions at the end this chapter and determine the Bloom's Taxonomy level for each. (*Hint:* Compare the action verbs in Exhibit 1 with the verbs used in the review questions.)

Companion Website

Creative Thinking

reative thinking, or the act of creating ideas for solving problems, is an integral part of education. Without creative thinking, there would be no inventions, new formulas, breakthroughs in technology and science, new art movements, advances in design and architecture—the list is endless. Without creative thinking, there would be no electricity, no indoor plumbing, no automobiles, and no zippers in our clothes. Just getting to your classes would be a totally different experience.

Harris (2002) contends that creative thinking is a skill, a process, and an attitude (pp. 1–2). In other words, creative thinkers are not born with special powers; they just use their imagination more regularly than others. The good news, though, is that you can learn to think creatively by following some basic guidelines.

Improve your imagination. Find ways to keep your mind sharp and your imagination flourishing. The puzzles that follow are just a sample of what you can do a few minutes a day to improve your thinking. Turning off the TV and picking up a book is another easy way to stimulate your imagination. If you enjoy kinesthetic activities, create something to get your mind active.

Creative thinking is a key part of science, art, technology, and any other discipline you can name.

Think in all directions. Thinking in all directions means you consider ideas that worked before, didn't work before, worked for other problems, and have not been paired with another idea. Some of the most creative ideas take ordinary solutions and reapply them to other problems. Creative thinking demands that all angles be considered as you generate ideas.

Suspend judgment. For creative thinking, evaluation is not necessary—save it for critical thinking and problem solving. The focus should be on getting ideas down, not on judging them for their practicality. "There is no wrong answer" is a common phrase at this point to keep you generating thoughts.

Keep it up. One main difference between people who think creatively and those who don't is perseverance, or the determination to see ideas through—and to keep generating them when the ones you come up with don't work.

Corbis

Harris (2002) says, "Creative thinking creates the ideas with which critical thinking works" (p. 5). To improve your critical thinking and problem-solving abilities, consider these guidelines, find ways to practice them, and maintain your curiosity and a positive attitude.

Keeping Your Mind Limber

As stated earlier, a key to thinking creatively is to play games and complete puzzles designed to stretch your mind's muscles. Some of the activities for maintaining intellectual flexibility include word searches, jigsaw puzzles, crossword puzzles, and logic problems. You can find books that contain countless activities, like the ones that appear below, in stores or on the Internet. Some appear regularly in newspapers and magazines. You may also participate in games of strategy to keep your mind sharp. You can benefit from the mental workout of board games, such as checkers and chess, that involve strategy and thinking about the effects of future actions.

Critical Thinking   **EXERCISE 3**

How many different uses can you think of for a plastic straw?

Companion Website

Cryptograms. Cryptograms are word puzzles that involve creating a "code" to be deciphered. Usually, a code, such as the following example, is given without any clues. The goal is to "break" the code by figuring out what letters have been replaced with other letters. For example, the letter A may appear as the letter T. Each time the letter T appears in the code, replace it with the letter A.

DECIPHERED CODE: HAPPY NEW YEAR
CODE: LGKKM VJS PJGU

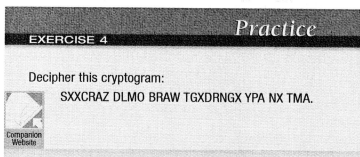

Wordplays. Wordplays are combinations of letters, symbols, and numbers that create a visual wordplay. See how quickly you can figure out the common phrase or saying that is represented. The answer to the first one is "six feet under ground."

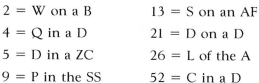

| GROUND / 6 FEET | MCE MCE MCE | R/E/A/D/I/N/G | OHOLENE |

Wordplays are also found on vanity license plates. The next time you see a license plate with an unusual arrangement of numbers and letters, see if you can decode the message. Here are four examples:

10SNE1   4U2NV   BCNU2   2M8OS

Numberplays. The purpose of this activity is to get your mind thinking in terms of what you know about the number of things. The words associated with the numbers are abbreviated to their first letters only. For example, the numberplay "88 = K on a P" is "88 keys on a piano." The numberplay "365 = D in a Y" is "365 days in a year." See if you can solve these numberplays.

2 = W on a B   13 = S on an AF
4 = Q in a D   21 = D on a D
5 = D in a ZC   26 = L of the A
9 = P in the SS   52 = C in a D

Analytical Thinking

Both creative and analytical thinking are part of problem solving. While creative thinking involves the *creation* of ideas,

Famous People in History Logic Problem

Middle States Community College has many professors and students who look like famous people in history. They decided to hold a contest to see who looks most like a famous figure in history. Dr. Longhorn and four of her students entered the contest and won 1st through 5th places out of 22 entrants. Using the clues below, determine who looked like whom and what place they won.

1. Sandy placed one position ahead of the Eleanor Roosevelt look-alike, who placed one position higher than Ms. Goodman in the final judging.

2. Jenny and Ms. Judd also placed in the top five.

3. Amy finished one place ahead of the Hillary Clinton look-alike.

4. Kathryn, who isn't the Eleanor Roosevelt look-alike, and Ms. Kirby both want to be scientists.

5. Debbie finished immediately ahead of the Marie Curie look-alike and two places ahead of Ms. Judd in the final standings.

6. Ms. Kirby, Ms. Young, and the Imelda Marcos look-alike were featured in an article about the event in the college newspaper.

7. The Harriet Tubman look-alike placed just ahead of Kathryn in the judging.

8. Ms. Goodman isn't the student who appeared as Hillary Clinton.

From All-Star Puzzles' Star Look-Alikes logic puzzle at www.allstarpuzzles.com/logic/00161.html. Used with permission.

Practice

Solve the logic problem in the box above.

Companion
Website

analytical thinking involves the *analysis,* or the breaking apart, of the problem and of the possible solutions to examine them fully. *Analytical thinking* is also defined by some disciplines as the scientific process of defining a problem, developing a hypothesis, gathering and examining facts, and proposing a solution. More recently, analytical and critical thinking were linked together as different parts of a process that ends with solving a problem. Analytical thinking is also found in such disciplines as literature, in which you break apart a poem and examine its parts, and computer science, in which you break apart a network and determine how each part comes together to create the whole.

To improve your analytical thinking skills, practice with basic logic problems that require you to break apart the problem and examine the different parts to arrive at an answer.

Critical Thinking

The term *critical thinking* is difficult to define, but has a long tradition. Critical thinkers such as Socrates and Thomas Aquinas, to name only two, had a tremendous effect on the way we think about the world we live in. But what makes them critical thinkers? What is a critical thinker? Diestler (1998) defines a critical thinker as "someone who uses specific criteria to evaluate reasoning and make decisions" (p. 2). Someone who thinks critically does not take information at face value; instead, the information is reviewed for accuracy, authority, and logic before it is considered useable.

Learning how to read critically is a start to making informed decisions about what you read, but you can also use critical thinking in other parts of your everyday life. There will be times when you have to make an important decision, and you should use critical thinking in order to make the best choice.

To illustrate the importance of using critical thinking skills, consider this scenario: You receive an e-mail from a friend who claims that she unknowingly sent you a virus. Her e-mail instructs you to search for the offending file and delete it immediately. Unaware of any problems usually associated with viruses, you nonetheless search for the file and find it, exactly where your friend said it would be on your computer. Your friend is a trustworthy person and you value her advice, so you delete the file. You get an e-mail from her the next day that says she is sorry she sent you a hoax, but you've already deleted a perfectly normal file from your computer.

Now, consider the next scenario: Your friend sends you a link to a pop-up blocker because he knows you hate those annoying intrusions while surfing the Internet. Because you have been deceived by free software before, you decide to search several reputable sites devoted to reviewing new software. You find that the pop-up blocker is a fraud; if you clicked on the link your friend sent, your computer would be overrun with pop-up advertisements of questionable origin.

In the first scenario, two people, at least, were deceived by what appeared to be legitimate, and helpful, information. Who doesn't want to rid his computer of a potentially dangerous virus? Unfortunately, you and your friend did not question the information. In the second scenario, however, you had encountered false claims before and realized that you should check every piece of information that comes to you, regardless of the friendly source. You became, in essence, a critical thinker. Thinking critically allowed you to review the information and search for authoritative sources that helped you make a decision about what action to take.

As the Information Age evolves, critical thinking skills are not just advantageous; they are essential to survival. Not only must you possess these skills, but others must also possess them so you do not have to evaluate every piece of information you receive. Can you imagine a world in which everything you read is suspect, and there is no sure way of determining what is true and accurate and what is not? For people who do not think critically, that imagined world is a reality.

Common Logical Fallacies

To evaluate information effectively (a part of critical thinking), familiarize yourself with some of the more common logical fallacies used when arguing a point. A *logical fallacy* is a mistake in reasoning. Although most people try to avoid fallacies when trying to persuade others, fallacies do appear even in the best of arguments. You should be aware of the many errors in reasoning that can lead to fallacies. Exhibit 2 summarizes common fallacies.

You read that left-brained people are better at analytical thinking and right-brained people are better at creative thinking. You consider yourself a left-brained thinker and your VARK learning style is kinesthetic. Your economics instructor asked the class to identify several ways the college economics club could earn money to send a group of students to Mexico for a week to study the impact of economic development. Your instructor said that the person who develops the most creative ideas will also go on the trip. You would like to go, but you don't think of yourself as creative. What can you do to generate creative ideas and go on the trip?

*PERSONALITY + LEARNING STYLE = UNDERSTANDING SITUATIONS

Connection Between Critical Thinking and Problem Solving

Although not all critical thinking leads to solving a problem, problem solving relies on critical as well as creative and analytical thinking. In order to think critically to solve a problem, you have to go through a process. Remember, the more minds that work on a problem, the more likely all sides of the problem will be addressed, which may make the solution better. Although you may not always have an opportunity to work on a problem in a group, you can ask others for their advice during the process.

Here are the basic steps for using critical thinking to solve a problem:

- Clearly identify the problem.
- Brainstorm possible solutions to the problem.
- Analzye possible solutions for their viability.
- Think through each solution and determine the benefits and drawbacks of each.
- Choose the solution that potentially works best.
- Evaluate the solution after it is in place.

Step 1: Identify the Problem Sometimes we assume we know what the problem is and try to fix it only to discover that the solution doesn't work because we fixed the wrong problem. Consider a crying baby who last ate two hours ago. If faced with the problem of a crying baby, you may assume

EXHIBIT 2 *Common fallacies.*

LOGICAL FALLACY	DEFINITION	EXAMPLE
Ad hominem	Literally means "at the man." It happens when someone attacks the person who is making the argument rather than the argument itself	What does she know about the economy? She didn't report her taxes for two years.
Beg the question	Assumes that what is being argued is actually true	Taxing the American public is akin to stealing from them. Therefore, taxes should be abolished.
False analogy	Creates a comparison between two items that are not in fact similar	Adolph Hitler's treatment of Jews is very similar to Saddam Hussein's treatment of the people of Iraq.
Hasty generalization	Jumps too quickly to a conclusion about an issue based on very little proof	I did not do well in my online class, so I believe that online classes are not as good as on-campus classes.
Non sequitur	Does not make sense	If I am in Boston, then I am in Massachusetts. Since I am not in Boston, then I am not in Massachusetts.
Post hoc	Assumes that if something comes before an event, then it must have caused the event.	I packed my lunch today and I got a speeding ticket. Therefore, the speeding ticket was caused by packing my lunch.
Straw man	Makes out the opposing argument to be weaker than it is and then counters that weaker argument; also refers to creating a weak argument for the purpose of making your argument look stronger	The city council doesn't want to build the bridge because they think it is unattractive. We shouldn't make important transportation decisions based on aesthetics.

the baby is still hungry and wants more to eat. When you try to feed the baby, he rejects the food. Now what? Is the baby not hungry? Did you offer something the baby doesn't like? Is the baby sick, too hot, too cold, tired? You can imagine how much time and energy you might spend trying to find a solution to the problem.

Identifying a problem's cause is the first logical step before you can begin to solve it. If you do not correctly identify the cause—or at least eliminate possible causes—before starting the next step, either you won't solve the problem or you might create a whole new problem to solve.

Step 2: Brainstorm Ideas This is the step where creative thinking is used. When you generate ideas, there are no rules except don't eliminate any ideas because they are too far-fetched or too odd. The goal of this step is to get the ideas recorded, and the more you can think "outside the box," the more likely you are considering all possibilities.

Use brainstorming, freewriting, clustering, and role-playing (if you can work with another person) to get ideas flowing. This is a good time to use your learning style strength to stretch your imagination.

PhotoDisc

Critical thinking is an integral part of problem solving— identifying, analyzing, choosing, and evaluating solutions.

Step 3: Analyze the Possibilities Both creative and analytical thinking, or breaking down the different ideas, help you at this stage. What are the different parts of the possibilities? Are any impossible, impractical, or illogical? Identify the least viable solutions and remove them from the list.

Step 4: Think Through Solutions Thinking through each solution involves exploring their benefits and drawbacks. Consider the possibilities, but don't completely discard them after the next step. You may need them after you evaluate your final solution and find it to be ineffective.

Step 5: Choose the Best Solution When choosing the best solution, consider the effects of the solution. Will it cause another problem? What kind of emotional, physical, and financial investment will it take? What do you need to do to implement the solution correctly? Use creative thinking to consider all sides of the solution before you make a final decision. Analytical thinking can help you list all the possibilities in a table to examine the consequences.

Step 6: Evaluate the Solution The final stage of problem solving is also the highest level in Bloom's Taxonomy: evaluation. The ability to evaluate allows you to use what you learned in the problem-solving process to solve other problems. Ask yourself if the problem is resolved adequately. Did the solution only partly solve the problem or was it a complete solution? What, if anything, would you do differently if you experience the same problem?

Putting Critical Thinking into Practice

What do you do in the following situations?

- You have an exam at 9:00 A.M. You get into your car at 8:20 to get to class on time, and your car won't start.
- You need a math tutor to help you get through elementary algebra successfully. The tutoring center's hours are not convenient for you because you work every evening the center is open late.
- You are worried that you may not be able to purchase your textbooks for next semester because the bookstore's prices are higher than you anticipated.

If your car won't start and you have to get to an exam, would you give up and go back into the house, hoping that you can make up the exam? If you cannot find a tutor for elementary algebra, would you plod through the course and pray that you make it? If you can't afford textbooks next semester, would you see how far you can get without buying them? What are other possible solutions to these problems? If you use the critical thinking steps for problem solving, you may realize that there are other alternatives, or possible solutions, to your predicaments. Here are one student's problem-solving steps for the first scenario:

1. Clearly identify the problem. I have two problems. The first is that my car won't start, and the second is that I need to get to school to take an exam.

2. Brainstorm possible solutions to the problem. To address my more immediate problem, getting to school to take my test, I can do one or more of the following:

- Call a friend to pick me up.
- Call a cab to take me to school.
- Catch a bus.
- Call my instructor to ask about taking a makeup exam.
- Run to school.
- Walk to school.

3. Evaluate the possible solutions for their viability.

- *Call a friend:* I can get Jessica to pick me up, but she will then be late for work.
- *Call a cab:* It costs $20 and I won't get to school until 9:15 A.M.
- *Catch a bus:* I don't know the bus schedule and will have to walk 1.2 miles to the bus stop.
- *Call my instructor:* She may not allow me to make up the exam; I may not be able to get a message to her.
- *Run to school:* I am not in shape to make it all the way.
- *Walk to school:* The distance to school is 3.5 miles. It will take me at least an hour to get there, which will give me only 30 minutes to take my exam.

4. Think through each solution and determine the benefits and drawbacks to each. I eliminated walking or running to school and catching the bus. I am left with three possible solutions: (1) call my friend Jessica to pick me up; (2) call a cab; and (3) call my instructor about making up the exam.

- *Option 1:* The benefit of calling Jessica is that she is a friend and would help me out. I would also make it to the exam on time. A drawback to calling Jessica is that she would be late to work if she takes me to school.
- *Option 2:* The benefit of calling a cab is that I would definitely get to school. A drawback is that it costs $20, which I don't need to spend. Also, I wouldn't get to school until 9:15.
- *Option 3:* The benefit of calling my instructor is that I could explain why I can't make it to class, and she might be sympathetic to my dilemma. Another benefit is that she might allow me to make up the exam. The drawbacks are that I might not be able to get a message to her, and she might not allow me to make up the exam.

5. Choose the solution that potentially works the best. My solution is to call my friend Jessica because it is the easiest solution. I won't have to pay to get to school, and I can get there on time. She may, though, be irritated at me for asking for a favor at the last minute. Then again, she may be very glad to return a favor to me, or she may not want to take me because it will make her late for work.

6. Evaluate the solution after it is in place. After I have Jessica take me to school, I can evaluate whether or not the solution worked. If Jessica agrees to take me and can get me to school on time even though it makes her late, then the solution will be a success for me. If she has trouble picking me up or if she gets mad because I made her late, then I have to consider other solutions if I have car trouble again.

Collaboration

EXERCISE 8

Working in a group, discuss a student issue (e.g., parking, student events, or computer access) on your campus. Use the critical thinking process to develop a viable solution. Share your ideas with the class.

Companion Website

Answers to Creative Thinking Puzzles

Cryptogram: KEEPING YOUR MIND FLEXIBLE CAN BE FUN.

Wordplays: (1) Three blind mice; (2) Reading between the lines; (3) A hole in one

License plates: (1) Tennis, anyone?; (2) For you to envy; (3) Be seeing you, too; (4) Tomatoes

Numberplays: 2 Wheels on a Bicycle; 4 Quarters in a Dollar; 5 Digits in a Zip Code; 9 Planets in the Solar System; 13 Stripes on an American Flag; 21 Dots on a Die; 26 Letters of the Alphabet; 52 Cards in a Deck

Logic puzzle.

First place: Sandy Longhorn as Imelda Marcos

Second place: Debbie Kirby as Eleanor Roosevelt

Third place: Jenny Goodman as Marie Curie

Fourth place: Amy Judd as Harriet Tubman

Fifth place: Katherine Young as Hillary Clinton

Reflection

How is critical thinking essential to surviving in the 21st century?

Companion Website

Learning Styles Application

This chart lists the four learning styles and tips based on the chapter's main ideas. Locate your learning style and read the corresponding tips to maximize your success in college.

VISUAL

Learners whose strength is visual need to see the causes of a problem and the consequences of possible solutions. You can use visual representations to determine what the best solution is.

AURAL

Aural learners can listen to or play music as a way to flex their creative muscles. Talking through or listening to possible solutions work better for you than writing down ideas.

READ/WRITE

Those who learn best by reading and writing can improve their creativity by reading books and articles about creative people and about creative solutions to problems. You also work through problem solving by brainstorming and writing out possible solutions.

KINESTHETIC

Kinesthetic learners can stretch their creative muscles by using their bodies. Exercise may clear your mind enough to think a little more clearly and creatively. Create physical models of possible solutions.

Chapter in Review

1. What kinds of thinking will you use in college?
2. Describe the critical thinking process for solving a problem.
3. Provide examples of uses for creative, analytical, and critical thinking.
4. Compare and contrast creative thinking and analytical thinking.
5. How effective is the critical thinking process? Would it be helpful in all situations? If not, describe the situations in which the critical thinking process might hinder a positive outcome. What other process would work better?

Case Scenarios

Read the following case scenarios and determine what each person should do. Refer to the information in this chapter as you write a description and plan of action for each student.

1. Joan was selected as a student ambassador for her college. One of her duties is to help prepare the fall orientation for new students. The advisors told the ambassadors that last year's new students rated orientation low because they had to wait in long lines to get registered and the information they received was too detailed and difficult to comprehend. Joan and her fellow ambassadors were asked to create a new way of providing orientation to students. What process should Joan and her fellow ambassadors follow to create a successful program for new students?

2. Sidra wants to earn money for college tuition next year, but she doesn't have the time to work 40 hours a week. If Sidra's creative thinking process results in the following ideas, explain what steps she should follow to determine the most viable solution: sell blood, tutor classmates, tattoo herself with a local company's logo and charge them for advertising, sell items on the Internet, work as a telemarketer, and house sit for friends and family members.

3. Kenya decided to apply for a loan forgiveness program that will pay all of her tuition as she completes a degree in computer networking. The loan forgiveness program requires that she find a job in networking within three months of graduation, or she will owe the full amount of her loans. After she completes a year of her degree program, she learns that the job market for networking specialists does not look promising for the next five years, which means she may have difficulty finding a job when she graduates in a year. What should Kenya do?

Research It Further

1. Using the keywords "critical thinking" and "creative thinking," search the Internet for tips on improving critical and creative thinking skills. Make a table of the different tips and present the information to your classmates.

2. Create a survey to distribute to fellow students that asks what the top concerns on campus are. Report your results to the class and choose one concern to solve using the critical thinking process.

3. Interview faculty members in different programs and ask them to provide a critical thinking scenario that a graduate in their programs would encounter at work. Ask them to work through the problem to a feasible solution. Share the different problem-solving scenarios with the class and ask them to compare and contrast the processes.

References

Diestler, S. (1998). *Becoming a critical thinker: A user friendly manual* (2nd ed.). Upper Saddle River, NJ: Prentice Hall.

Harris, R. (2002). *Creative problem solving: A step-by-step approach.* Los Angeles: Pyrczak Publishing.

Soto, M. (2005). "Bloom's Taxonomy." Retrieved Sept. 27, 2005, from www.officeport.com/edu/blooms/htm.

StockByte Royalty Free CD/Getty Images

ETHICS AND POLITICS

9

OBJECTIVES

▶ Define *ethics* and its impact both personally and professionally

 Identify the importance of maintaining *confidentiality*

Define and identify the appropriate use of *power* and power bases

▶ Understand the topics of *politics* and *reciprocity* and their appropriate use in the workplace

▶ Understand the importance of ethical decision making

I hope I shall possess firmness and virtue enough to maintain what I consider the most enviable of all titles, the character of an honest man.

George Washington (1732–1799)

▶ ETHICS DEFINED

Throughout our school days, we are told to behave ethically. In education, ethics typically refers to not cheating on homework and exams. At work, cheating can occur in all areas of a job. From the time we clock in to the time we leave the office—and even extending into the weekend, we must behave in an ethical manner. Ethical behavior is a twenty-four-hour process. Our behavior reflects our ethical values. In turn, our ethical behavior reflects and represents our company.

Ethics is a moral standard of right and wrong. Although the meaning of ethics is a simple statement, it is important to identify who and what determines what is morally right and wrong. Just as your personality is shaped by outside influences, so is your ethical makeup.

Your ethical behavior is a reflection of the influences of coworkers, friends, family, religion, and society. For example, if you associate with people who shoplift, you most likely will not view shoplifting as being unethical. As a result, you may shoplift without remorse. If your family routinely lies about a child's age to pay a lower admission fee to a movie theater or amusement park, the child is being taught that it is okay to cheat. Common religions teach that lying, cheating, and stealing are wrong. Finally, consider the influences our society and culture have on our ethical behavior. Corporate America has been bombarded with ethical scandals, and many of the marketing messages we receive on a daily basis influence our ethical behavior.

Although the preceding factors all have an enormous influence on the makeup of one's ethics, it is important to note that ethical behavior starts with the individual. As we explore the concept of ethics at work, you must remember that ethics begins with you.

▶ INFLUENCES ON ETHICS AT WORK

At work, you will be confronted with ethical issues. Many issues must be kept **confidential.** These issues include private matters such as client records, employee information, business reports, documentation, and files. Whether you are overtly told or not told to keep information within your department confidential, you have an obligation to not share information with individuals with whom the business is of no concern. This is called **implied confidentiality.** Sometimes, you may be tempted or even asked to share confidential information. Do not fall into that trap. If you are uncertain about sharing confidential information with someone, check with your boss. Doing so will demonstrate to your boss that you want to not only maintain the privacy of your department but also behave in a professional manner.

Your ethical behavior extends beyond the professionalism of how you deal with others. It is also reflected in your dependability and how you conduct yourself on company time. Remember that the company is paying you to work when you are on the job. Although at times it may be necessary to conduct personal business on company time, it is inappropriate to consistently spend your time on noncompany activities. The following activities should not be done during your work time:

- ▶ Surfing the Internet for personal business
- ▶ Taking personal telephone calls
- ▶ Making personal telephone calls (including family, personal appointments)
- ▶ Routinely exceeding the allotted break and lunch periods
- ▶ Playing computer games
- ▶ Using company supplies and equipment for nonbusiness purposes

If you must conduct personal business during work time, only do so during your break or lunch hour. Whenever possible, conduct the business before or after work hours and in a private manner.

Cory is responsible for the department's petty cash box. Cory is planning on going to lunch with friends but does not have time to stop by the ATM until later in the afternoon. Cory struggles with the thought of temporarily borrowing $10 from the petty cash box and returning the money later in the day (after a visit to the ATM). No one would ever know. Technically, it is not stealing. It is just borrowing. Cory decides the behavior is wrong, does not take the petty cash, and skips going out to lunch with friends.

◀ **EXERCISE 1: Legal Behavior:** *Based on Cory's dilemma, is Cory borrowing money from the petty cash box legal?*

Yes ☐   No ☐

Is this behavior fair?

Yes ☐   No ☐

Whom could it harm and why?

_____

_____

_____

▶ # POWER AND ETHICS

Power is one's ability to influence another's behavior. Whether you recognize it or not, everyone at work has some power. Some people understand this ability to influence others' behavior and use it appropriately. Let us first review the different types of power, what they are, and how you can increase this use of power at work. There are seven bases of power: legitimate, coercive, reward, connection, charismatic, information, and expert.

Legitimate power is the power that is given to you by the company. It includes your title and any other formal authority that comes with your position at work. **Coercive power** is also power that is derived from your formal position. However, the difference between legitimate and coercive power is that coercive power uses threats and punishment. In contrast to coercive power is **reward power.** Reward power is the ability to influence someone with something of value. Those with legitimate power can reward others with promotions, pay increases, and other incentives. You do not have to have legitimate power to reward others in the workplace. **Connection power** is based on using someone else's legitimate power. Consider the department assistant that arranges meetings based on his boss's power. This is because the department assistant has connections to a powerful individual.

◀ **EXERCISE 2: Identify What Power Can Do:** *Identify four ways employees without legitimate power can reward others.*

1. _____

2. _____

3. _____

4. _____

The last three types of power come from within. They are often referred to as types of personal power. **Charismatic power** is a type of personal power that makes people attracted to you. We all know someone who walks into a room and immediately people are attracted to her. This is because the individual with charismatic power or charisma shows a sincere interest in others. **Information power** is based upon an individual's ability to obtain and share information. Doing so makes you more valuable to those with whom you interact. **Expert power** is power that is earned by one's knowledge, experience, or expertise. Consider the company's computer repair person. On the company's organization chart, he or she is not very high in the formal chain of command. However, this individual wields a lot of power.

▶ INCREASING YOUR POWER BASES

As mentioned earlier, everyone possesses some power. The trick is to recognize, utilize, and increase your power. The easiest way to increase your legitimate power is to make people aware of your title and responsibilities. Because coercive power utilizes threats and/or punishment, coercive power should only be used when an individual is breaking policy or behaving inappropriately.

Reward power should be used daily. Whenever possible, dispense a sincere word or note of appreciation to a coworker who has assisted you or has performed exceptionally well. Doing so will develop and enhance relationships not only within your department but also outside your immediate work space. Just remember to be sincere. Increase your connection power by strengthening your network. **Networking** means meeting and developing relationships with individuals outside your immediate work area. It is important to network with individuals within and outside of your organization.

Charismatic power is increased when you focus attention on others. Make eye contact, initiate conversation, and focus the conversation on the other individual instead of on yourself. Information power is developed by attending meetings and networking. Whenever possible and without overcommitting, join committees and attend meetings. Doing so exposes you to other people and issues throughout the company. You, in turn, not only learn more about what's going on within the organization but also increase your connection or network power. Increase your expert power by practicing continual learning. Read books and business-related magazine articles and attend workshops and conferences when possible. Whenever you learn something new that can assist others at work, share this information. Coworkers will see you as the expert in the respective area.

▶ POLITICS AND RECIPROCITY

When you begin to obtain and utilize your power, you are practicing politics. **Politics** means to obtain and use power. People generally get a bad taste in their mouth when someone accuses them of being political, but this is not necessarily a bad thing. As we have discussed, it is important to recognize, increase, and utilize the various power bases at work. It is when one expects reciprocity that politics at work gets dangerous. **Reciprocity** means creating debts and obligations for doing something. Suppose you are on a time crunch and must get a report out in two hours but you need help. You ask a coworker to help you. She stops what she is doing and assists you with an hour to spare. You have just created a reciprocal relationship with the coworker. When she is in a crunch, she will not only ask you but expect you to help her out. The workplace is comprised of reciprocal relationships. Unfortunately, sometimes the phrase "you owe me" encroaches on our ability to behave ethically.

Cory has a coworker who helps Cory out with special projects when time is short. When the coworker tells Cory she needs help with something, Cory immediately responds, "Sure, no problem." Unfortunately, there is a problem. The coworker wants Cory to attend a meeting for her and tell people at the meeting that she is home sick when Cory knows she would actually be taking a miniholiday with friends. Cory tells the coworker that it would be unethical to cover for her. "But you owe me!" says the coworker. Cory is unsure what to do. After some thought, Cory tells the coworker that Cory wants to repay the favor and appreciates all the help the coworker provides but Cory's ethics cannot be compromised. Cory should expect some tension between the two, but, in the long run, the worker will respect Cory.

▶ CORPORATE VALUES/CULTURE

Each company has a corporate culture. A corporate culture is the way a company's employees behave. It is based upon the behavior of its leaders. This culture can be viewed from a corporate level and also from a departmental level. For example, if all the executives within the company are very laid-back and informal, most employees throughout the company will also be laid-back and informal. If a department supervisor is always stressed out and unprepared, the department members will most likely be stressed out and unprepared as well. This behavior also reflects an organization's ethical behavior. Companies that want to be proactive and decrease any type of unethical temptation will have and enforce an **ethics statement.** This is a formal corporate policy that addresses the issues of ethical behavior and punishment should someone behave inappropriately. As Corporate America recovers from its recent scandals, more and more companies are placing great importance on ethics statements. Included in a corporate ethics policy will be a statement regarding **conflict of interest.** A conflict of interest occurs when you are in a position to influence a decision from which you could benefit directly or indirectly.

Cory's company is looking for a flower vendor for an upcoming company event. Cory's uncle owns a local flower shop, and getting this contract would be a big financial boost to his store. Cory wonders if it would be unethical to tell his uncle about the opportunity. After some thought, Cory decides to ask the boss about the dilemma. Cory's boss explains that there is no conflict of interest if Cory does not financially benefit from the contract and encourages Cory to contact the uncle.

If there is ever any possibility that someone could accuse you of a conflict of interest, excuse yourself from the decision-making process. If you are uncertain that there is a conflict, check with your boss or the respective committee. Explain the situation and ask for your boss's or committee's opinion. To avoid a conflict of interest, many companies have strict policies on gift giving. Check with your employer to see if you are able to accept gifts from customers and/or vendors. Most companies do not allow the acceptance of gifts or have a dollar limit on the value of the gift.

◀ **EXERCISE 3: Receiving a Gift at Work:** *Your company has a strict policy on not accepting gifts valued over $15. One of the key vendors for your company sends you flowers on your birthday. The arrangement is quite large, so you know it clearly exceeds the $15 limit. What do you do?*

_____

_____

_____

_____

_____

▶ MAKING ETHICAL CHOICES

As you attempt to make ethical choices at work, it is easiest to do so by remembering the three **levels of ethical decisions.** *The first level of ethics is the law.* When confronted with an ethical issue, you must first ask if the action is legal. If the action is illegal, it is unethical.

Sometimes, a behavior is legal but may be considered unethical (i.e., just because it is legal does not mean it is right). Take the case of an individual who has a romantic relationship with someone who is married to someone else. There is no law that says having an extramarital affair is illegal. However, many consider this behavior unethical. This scenario takes us to *the second level of ethics—fairness.* Your actions/behavior should be fair to all parties involved. If, when making a decision, someone is clearly going to be harmed or is unable to defend himself or herself, the decision is probably not ethical. Note that the concept of "fairness" does not mean that everyone is happy with the outcome. It only means that the decision has been made in an impartial and unbiased manner.

It is understandable that not everyone agrees on what is right and fair. This is where *the third level of ethics—one's conscience—*must be considered. This is also when an ethical decision gets personal. In the classic Disney movie, *Pinocchio,* there was a character named Jiminy Cricket. He was Pinocchio's conscience. He made Pinocchio feel bad when Pinocchio behaved inappropriately. Just like Pinocchio, each individual has a conscience. When one knowingly behaves inappropriately, he will ultimately feel bad about his poor behavior. Some people take a bit longer to feel bad than others, but most everyone at some point feels bad when they have wronged another. Sometimes a behavior may be legal and it may be fair to others, but it still may make us feel guilty or bad. If it does, the behavior is probably unethical.

◀ **EXERCISE 4: Honesty, Part I:** *It is 9:00 p.m., it is raining, and you are hungry. You are on your way home from a long workday. You only have $5 in your wallet, so you decide to go to a fast-food drive-through restaurant to get dinner. You carefully order so as not to exceed your $5 limit. You hand the drive-through employee your $5, and he gives you change and your meal. You place it all in the passenger's seat and go home. When you get home, you discover that the fast-food employee gave you change for $20. What do you do?*

_____

_____

_____

_____

Review the scenario; apply the three levels of ethical decision making to the following questions. Is the behavior legal? Is it fair? How do you feel about keeping the money?

Is it legal to keep the money?

Yes ☐   No ☐

Is it fair to keep the money?

Yes ☐   No ☐

How do you feel about keeping the money?

_____

_____

_____

◀ **EXERCISE 5: Honesty, Part II:** *Typically, in the fast-food business, employees whose cash boxes are short or over more than once are at risk of being fired. If you initially were going to keep the money, but now you know the employee who gave you too much cash could get fired because you decided to keep the money, would you still keep the money?*

_____

_____

_____

▶ WHEN OTHERS ARE NOT ETHICAL

This chapter discusses how you should behave ethically at work. But what should you do when others are not behaving ethically? Let us go back to the three levels of ethical decision making. Everyone must abide by the law. If someone at work is breaking the law, you have an obligation to inform your employer immediately. This can be done confidentially to either your supervisor or the human resource department. If the accused are executives within the company, you are protected by the **whistle-blower law.** You cannot be fired for informing authorities of a coworker's or an employer's illegal conduct. Whenever you accuse anyone of wrongdoing, make sure you have documented facts and solid evidence. Keep track of important dates, events, and copies of evidence. Your credibility is at stake. Remember, depending on the enormity of the situation, you, as an employee, have three choices: (1) alert outside officials if the offense is illegal and extreme; (2) if the offense is not extreme and is accepted by management, accept management's decision; or (3) if the inappropriate behavior is accepted by management and you are still bothered, you must decide whether you want to continue working for the company.

Cory finds out that a certain coworker received a laptop computer from a vendor for personal use. No other employees received a laptop. The coworker said the laptop was an incentive for the company's good standing with the vendor and, because he was the employee who made the purchases, it was his right to keep the laptop. Cory thinks this is not fair and is unethical. Cory politely checks with the human resource department, and they tell Cory that the coworker can keep the laptop. Cory must accept the company's policy. Although construed as being unethical in Cory's mind, the company found no conflict with its policies. Cory decides the offense is not extreme; and, because it was accepted by management, Cory accepts management's decision.

Another common ethical issue at work occurs in the area of company theft. Company theft is not always large items such as computers or equipment. More often, it is smaller items such as office supplies. Time can also be stolen from the company. If you use company time to surf the Net, make personal calls, or take extra long breaks, you are stealing from the company. You may not realize that taking a pen or pencil home is stealing from your company. Office supplies should only be used for business purposes. Although it is heavily influenced by the company and how others view right behavior from wrong, ethical behavior starts with the individual.

◀ SUMMARY OF KEY CONCEPTS

▶ Your ethical behavior is a reflection of the influences of friends, family, religion, and society
▶ Ethical behavior starts with the individual
▶ You have an obligation to not share confidential information with individuals with whom the business is of no concern
▶ Power and power bases are effective tools to use in the workplace
▶ Be cautious to not use power and reciprocity in an unethical manner
▶ A conflict of interest occurs when you are in a position to influence a decision from which you could benefit directly or indirectly
▶ There are three levels to consider when making ethical choices: the law, fairness, and your conscience
▶ Reporting unethical behavior that is occurring within your company is called whistle blowing. Whistle blowers are protected by the law

◀ KEY TERMS

charismatic power	ethics statement	networking
coercive power	expert power	politics
confidential	implied confidentiality	power
conflict of interest	information power	reciprocity
connection power	legitimate power	reward power
ethics	levels of ethical decisions	whistle-blower law

◀ REFERENCES

Etzioni, Amitai A. *Comparative Analysis of Complex Organizations*, 4–6. (New York: The Free Press), 1961, 4–6.

French, John R. P., and Bertram Raven. "The Bases of Social Power." In *Studies in Social Power*, (Ann Arbor: University of Michigan Press, 1959), 150–67.

Kotter, John P. "Power, Dependence and Effective Management." *Harvard Business Review* (July–August 1977); 131–36.

Peale, Norman V., and Kenneth Blanchard. *The Power of Ethical Management*, (New York: William Morrow, 1988).

◀ IF YOU WERE THE BOSS

1. You have just been promoted to boss. What are the first five things you should do?
2. What is the best method of dealing with an ethical decision regarding the performance of an employee?

◀ WEB LINKS

http://www.discriminationattorney.com/eeocdfeh.shtml

http://www.whistleblowerlaws.com/protection.htm

http://www.mapnp.org/library/ethics/ethxgde.htm

◀ WORKPLACE DOs AND DON'Ts

Do always behave in an ethical manner.	*Don't* behave one way at work and another around your friends.
Do keep information confidential.	*Don't* break the company's trust.
Do recognize and increase your workplace power bases.	*Don't* use your workplace power in a harmful or unethical manner.
Do remember the three levels of ethical decision making.	*Don't* forget the impact your conscience can have on making the right decision.
Do report your company's unlawful behavior to authorities.	*Don't* constantly complain and point out others' errors.

▶ **ACTIVITIES**

ACTIVITY 1

Is it ever ethical to take paper clips, copy paper, and pens home from work?

Yes ☐   No ☐   Sometimes ☐

Support your answer.

_____

_____

_____

_____

ACTIVITY 2

List three examples you have observed in which an individual has conducted personal business in the workplace or at school that could be considered unethical. Why do you believe this behavior is unethical? What type of power was used?

BEHAVIOR	WHY IS IT UNETHICAL?	WHAT TYPE OF POWER WAS USED?
1.	1.	1.
2.	2.	2.
3.	3.	3.

ACTIVITY 3

Research a company's conflict of interest policy.

Name of company: _____

Policy: _____

_____

What would you add to the policy to make it better?

_____

_____

(*Continued*)

ACTIVITY 3 (*Continued*)

What would you eliminate?

_____

_____

What should you do if you work for a company that does not have a policy?

_____

_____

ACTIVITY 4

List a time when you overheard confidential information that should not have been shared—for example, sitting in a physician's office or overhearing a private conversation while shopping.

_____

_____

How should this situation have been better handled?

_____

_____

_____

ACTIVITY 5

Identify at least four potential areas for employee theft on a small scale.

1. _____

2. _____

3. _____

4. _____

Identify at least two potential areas for employee theft on a large scale.

1. _____

2. _____

▶ SAMPLE EXAM QUESTIONS

1. _____ is a moral standard of right and wrong.

2. _____ is your obligation to not share information with individuals with whom the business is of no concern.

3. Everyone at work has some _____. The difference is that some people understand this ability to _____ and use it appropriately.

4. A/An _____ is a formal corporate policy that addresses the issue of ethical workplace behavior.

5. _____ means creating debts and obligations for doing something.

6. A/An _____ occurs when you are in a position to influence a decision from which you could benefit directly or indirectly.

7. The first question for ethical decision making is: Is it _____?

8. The second question for ethical decision making is: Is it _____?

9. The third question for ethical decision making is: How does it _____ _____?

10

ETIQUETTE/DRESS

StockByte Royalty Free CD/Getty Images

ETIQUETTE/DRESS

OBJECTIVES

▶ Describe and discuss the importance of professional behavior in your career

▶ State the impact dress can have on others' perception of you

▶ Demonstrate a professional and correct introduction and handshake

▶ Demonstrate appropriate professional behavior in business dining situations

▶ Recognize and apply the appropriate use of technology in business/social situations

▶ Utilize professional *etiquette* in appropriate business situations

*Winning is
accomplished
in the preparation
phase, not the
execution phase.*

Anonymous

▶ EXECUTIVE PRESENCE

The way you look and behave is a reflection of the organization for which you work. You should have the attitude of an executive; this is referred to as an **executive presence**. Projecting an executive presence is important because one of the biggest concerns employers have when hiring is the employee's lack of knowledge regarding basic workplace behavior.

The purpose of this chapter is to provide basics on expected professional behavior on topics including attire, social etiquette, dining, and the appropriate use of technology. There is a reminder of what our parents taught us early in life that some have forgotten, such as smiling and saying please and thank-you. You will encounter many of these social situations daily at work, while other situations may not be as common. All are important.

Some of this information may be new to you, and you may feel awkward when you first implement these positive behaviors. The purpose of this chapter is to prepare you for many of the social experiences you will face in the workplace. Remember, practice makes perfect.

▶ INFLUENCES OF DRESS IN A PROFESSIONAL ENVIRONMENT

Both your maturity and the importance you place on your job are reflected in the way you behave and dress at work. Because impressions are often made in the first few minutes of meeting someone, individuals rarely have time to even speak before an impression is made. The majority of first impressions are made through your visual **appearance**. This means that your coworkers, bosses, and customers form attitudes based on how you look. Appearance has an impact on how you perform at work. If you dress professionally, you are more apt to act in a professional manner. The more casual you dress, the more casual you tend to behave. Think of your appearance as a frame. A frame is used to highlight a picture. You do not want the frame to be too fancy, because it will take away from the picture. You just want a frame to complement the picture. This appearance frame highlights not only your physical features, including your face, but also your attitude and potential.

◀ **EXERCISE 1: Define Your "Frame":** *What does your frame look like? Be honest with these answers.*

Is it trendy, outdated, professional, or inconsistent?

_____

Does it complement your desired appearance as a professional?

_____

If your current frame is not yet professional, what changes need to occur?

_____

_____

_____

For many students, one of the toughest transitions to make when entering the workplace is appropriate dress. Dressing professionally does not have to conflict with current fashion trends. The trick is to know what is acceptable. A basic rule of thumb is to make it a habit to dress one position higher than your current position (i.e., dress like your boss). Doing so communicates that you are serious about your career and how you represent the company. Dressing professionally may not always put you on the cover of a fashion magazine, but it will certainly assist you in projecting a favorable image at work and position you for advancement.

Know the workplace policies. One of the first steps to determining appropriate attire for work is to identify your company's **dress code**. Many organizations have policies regarding appropriate workplace attire. These policies address issues such as required attire, uniforms, hairstyle, undergarments, jewelry, and shoes. Frequently, these policies are included in the employee handbook. If there is no policy, ask your boss if there is a formal dress code and secure a copy. Another important cue to workplace attire is how managers dress. Suits are not always the preferred attire. In some situations, pants are acceptable for women, while in other situations they are not. Please note that sweats (shirts and/or pants) are not appropriate for work.

Once you have identified what your organization considers proper attire, you must begin to create a **work wardrobe**. These are clothes that you primarily wear only to work and work-related functions. You need not invest a lot of money when building a work wardrobe. Start with basic pieces and think conservative. For women, this means a simple, solid skirt in a dark color and a blazer. Skirts should not be above the knee. No one at work asks to see the tags of clothes; therefore, purchase items that fit properly. Men should select dark slacks, a matching jacket, and a tie. Frequently, these items can be found inexpensively at thrift and discount stores. If these items are purchased at a thrift store, take them to the dry cleaners for cleaning and pressing. You will be surprised how professional these items will look. Select items that are made of quality fabrics that will not wear out quickly. Also, make your selections based on fit and comfort. As you begin to earn money, continue building your wardrobe and develop a style that conforms to both company policy and your taste.

► TIPS FROM HEAD TO TOE

A woman's outfit should be a reflection of her style and personality—within reason. When dressing for work, your goal is to appropriately frame yourself in a manner that draws attention to your face (i.e., your brains and inner beauty). Regardless of your company's dress code, it is important that women heed several unspoken rules regarding professional dress at work:

► *Shower daily.* If needed, use deodorant. If you wear perfume or lotion, use it sparingly. Scent should not be overpowering.
► *Clothes should be clean and ironed, and they should fit properly.*
► *Hair should be clean, well kept, and a natural color.* Your hairstyle should reflect your profession. Fad hairstyles and unnatural color are inappropriate in many workplaces.
► *Makeup should be for day wear.* Makeup is appropriate for work. Makeup that makes people think you are going to a bar after work is not. Do not wear heavy eyeliner, eye shadow in colors that draw attention, or lipstick in bold colors.
► *It is not acceptable to wear suggestive clothing.* This means no cleavage and bare midriffs. No matter the current fashion trends, undergarments (bras, panties, and thongs) should not be visible. Remember, skirts should not be above the knee.
► *Hands and nails should be well groomed.* Should you use polish, it should be neat and color/artwork conservative. Nails that are too long are inappropriate.
► *Jewelry should be kept to a minimum.* Your jewelry should complement your outfit. Do not wear anything that is distracting or that makes noise.
► *Shoes should be in good condition.* Keep your shoes polished and free of scuffs. Heels should be in good condition; if not, get them repaired or replaced. Heels should not be too high. Heels that are too high are not appropriate for the workplace, nor are flip-flops. Nylons should be free of runs and snags.

Just like a woman's outfit, a man's outfit should be a reflection of his style and personality. For some positions, a suit may not be appropriate. The biggest wardrobe blunder men make is wearing clothing that is not clean and/or pressed. After checking with your company's dress code, heed these unspoken rules regarding professional dress at work for men:

► *Shower daily.* If needed, use deodorant. If you wear aftershave or cologne, the scent should not be overpowering.
► *Hair should be clean, neatly trimmed, and a natural color.*

- ▷ *Shave and/or trim facial hair.*
- ▷ *Clothes should be clean, ironed, of proper fit, and not torn or tattered.*
- ▷ *In an office environment, dress pants are the only pants that are professional.* With the exception of casual workdays, jeans are inappropriate. Baggy pants that reveal underwear are also inappropriate. Whenever possible, wear a neutral, plain belt that does not draw attention.
- ▷ *Shirts should be tucked in.* A polo shirt or a dress shirt with a tie is best. Shirts should not display excessive wear (check around the collar line). Shirts with inappropriate logos or offensive phrases should not be worn at work.
- ▷ *Shoes should be clean and in good condition.* Flip-flops are not appropriate for the workplace. Sock color should match shoe or pant color.
- ▷ *Hands should be clean and well groomed* (i.e., clean, trim nails).
- ▷ *Hats should not be worn inside buildings.*

◁ **EXERCISE 2: Professional Dress List:** *What do you have?*

Take inventory of your current wardrobe.

_____

_____

_____

List clothing you own that you can use for your professional wardrobe.

_____

_____

_____

List the necessities that you are missing.

_____

_____

_____

▷ JEWELRY, BODY PIERCING, AND TATTOOS

Although body piercing and body rings/jewelry appear to be current fads, they are offensive to some individuals. For this reason, it is important that you check with your company regarding its policies. However, in general:

- ▷ Nose rings, lip rings, and/or tongue rings are not professional and should not be worn in a professional setting.
- ▷ Any other body piercing/body jewelry should not be visible at work.
- ▷ More than two earrings worn on each ear is considered unprofessional.
- ▷ Earrings and other jewelry should not draw attention. This includes symbols or words that could be considered offensive to others.

Hiding a tattoo is difficult. If you are thinking about getting a tattoo, consider the long-term consequences. They are painful and expensive to remove and are designed to last a lifetime.

▶ CASUAL WORKDAYS AND SPECIAL EVENTS

Many companies offer something called **casual workdays**. These are days when companies relax their dress code. Unfortunately, too many employees attempt to stretch the term *casual*. If your company has a casual Friday, remember that you are still at work and should dress appropriately. Of course, you can wear jeans if jeans are the preferred attire; just adhere to the *head-to-toe tips* recently presented. Do not wear clothing that is tattered, stained, or torn (even if it is considered stylish).

Your company may also play host or invite you to attend a special function. Holiday parties and receptions are such examples. In these situations, instead of daily work attire, more formal attire may be required. Just as with casual Fridays, stick with the basics provided in the *head-to-toe tips*. Women, if appropriate, wear something in a more formal fabric. Although you have more freedom and flexibility regarding style and length, this is still a work-related function, so remember to dress conservative and not suggestive. Men, check ahead of time and see if tuxedos are preferred. Although seldom required these days, if one is required, you may need to rent one. For most occasions, a suit will suffice.

As a reward for winning Employee of the Month, Cory was invited to attend a one-day conference/luncheon with several managers from Cory's company. Cory had not attended a function like this before and was a little nervous about how to dress and behave in this new business situation. Cory did some preparation and found that dress and behavior are as important in public situations as they are at work. Cory decided dressing more formal would be most appropriate. Cory made sure to shower, clean and trim fingernails, wear polished shoes, and not wear inappropriate jewelry.

▶ BUSINESS ETIQUETTE

Because we live in a modern society, human interaction is unavoidable. Our society has a standard of social behavior that is called **etiquette**. Typically, when individuals think of etiquette, they think it only applies to the wealthy, high society. This is not true. Socially acceptable behavior should penetrate all demographic and economic groups. Individuals wanting to succeed in the workplace need to heed this protocol and consistently utilize it not only at work but in all areas of their life.

Before we study common areas of business etiquette, we need to define a few terms. Understanding these terms and implementing them into your daily behavior will make it much easier to carry out the desired and appropriate workplace behavior. The first word is **courtesy**. When you display courtesy, you are exercising manners, respect, and consideration toward others. The second word is **respect**. Respect is defined as holding someone in high regard. This means putting others' needs before your own needs. Both courtesy and respect are the keys in becoming ladies and gentlemen at work.

Some of the first words parents teach young children are *please* and *thank-you*. Although they are not used as frequently as they should be, they are extremely powerful words that can actually create power for you at work. Think about it; when someone says "please" and "thank-you" to you, you are more likely to repeat a favor or gesture because your deed was acknowledged. When someone does something nice, verbally say "thanks." Not doing so makes you appear selfish and unappreciative. When you express thanks, individuals will be more likely to continue performing kind acts for you.

Make it a habit to write a thank-you note when someone does something for you that takes more than five minutes or when someone gives you a gift. Do not wait more than three days to write the thank-you note. Write the note as soon as possible. Always send a thank-you note within twenty-four hours of completing a job interview, and remember to send thank-you notes to individuals who agree to be job references for you.

In addition to saying "please" and "thank-you," do not underestimate the value of a simple smile and eye contact. If you have a positive attitude, it will be reflected in your demeanor. When encountering people in the hallways, elevators, and/or meeting rooms, make eye contact and smile.

At times, you will be with individuals who do not know each other. When you are with two people who do not know each other and you know both people, it is your responsibility to introduce the two individuals to each other. This is called an introduction. Politely introduce the least important person to the most important person. For example, "Roger, this is Tim Wilson, the president of our company." "Tim, this is Roger Hue, my next-door neighbor." This rule should be applied in all social situations including dining, meetings, receptions, and parties.

A daily element of business is making and keeping appointments. Always be kind to the receptionist and/or administrative assistant. These individuals are not only the gatekeepers to their bosses; they also control schedules and often wield great power in decisions. When scheduling an appointment, always state your name, the purpose of the meeting, and the desired date/time. If possible, avoid scheduling appointments on Monday mornings. Others are attempting to schedule their own week and are less likely to accommodate you. When keeping an appointment, arrive five minutes early. When you enter the office, greet the receptionist and politely introduce yourself. Then state whom you have an appointment with and the time of the meeting. When entering an office for a meeting, wait to be invited to sit down. After the meeting, extend a handshake and thank the individual for his or her time. If you will be arriving late to an appointment, call and let the other party know you are running late. If you must cancel an appointment, do so immediately and apologize for any inconvenience. Do not just ignore an appointment.

▶ HANDSHAKES

A good handshake conveys confidence. Approach the individual you are greeting and extend your right hand as you verbalize a greeting. For example, "Hello Ms. Jones, my name is Danielle. We met at last week's meeting. It's nice to see you again." Ms. Jones will extend her right hand. Your two hands should meet at the web (see Figure 1). Grip the other person's hand and gently squeeze and shake hands.

▶ Do not squeeze the other hand too firmly.
▶ Make certain you shake the entire hand and not just the other person's fingers. Doing so is insulting and implies that you feel you are better than the other person.

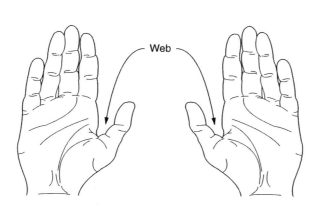

◀ **FIGURE 1** Proper Handshake

▶ Do not place your hand on top of the other person's hand or pat the hand. Once again, doing so is insulting.

▶ If your palms are sweaty, discretely wipe your palm on the side of your hip prior to shaking.

Remember to always make eye contact and smile while extending your hand. A good handshake takes practice. Get into the habit of being the first to greet and introduce yourself to others. Practice makes perfect. The more frequently you initiate a good handshake, the more comfortable and confident you will become. See Figure 1.

◀ **EXERCISE 3: Shake Hands:** *Pair up with a classmate and practice initiating an introduction making sure to include a professional handshake. Rate the quality of the introduction and handshake on a scale of 1 to 5 with 5 being the best. Discuss what improvements should be made.*

▶ DINING

Apart from fast food, few college students are generally comfortable eating in a formal dining situation. Here are a several rules of thumb regarding dining etiquette:

▶ As soon are you are seated, place your napkin on your lap. If you need to leave the table, place your napkin to the side of your plate. Do not place your napkin on your chair.

▶ Utensils are set to be used in order of necessity. As your courses are served, start with the outside utensil and work in, toward the plate. The utensils set at the top of the plate are for your dessert.

▶ When serving coffee, water, tea, or any other beverage available at the table, first offer and serve others at your table.

▶ Do not order alcohol unless others at your table first order an alcoholic beverage. Abstaining from alcohol is the most desired behavior. If you choose to drink, limit consumption to one drink.

▶ When bread is available, first offer bread to others at your table before taking a piece.

▶ Place your bread on the bread plate (located at the top left corner of your dinner plate). Place your serving of butter on the bread plate. Do not butter the entire piece of bread at one time. Tear a piece of bread, and butter only that piece of bread before eating.

▶ Do not take the last piece of bread or appetizer unless it is first offered to others at your table.

▶ When your meal arrives, do not begin eating until everyone at your table has been served. If everyone receives their meals except you (you are the last to be served), give others at your table permission to begin eating without you so that their food does not get cold.

▶ Do not eat your meal with your fingers unless your main course can be eaten without utensils.

▶ Burping and slurping are inappropriate while dining. If you accidentally burp or slurp, make sure you immediately apologize and say "excuse me."

▶ When you are finished eating, place your knife and fork together, with the blade facing in and the tines up. When you are only resting and you do not want the server to take your plate away, cross your utensils with the tines facing down.

▶ It is inappropriate to use a cell phone while dining. If you must take a call, excuse yourself from the table.

In business, you will encounter a variety of dining situations. Some dining experiences will be less formal than others. You will most likely encounter some form of the table setting illustrated in Figure 2. Take time to study and review a common place setting to help you understand proper use for utensils, plates, and cups. As you eat, you should use the utensils from outside toward the plate.

1	napkin
2	plate
3	salad fork
4	dinner fork
5	dinner knife
6	teaspoon
7	soup spoon
8	salad plate
9	bread plate
10	butter knife
11	dessert spoon
12	dessert fork
13	water glass
14	beverage/wine glass
15	coffee cup and saucer

◀ **FIGURE 2** Table Setting

When Cory arrived at the conference, Cory was glad to be dressed professionally. Everyone there was dressed as a business professional. Cory was introduced to many business professionals. Cory was sure to make eye contact, smile, and properly shake hands when meeting new people. Cory was also careful to follow dining etiquette during lunch. At work the next day, Cory immediately wrote a thank-you note to the managers for being included in the event. At the end of the day, Cory's manager invited Cory into the office and let Cory know what a great impression Cory made at the conference. Several colleagues had mentioned to Cory's manager how impressed they were with Cory's professionalism. Cory realized that doing a little research and being professional were well worth the effort.

A major area of business involves attending social functions. Many invitations request an RSVP, which is French for "répondez s'il vous plaît" (i.e., please respond). As soon as you receive an invitation, send a reply—whether it is an acceptance to attend or regrets. Not acknowledging the invitation and failing to respond are rude.

When you attend a social function, remember that you are attending the function to meet with other professionals, not to receive your last meal.

▶ Refrain from or limit the consumption of alcohol.
▶ Only serve yourself a small plate of hors d'oeuvres and move away from the food table.
▶ Hold your hors d'oeuvres in your left hand, leaving your right hand free to shake hands and greet others.
▶ Do not talk with food in your mouth.

▶ TECHNOLOGY AT WORK

Cell phone usage, messages, voice mail, e-mails—it all gets so confusing! This section provides some basic rules for the appropriate use of communications.

CELL PHONES AND OTHER PORTABLE DEVICES

➤ Turn off cell phones when you are attending a meeting (business, education, religious, or others).
➤ If you are anticipating an emergency call, turn off the ringer of your phone.
➤ Do not use your phone while dining or while attending meetings and performances (including movies).
➤ Do not take or make a call in front of others. Excuse yourself and step away for privacy. Taking or making a call in front of others implies that they are not important.
➤ It is inappropriate to use or display portable music devices when with others.

TELEPHONE MESSAGES

Voice-mail messages are a routine part of conducting business. It is important to remember that a voice-mail impression is equally as important as how you answer the telephone. The following are tips regarding telephone messages:

➤ Keep telephone messages brief.
➤ State your name, purpose of the call, and return telephone number.
➤ Speak slowly and clearly.
➤ Repeat your name and return number at the end of your message.
➤ Promptly return telephone messages.
➤ Keep your voice-mail greetings professional. Cute voice-mail greetings are not professional. Musical introductions or bad jokes do not form favorable impressions when employers or customers are attempting to contact you.

E-MAIL AND COMPUTER USAGE

In addition to all other workplace tools and equipment, your computer at work is the property of the company. Therefore, only use it for company business. This includes Internet use and electronic messaging.

➤ Emoticons (faces made and embedded in e-mail messages) are inappropriate at work.
➤ Do not forward messages that do not involve work-related issues.
➤ Check all messages for spelling and grammar before responding.
➤ Do not send e-mail with large and colorful letters or all capital letters. This is interpreted as yelling and is considered rude.
➤ If you receive a work-related message that requests a reply, respond to the message. Ignoring the message is not only rude, it communicates to the sender that you do not care. You also run the risk that you will be excluded from future messages.
➤ Always include the business subject in the subject line to let the receiver know it is not junk e-mail or a virus. The subject "hello" or "hi" is not appropriate.
➤ Carefully proofread and think about a message before you press Reply to ensure that it cannot be interpreted improperly.

➤ OTHER ETIQUETTE BASICS

➤ *Knock before entering an office.* Do not enter an office until you are invited. If the individual you want to see is with someone else, wait your turn. If the matter is urgent, apologize for interrupting.
➤ *Put others first.* When you are with colleagues and you are taking turns (in line, to order, etc.), allow your colleagues go to first.
➤ *Interruptions.* In today's society, we have so many inputs trying to attract our attention. As a result, we often get anxious to share our point of view in a conversation and fail to allow

others in the conversation to complete their sentence. Interrupting is a bad habit and is considered rude behavior. If you accidentally interrupt someone, immediately apologize and ask him or her to continue his or her statement.

▶ *Apologies.* Everyone is human. Therefore, everyone makes mistakes. When you realize that you may have said or done something hurtful to someone, apologize immediately. Apologizing is not a sign of weakness; it is a sign of strength and maturity. Even if you are not sure whether you have offended someone, apologize to avoid any potential misunderstandings. However, do not unnecessarily and continually apologize. Doing so gives you the appearance of being needy and insecure.

▶ *Dominating a conversation.* There is a key to carrying on a successful conversation. The key is listening. Listening means that you value the information the other individual is providing. Too frequently, individuals dominate the conversation with their own personal accounts. In general, this is not appropriate. This behavior becomes annoying when you begin to turn the conversation to yourself. Next time you are in a conversation, listen to how many times you state the words *me, I,* and *my.* Try to minimize the use of these words in your conversation.

◀ SUMMARY OF KEY CONCEPTS

▶ Projecting an executive presence is important in demonstrating knowledge of basic workplace behavior
▶ The majority of first impressions are made through your visual appearance
▶ Both your maturity and the importance you place on your job are reflected in the way you behave and dress at work
▶ You must begin to create a work wardrobe now
▶ Body piercing and body rings/jewelry appear to be current fads; they are offensive to some individuals. Consider the long-term consequences of getting a tattoo
▶ To succeed in the workplace, you need to follow etiquette protocol and consistently utilize it in all areas of your life
▶ Make a habit of thanking individuals either verbally or in writing
▶ Appropriate etiquette at social functions and while dining is as important as professional behavior at work

◀ KEY TERMS

appearance	dress code	respect
casual workdays	etiquette	work wardrobe
courtesy	executive presence	

◀ REFERENCE

Post, Peggy, and Peter Post. *The Etiquette Advantage in Business: Personal Skills for Professional Success.* New York: HarperCollins Publishers, Inc., 1999.

◀ IF YOU WERE THE BOSS

1. As the manager of a bank, one of your employees comes in on a Monday morning with a pierced tongue and purple hair. What should you do?
2. You have just hired a new employee who clearly has no concept of business etiquette. What specific steps would you take to teach your new employee how to behave professionally?

◀ WEB LINKS

http://www.ravenwerks.com/practices/etiquette.htm

http://www.youngmoney.com/careers/monstertrak/on_the_job/095

http://www.yorktech.com/department/jobplacement/Profdress.htm

◀ WORKPLACE DOs AND DON'Ts

Do wear professional clothes to work.	*Don't* wear sweats, tennis shoes, or suggestive apparel at work.
Do shower and make sure you are always clean.	*Don't* overdo the cologne (or any body sprays).
Do make sure you make eye contact and offer a gentle but firm handshake.	*Don't* grasp just the fingers when shaking hands.
Do follow formal dining etiquette at work-related functions.	*Don't* reach, grab, or overload your plate at the hors d'oeuvres table.
Do say "please" and "thank-you" when appropriate.	*Don't* assume that the other person knows you are thankful for his or her act of kindness.

► ACTIVITIES

ACTIVITY 1

Assume you are starting a new job as an accounting clerk next week and you need some professional clothes. You need to go shopping for your work wardrobe and are limited to a $50 budget. Make a list of what you need and could buy to get you through your first week of work. Include the cost.

WHAT YOU NEED TO BUY	COST
	$
Total Cost	$50

Prior to being faced with this scenario, what items can you purchase today to begin building your professional wardrobe?

ACTIVITY 2

Pretend you are at a business reception and you do not know anyone else in the room. Role-play formal introductions with a classmate, then evaluate your partner's performance by identifying strengths and weaknesses.

Student Name	
STRENGTHS	**WEAKNESSES**

Student Name	
STRENGTHS	**WEAKNESSES**

ACTIVITY 3

Visit a (non fast food) restaurant to practice proper dining etiquette. While you are doing so, identify five acts of inappropriate behavior others are exhibiting.

	INAPPROPRIATE BEHAVIOR	WHY BEHAVIOR IS INAPPROPRIATE
1.		
2.		
3.		
4.		
5.		

▶ SAMPLE EXAM QUESTIONS

1. The majority of first impressions are made by _____.

2. One of the first steps to determining appropriate attire for work is to identify _____.

3. Give five tips for women for dressing professionally from head to toe. _____, _____, _____, _____, _____.

4. Give five tips for men for dressing professionally from head to toe. _____, _____, _____, _____, _____.

5. A standard of social behavior is called _____.

6. When someone does something nice for you, you should _____.

7. A good handshake conveys _____.

8. Give five rules of thumb regarding dining etiquette. _____, _____, _____, _____, _____.

Getty Images, Inc./Photodisc/Spike Mafford

CUSTOMER SERVICE/QUALITY

11

OBJECTIVES

► Define *productivity* and its impact on organizational success

► Identify and define *directional statements*

► Know the various types of plans used in an organization

► Define the primary business functions and their purpose in an organization

► Define *quality* and its importance in business

► State the difference between a *product* and a *service*

► Identify and describe the importance of *customers* and *customer service*

► Describe how to handle a difficult customer

There are only two qualities in the world: efficiency and inefficiency, and only two sorts of people: the efficient and the inefficient.

George Bernard Shaw (1856–1950)

▶ PRODUCTIVITY IN THE WORKPLACE

Part of your workplace success will be based upon your understanding of the business, the way it is organized, and its overall purpose. Without an understanding of the business as a whole, it is difficult for you to be a good employee. This chapter addresses these issues.

The purpose of a business is to make a profit. Moreover, the business has hired you to be productive. Workplace **productivity** means to perform a function that adds value to the company. Whatever you produce (called *output*) should always assist the company in achieving its mission. It is your responsibility to help the company be successful. There are several ways of doing this. First and foremost, you must behave ethically. You should always make ethical choices that serve the best interest of the company. It is your responsibility to take care of company resources that have been entrusted to you. This includes eliminating waste and producing quality products. Your attitude assists the company with becoming successful. Maintain a positive attitude. Be an active team member and work to create positive workplace relationships. You should be open to learning new skills.

A company's **mission statement** is its statement of purpose. It identifies why everyone comes to work. An example of a college's mission statement is to make students successful. This means not only providing a solid education but also preparing students to succeed on the job or with their continuing education. If all college employees know their ultimate purpose is to make students successful, every activity they perform on the job should contribute to student success. Either prior to starting your job or within your first week at work, secure a copy of your company's mission statement. If possible, memorize it. A copy should be included in your employee handbook and/or provided to you during the employee orientation. If this information is not provided, ask your supervisor or the human resource department for a copy.

A company will not survive without being profitable; even nonprofit organizations need to make a profit to accomplish their mission. However, a company is not successful just because it turns a profit. There are several important elements that contribute to a company's success. These include satisfied customers who have purchased a quality product produced by motivated employees. Moreover, successful companies are accountable to various stakeholders including their investors, the community at large, the environment, and their employees. Factors within the business environment are always changing, so it is important that companies constantly monitor changes and be proactive in meeting the needs of various stakeholders.

Once a company has identified why it exists, it must identify where it wants to be in the future. This is called a **vision statement**. A company's vision statement is its viable view of the future. For example, a college may want to be the top-ranked college in the nation. It will take work, but it is achievable. In addition to the company's mission and vision statements, every company should have a values statement. The **values statement** defines what is important to (or what the priorities are) for the company. This could include providing a healthy return to investors, taking care of the environment, taking care of its employees, or keeping customers satisfied. Included in the company values statement will typically be the company's code of conduct or ethics statement. These statements discuss the importance of behaving ethically in all areas of business.

Together, the company's mission, vision, and values statements comprise the organization's **directional statements**. These statements create the foundation of why the company exists and how it will operate.

For example, Cory's company was updating its strategic plan and was asking for volunteers to sit on various committees. Cory questioned if new employees were qualified to sit on these committees. Cory decided to ask a coworker. The coworker encouraged Cory to participate and said it would be a great way for Cory to learn more about the company, get to know people throughout the organization, and help make positive changes for the company's overall success. Cory's coworker then showed Cory the back side of Cory's name badge. On it was printed the company's mission statement. "This," Cory's coworker proudly said, "is why we come to work everyday." Cory signed up for a committee that afternoon.

Each company should have a strategy. The company's **strategy** is its road map for success. Typically, a **strategic plan** is a formal document that is developed by senior management. The strategic plan identifies how the company will secure, organize, utilize, and monitor its resources. **Company resources** include financial (fiscal), human (employees), and capital (long-term investments).

The formal strategic plan is generally not available to all employees. However, many companies provide brief summaries or overviews to all employees to keep everyone focused on priorities and goals. Just as you created a personal plan earlier in this text, all areas of the company will have smaller plans with stated **goals** and **objectives** that identify how their respective areas will assist in achieving the company's strategy. A goal is a broad statement or aim while an objective supports the goal. Remember that an objective must be short-term and measurable. Each area of the company will utilize its respective resources and have its performance monitored based upon the company strategy and goals.

◀ **EXERCISE 1: Create Job Goals:** *Assume you started your new job today as a receptionist for a law firm. Write one goal and two objectives for your new job.*

Goal	
Objective 1	
Objective 2	

▶ LINES OF AUTHORITY

Company functions and resources within the business are organized according to the company's mission and strategy. The way a company is organized is called its **organizational structure**. The graphic visual display of this structure is called the company **organizational chart**. This chart not only identifies key functions within the company but also shows the formal lines of authority for employees. These formal lines of authority are also referred to as the *chain of command*. The formal lines of authority will identify who reports to whom within the company. It is important to remember that you must respect and follow the formal lines of authority within your company. For example, using the organizational chart in Figure 1, it is inappropriate for the accounts

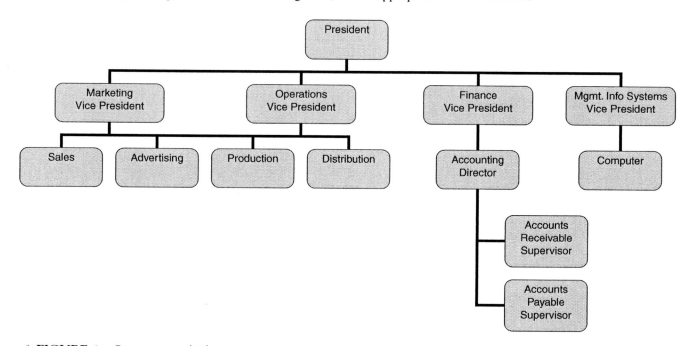

◀ **FIGURE 1**   Organizational Chart

payable supervisor to directly approach the marketing vice president for a request without prior approval from the accounting director.

This story is a good example of why you should know your organizational structure and identify your superiors. One day Cory was left alone in the department while everyone was away at an important meeting. A tall man walked through the doors and asked to see Cory's boss. Cory explained that the boss was currently out. The gentleman began asking about how Cory felt about the company, including how long Cory had worked for the company and if Cory were able to change one thing in the company what it would be. Cory found the questions strange but interesting. Cory was honest in the answers provided, always keeping the conversation polite and positive but constructive. The gentleman thanked Cory for the input and left. Two weeks later, Cory's boss returned from a meeting and told Cory that the CEO of the company had shared Cory's comments with key executives in identifying ways to improve employee morale. It was then that Cory realized that the earlier conversation was with the CEO of the company. Cory was relieved to have been polite and positive in the CEO conversation but regretted not recognizing the CEO when he first walked into the office.

Each company has a leader (see Figure 2). The leader is typically called the **president or chief executive officer (CEO)**. The president or CEO reports to the company **board of directors**. This group of individuals is responsible for developing the company's overall strategy and major policies. The people who become the company's board of directors are elected by shareholders or investors. Smaller companies may not have such a formal structure and/or titles, but every business has investors (owners) and a leader (president). It is important to become familiar with your leaders' names and titles and the formal lines of authority. This will allow you to determine whom you can go to if there is a question or problem. If possible, try to view updated photos of these individuals so that, if the appropriate opportunity arises, as with Cory's experience, you can introduce yourself to them.

Within a typical company structure are three different levels of management (see Figure 3). These levels include senior management, middle management, and operations management. **Senior managers or executives** typically have the title of *vice president*. These individuals work with the president in identifying and implementing the company strategy. The time line for **strategic issues** typically ranges from three to five years or more. **Middle managers** typically have the title of *director* or *manager*. These individuals work on tactical issues. **Tactical issues** identify how to link the strategy into the reality of day-to-day operations. The time line for tactical issues is one to three years. **Operations managers**, typically *supervisors* and *assistant managers*, work on **operational issues**. These are issues within the company that occur on a daily

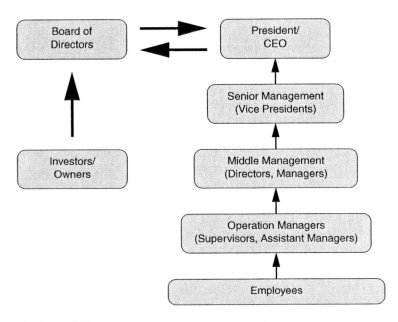

◀ **FIGURE 2** Formal Structure

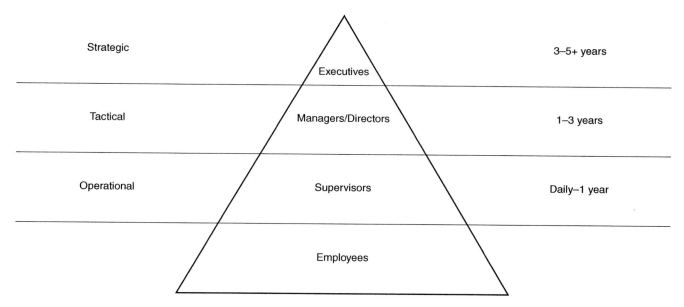

◀ FIGURE 3   Management Levels

basis and/or no longer than one year. As you begin to develop your career, you will have the opportunity to advance into a position of leadership. Your first step into a management position will be that of a **supervisor**. And, although supervisors only concern themselves with operational issues, successful employees and supervisors understand the bigger picture of the company's overall tactics and strategy.

As displayed in a typical organizational chart, companies are typically arranged by major functions. These major functions are frequently referred to as **divisions**. Within these divisions are **departments**. The departments carry out specific functions respective of their division. A number of major functions (divisions) are necessary in business. These include finance and accounting, human resource management, operations, information systems, marketing, and legal counsel.

The **finance and accounting** department is responsible for the securing, distribution, and growth of the company's financial assets. These individuals handle everything within the company that has to do with money. Any invoices (company bills) or incoming cash or checks must be recorded through the accounting department. The accounting department will work with the human resource department on payroll issues regarding your paycheck. Because the primary purpose of every company is to make a profit, you, as an employee, are accountable for how you utilize the company's financial resources. Just as you have a personal budget, every company utilizes **budgets**. A budget is a plan used to allocate money. There are several types of budgets including a **capital budget** and an **operational budget**. The capital budget is used for long-term investments including land and large pieces of equipment. An operational budget is used for short-term items including payroll and the day-to-day costs associated with running a business.

Here is an example that shows the importance of budgeting. One of Cory's coworkers went on vacation. Before leaving, Cory's coworker showed Cory how to order office supplies online and asked Cory to order more supplies if the department fell short. Cory noticed that the department was running low on a few items and decided to place an order. As Cory clicked through the online catalog, Cory saw a lot of items that would be nice to have around the office, including a new hole punch, a label maker, and multicolored vinyl file folders. Cory also thought it would be nice to have a pair of new scissors, a tape dispenser, and other personal desk items. As Cory was about to place the order, Cory was shocked to see that the total was over $1,000. Cory realized that the coworker never gave Cory a budget. Cory decided to order only the necessities and wait to ask the coworker about the other items.

As illustrated in the Cory example, too frequently, nonmanagement employees do not think before they spend the company's money. Before you spend the company's money, ask yourself a simple question: "If I owned this company, would I spend my money on this item?" Answering that simple question makes you more accountable for your actions and makes you think like a business owner. You most likely will not spend your money on frivolous, unnecessary items and will pay more attention to not only adhering to a budget but also identifying ways to save money.

The **human resource management** department deals with recruiting, hiring, training, evaluating, compensating, promoting, and terminating employees. This function deals with the employee (people) side of business. Your first contact with this function will be when you apply and interview for a job. You will also interact with the human resource department for any issue regarding company policy, complaints and grievances, and your terms of employment.

The **operations** function deals with the production and distribution of the company's product or service. It is the core of the business. Even if your position does not directly contribute to the primary purpose of the company, it is your job to support individuals whose job it is to produce and distribute the product or service.

The **information systems** department deals with the management of information within the organization. This division is responsible for ensuring that the company appropriately utilizes its computer/technology resources. As an employee, you assist and support the information systems department by only utilizing company technology for work-related business. You should report any computer virus and system problems immediately.

Marketing is responsible for creating, pricing, selling, distributing, and promoting the company's product or service. As is discussed later in this chapter, there are internal and external customers and it is every employee's responsibility to assist in satisfying the customer's needs. Therefore, regardless of your position, it is your job to contribute to producing a high-quality, high-value product. You are a walking billboard for your company. Remember that your behavior both at and away from work represents the company. Never speak poorly of your company, coworkers, or the company's product or service.

Finally, the company's **legal counsel** handles all legal matters relating to the business. You should always check with the company's legal department prior to engaging in a contract on behalf of the company.

Large companies may have separate divisions for each of these functions, while smaller companies combine several functions into a single division, department, or position. Note that not all companies have all the formal departments, titles, or organizational charts described in this chapter. Most small businesses will not have such formal structures. However, to be successful, they will have someone who performs these important functions for the business.

▶ QUALITY AND THE COMPANY

If someone asked you to describe a company, you would most likely describe a building, its employees, and the product produced. In some respects, you are right. These are major elements that define a company, but a company needs customers to succeed. Excellent service, quality, and innovation are what will persuade customers to purchase a company's product or service. More important, a successful company's employees and products must make customers want to make a repeat purchase.

As an employee, you are an important part of the company. Every job in the company has a purpose; therefore, every employee is important to a company. Although administration may lead what is being done in the company, your job is necessary to help run the company. This is what makes you an important part of the company. Therefore, you must do your best at all times. **Quality** is a predetermined standard that defines how a product is to be produced or a service is to be provided. Customers demand quality not just in the product they purchase but also from the company employees. If customers do not perceive that they have received a quality product or service, they will not make a repeat purchase.

Customer loyalty is another important element that contributes to the success of a company. If a customer perceives she has received value and a quality product, she will display loyalty to your company by making a repeat purchase. Companies want to build brand loyalty with customers. This means that the customer will not substitute your product for that of a competing product. Customers will be loyal to a company and its products when quality products and service are consistently provided.

Employee loyalty is an employee's obligation to consistently support a company and its mission. Displaying loyalty contributes to a company's success. Employees can show their loyalty in several ways. The most obvious is for you to do your job and do it well. Another way to show loyalty to the company is to show respect for company policies, your coworkers, and the company's customers. Also, you should make every effort to promote the company and its products. To do this, you must understand the company and know the mission, strategy, and business structure of the company you work for.

The success of a company depends on profit. **Profit** is revenue (money coming in from sales) minus expenses (the costs involved in running the business). You can help create profit for your company by monitoring and decreasing expenses and identifying ways to increase sales. You should be aware of expenses you incur at work and make every effort to eliminate waste. You should also find ways to be involved with and take responsibility toward better knowing your customers and the community. As profits increase, the company can grow. This means a company can expand into a larger space, add more sites, offer more services and/or products, increase your pay and benefits, and/or hire additional employees. For you, as an employee, this could result in raises or promotions.

Some companies sell only products, some sell only services, and some sell both. A **product** is a tangible item, that is, something that you can physically see or touch. Appliances, toys, or equipment are examples of tangible products. A **service** is an intangible product. In other words, you cannot always touch or see the product. Examples of services include haircuts, banking, golf courses, and medical services. You need to differentiate between a company's service and customer service. This is explained in more detail later in this chapter.

◀ **EXERCISE 2: Compare Product Businesses to Service Businesses:** *Identify the following items as either products or services.*

Item	Product	Service
Movies		
Gasoline		
Photography		
Restaurant		
College class		

▶ WHO IS THE CUSTOMER?

All functions of a company are important. However, what you must remember is that a company cannot survive without customers. This makes it extremely important to know who your customers are and how to treat them. A **customer** is one who buys a service or product. It can be anyone with a want or need who is willing to pay for a product or service that fills that want or need.

A company has internal and external customers. Internal customers are fellow employees and departments that exist within a company. External customers are individuals whom the company serves outside. These include customers, vendors, and investors. You may have a job that never allows you to interact with the company's external customers, but you must serve and treat your internal customers as well as the company expects employees to treat its external customers. Doing so makes it easier for employees who interact with external customers to do so successfully.

◀ **EXERCISE 3: Identify Professional Treatment in the Workplace:** *As a customer, how do you expect to be treated?*

_____

_____

How do you want your coworkers to treat you?

_____

_____

A satisfied customer will make a repeat purchase. More important, maintaining satisfied customers is one of the best ways to sell your product or service because they will encourage others to buy your product. In contrast, unsatisfied customers will spread the word about their dissatisfaction even faster than satisfied customers spread the word about their satisfaction. Think about how many times you have been satisfied or unsatisfied about a product or service. When others ask you if you know about a particular product, you will tell them whether your experience was good or bad. The reason satisfaction is important is that most people will tell about the problems and bad experiences without prompting, or without anyone asking. You do not want people bad-mouthing your company or product.

To create a satisfied customer, you need a high-quality product or service and excellent customer service. This can only occur with quality employees producing their product with quality materials (inputs). This concept is best expressed in the equation found in Figure 4.

▶ QUALITY

When it comes to quality, the expectation of customers is high. With increased technology and competition, customers demand high-quality products and services. Customers expect that a product will last. Customers also expect **value**, which means customers believe they are getting a good deal for the price they have paid. Companies that cannot compete on this issue cannot experience long-term success.

If your job is to help create a product, keep in mind that if you do your job well and the product is of high quality, customers will be happy and keep buying the product. Good-quality products can only be achieved if you, as an employee, are doing your job well.

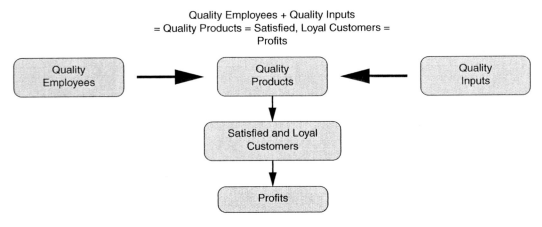

◀ **FIGURE 4**   Quality

◀ **EXERCISE 4: Taking Responsibility for Quality:** *As an employee, list five ways you can take personal responsibility for quality at work.*

1. _____

2. _____

3. _____

4. _____

5. _____

Customers measure product quality by comparing your product to similar products. They also measure quality by how satisfied they are after consuming or using a product. Successful companies include performance monitors in their strategies. Performance monitors identify how success will be measured. An example would be employee evaluations. The evaluation can identify how an employee's performance contributes to customer quality. Monitors, or standards, may include defect rates, expenses, or sales quotas. This evaluation can include areas of quality and service that are done well and those that need improvement. Evaluation criteria can also include areas such as response time, attitude toward customers, and the right use of resources.

As mentioned earlier in this chapter, the marketing department is responsible for the pricing, development, distribution, and promotion of a product. Although these functions are the primary responsibility of the marketing department, projecting a positive image and selling the company's product are the jobs of every employee within the organization. The premise that marketing is everyone's job is commonly referred to as the *marketing concept*.

▶ EXCELLENT CUSTOMER SERVICE DEFINED

An important concept you must remember in regard to workplace quality is the definition of customer service. **Customer service** is the treatment an employee provides the customer, whether the customer is purchasing a service or a product.

Customers expect excellent customer service. They want to be treated with respect and kindness. They not only want but expect employees to be competent, dependable, and responsive. They also expect the business environment to be clean, safe, and organized.

As a **competent** employee, you should know the product(s) your company offers. You should be able to answer questions when the customer asks. Customers expect you to be able to help them decide on a purchase by giving them correct information about the product. If you cannot answer a question, you should be able to direct the customer to another employee who can.

Dependable means that you are capable and honest when assisting a customer. Always speak the truth. Do not pretend to know something when you do not know the answer to a customer's question. Customers expect you to help them solve their problems. There is no shame in admitting that you do not know an answer. You will gain respect in admitting that you do not know all the answers but are willing to find someone who can assist the customer. If there is ever a situation in which you seek assistance from another employee when helping a customer, do not just hand the customer over to the other employee. Whenever possible, stay with the customer and learn from your coworker so that, in the future, you will know the answer the next time someone asks.

A **responsive** employee will provide a customer personal attention. This means that you need to be aware of the customer's need, often before the customer even realizes that need. Some customers like to be left alone to shop for a product but want you near if questions arise. Some customers would like you to guide them step by step when purchasing a product. When a customer approaches your area, make every effort to acknowledge the customer as soon as possible.

Greet him or her and ask the customer if he or she needs assistance. Watch the customer's body language. The customer will let you know if he or she wants to be left alone or wants you to stay nearby. Use the customer's name if you know it. Using the customer's name creates a more personal and friendly atmosphere. Remember, all customers are different and need to be treated differently according to their needs. You need to learn how to satisfy these needs.

A customer also expects a welcoming, convenient, and safe environment. This includes the appearance of the building, as well as the appearance of the employees. As soon as a customer comes in contact with a business, an opinion is formed about that business. There is only one first impression, so it must be good. The appearance of the building and/or employees can be the reason a customer comes to your company in the first place. Keep your workplace clean, and immediately address any potential safety hazards. If there is trash on the floor or a spill of water, clean it up. Take responsibility for keeping your workplace clean and safe. Make every effort to maintain a professional appearance from head to toe. Your attitude, language, and attire are a total package that creates an image for your customers.

▶ THE IMPACT OF CUSTOMER SERVICE

Get to know your customers. Good customers will keep coming back to purchase your product. These customers will tell others about your product. Excellent customer service is the biggest reason customers return. With so much competition, the same product can be purchased at many different places. With so many choices and increased competition, often times, the only thing that keeps customers coming back to your business may be the personal service that you have provided them. Your goal is to build a relationship with customers that will make them loyal to you and your business. This is why so many businesses now keep records of their customers. The more information businesses maintain on their customers, the more they are able to provide personal service. With the increased use of technology, many companies maintain databases with such information as past purchases, birthdays, special interests, and return/exchange practices. This helps the company to establish a more personal relationship with the customer and to follow up on sales. It is common to notify customers of upcoming sales of frequently purchased products, send notification of upcoming events, or mail discounts and coupons.

For example, when Cory moved to a new neighborhood and wanted to order pizza, Cory found there were many different pizza parlors. The only way to determine which one to try was to ask others for a recommendation or to just randomly try each one. Because Cory was new to the area and did not know many people, Cory called one of the pizza shops. When Cory called, the employee was friendly and sounded happy to assist with the order. Cory automatically formed a good impression about the pizza shop. When Cory went to pick up the pizza, the inside of the shop was clean, as were the employees. The pizza also tasted good. So the next time Cory wanted a pizza, Cory called the same place. Cory was really impressed when an employee at the pizza shop remembered what was previously ordered and called Cory by name. Cory experienced excellent service.

The success and profitability of a company depends on how you treat your customers. The happier the customers are, the more likely they are to come back. A business needs satisfied customers to not only make repeat purchases but also tell others about their favorable experience. Unhappy customers will tell others to avoid your business. It is important to note that all customer information and records should be kept confidential and should only be used for business purposes.

▶ THE DIFFICULT CUSTOMER

Customers can sometimes be difficult to deal with. Historically, companies have had the motto "The customer is always right." But, in many instances, the customer may not be right. Although the customer may be wrong, you need to adopt the attitude that the customer is unhappy and do all you can to help the customer solve his or her problem. Have patience, and sympathize with the customer.

Many times, a difficult customer will be unfriendly and may even begin yelling at you. You need to stay calm and not take the customer's inappropriate behavior personally. By remaining calm, you are better able to get the customer to identify the real problem and logically get the problem solved as quickly as possible in a manner that is fair to both the customer and your company.

In order to successfully resolve a difficult customer's complaint, you need to do the following:

1. *Stay calm, let the customer talk, and listen for facts.* This may mean letting the customer vent for a few minutes. This is not easy when someone is yelling at you. However, do not interrupt or say "please calm down." This will only fuel the fire. Pay attention, nod your head, and take notes if it helps you keep focused. Remember, even though the person may be yelling at you, you should not take harsh words personally.

2. *Watch body language.* This may include the tone of voice, eye contact, and arm movement. If a customer avoids eye contact, he or she may be lying to you or not fully conveying his or her side of the story. You should never allow a customer to touch you, especially in a threatening manner. If you feel a difficult customer has the potential to become violent or physically abusive, immediately seek assistance.

3. *Acknowledge the customer's frustration.* Say, "I can understand why you are upset." Let the person know you have been listening to his or her concern by paraphrasing what you have understood the problem to be. Do not repeat everything, just a summary of the concern.

4. *Make sure the problem gets solved.* Whenever possible, take care of the problem yourself; do not just send the customer to someone else. While it is tempting to just call your supervisor or someone else, whenever possible, take care of the customer by staying with him or her until you know the problem is resolved.

5. *Know company policy.* Some difficult customers are dishonest customers and attempt to frazzle employees by intimidation and rude behavior. Know the company policies and do not be ashamed to enforce them consistently. If a customer challenges a policy, calmly and politely explain the purpose of the policy.

6. *Expect conflict, but do not accept abuse.* Difficult customers are a fact of life. Although customers may occasionally yell, you do not have to take the abuse. If a customer shows aggressiveness or is cursing, politely tell him or her that you cannot help him or her until he or she is able to treat you in a respectable manner. If the customer continues the inappropriate behavior, immediately call a supervisor.

◀ SUMMARY OF KEY CONCEPTS

▷ Directional statements include the company's mission, vision, and values statements

▷ The company's strategic plan identifies how a company will secure, utilize, and monitor resources for success

▷ A company's organizational chart is a graphic display of the major functions and formal lines of authority within an organization

▷ Major functions (divisions) that are necessary within a business include finance and accounting, human resource management, operations, information systems, marketing, and legal counsel

▷ Excellent service, quality, and innovation are what will persuade customers to purchase a company's product or service

▷ Customers can be internal customers (other employees) or external customers (individuals outside of your company). A successful company has concern for both internal and external customers

▷ Employees that provide excellent customer service are competent, dependable, and responsive

▷ The customer is not always right, but you need to adopt the attitude that the customer is unhappy and do all you can to help the customer solve his or her problem

◄ **KEY TERMS**

board of directors
budget
capital budget
company resources
competent
customer
customer service
departments
dependable
directional statements
divisions
employee loyalty
finance and accounting
goals
human resource
   management

information systems
legal counsel
marketing
middle managers
mission statement
objectives
operational budget
operational issues
operations
operations managers
organizational chart
organizational structure
president or chief
   executive officer (CEO)
product
productivity

profit
quality
responsive
senior managers or
   executives
service
strategic issues
strategic plan
strategy
supervisor
tactical issues
value
values statement
vision statement

◄ **REFERENCE**

Deming, W. E. *Quality, Productivity and Competitive Position*, Cambridge, MA: MIT Press, 1982.

◄ **IF YOU WERE THE BOSS**

1. How can you get your employees to better relate their workplace productivity to the department's budget?
2. You are the supervisor for a team of employees who have a high number of product defects. They also waste materials. You recognize that product defects and wasted materials impact your department's budget. You have told your team to decrease the amount of wasted materials, but your employees do not seem to care. How can you get them to increase their quality and decrease waste?
3. One of your best customers verbally abuses two of your employees every time she visits your store. Your employees have complained to you several times about this customer. What should you do?

◄ **WEB LINKS**

http://www.inc.com/resources/startup/articles/20050201/missionstatement.html

http://www.smartdraw.com/tutorials/orgcharts/tutorial1.htm

http://www.personnelinsights.com/customer_service_profile.htm

http://www.cathcart.com/art_grow_business.html

◀ WORKPLACE DOs AND DON'Ts

Do read the company mission statement so you remember why the company pays you to come to work each day.	*Don't* ignore the company's directional statements and their application to your job.
Do know your internal and external customers. Also know what role you play in ensuring quality and how you contribute to your company's success.	*Don't* assume that your only customer is outside of the company and that you have no influence on the company's overall success.
Do take responsibility for producing and/or providing quality. Be a role model for other employees by eliminating waste and showing constant concern for quality.	*Don't* ignore quality by allowing wasted materials and productivity, and *don't* allow bad attitudes to affect your performance.
Do display competence by knowing your company products and policies.	*Don't* lie to customers and make up information you don't know regarding company products and policies.
Do make every effort to build a professional relationship with your customers by learning their likes and dislikes.	*Don't* become overbearing or intrusive when gathering or recording customer data.
Do remain calm when dealing with a difficult customer, and seek assistance immediately if a customer becomes abusive.	*Don't* tolerate foul language or violence.

▶ ACTIVITIES

ACTIVITY 1

Review the following organizational chart and answer these questions.

1. Whom should Linda go to if there is a question about employee benefits?
_____

2. Who is Joyce's immediate supervisor?
_____

3. If Joyce's immediate supervisor is not available, whom should she seek assistance from?
_____

4. Who is ultimately responsible for creating, pricing, selling, distributing, and promoting the company's product?
_____

5. What is Brandon's title?
_____

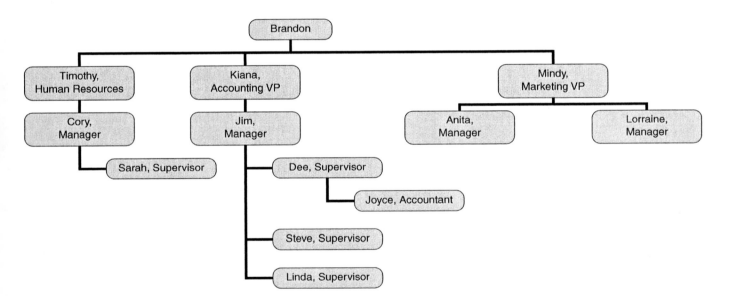

ACTIVITY 2

How would you measure performance in the following jobs?

JOB	PERFORMANCE MEASURES
Receptionist	
Customer service clerk	
Forklift driver	
Janitor	
Manager trainee	

ACTIVITY 3

What could you specifically do to communicate to your coworkers the importance customer service has on performance and profits?

_____

_____

ACTIVITY 4

Thinking about both internal and external customers, identify who the customer would be for the following jobs.

JOB	CUSTOMER
Accounting clerk	
Medical assistant	
Warehouse stockperson	
Mail sorter	
Printing press operator	

ACTIVITY 5

When is it appropriate to ask your boss to assist you with a difficult customer?

_____

_____

ACTIVITY 6

Describe two different times when you received exemplary customer service. Be specific in identifying how employees behaved toward you.

EXEMPLARY SERVICE ACT	BEHAVIOR TOWARD YOU
1.	
2.	

► SAMPLE EXAM QUESTIONS

1. A company's _____ is its statement of purpose and identifies why everyone comes to work.

2. The _____ identifies how the company will secure, organize, utilize, and monitor its resources.

3. The _____ department is responsible for the securing, distribution, and growth of the company's financial assets.

4. _____ is a predetermined standard that defines how a product is to be produced or a service is to be provided. Customers demand _____ not just in the product they purchase but also from company employees.

5. Profit is _____ (money coming in from sales) minus _____ (the costs involved in running the business).

6. A/An _____ is one who buys a service or product.

7. Quality employees + quality inputs = _____ = satisfied, loyal _____ = _____.

8. _____ is when customers believe they received a good deal for the price they paid.

9. _____ is the treatment an employee provides the customer.

10. When dealing with a difficult customer, the first step is to _____, let the _____, and _____ for facts.

StockByte Royalty Free CD/Getty Images

ACCOUNTABILITY AND WORKPLACE RELATIONSHIPS

12

OBJECTIVES

- Define and link the relationship among *empowerment*, *responsibility*, and *accountability*

- ▶ Describe how best to deal with your boss

- ▶ Describe how to respond when a workplace relationship turns negative

- ▶ Identify appropriate and inappropriate relationships with your boss, colleagues, executives, and customers

- ▶ Identify basic workplace expectations regarding social functions and gift giving

You cannot escape the responsibility of tomorrow by evading it today.

Abraham Lincoln (1809–1865)

▶ EMPOWERMENT

In politics, business, and education, everyone should be held accountable for their actions. Unfortunately, too many people do not know what it means to be accountable. This chapter discusses the concepts of accountability and workplace relationships. The concepts of empowerment, responsibility, and accountability are all about choices. These personal choices not only impact how successful you will be at work but have a tremendous impact on workplace relationships.

Workplace power affects politics and ethical behavior. Everyone in the workplace has power. Unfortunately, everyone in the workplace does not use their power appropriately or at all. As companies put an increased focus on quality, correct decision making by employees becomes more and more important.

Empowerment is pushing power and decision making to the individuals who are closest to the customer in an effort to increase quality, customer satisfaction, and, ultimately, profits. The foundation of this basic management concept means that if employees feel like they are making a direct contribution to the company's activities, they will perform better. This will then increase quality and customer satisfaction.

Consider the case of a manager of a retail customer service counter telling his employee to make the customer happy. The manager feels he has empowered his employee. However, the next day, the manager walks by the employee's counter and notices that the employee has given every customer refunds for their returns, even when the return did not warrant a refund. The boss immediately disciplines the employee for poor performance. But did the employee not do exactly what the manager asked the employee to do? Did the manager truly empower his employee? The answer is no. Telling someone to do something is different than showing someone the correct behavior. The employee interpreted the phrase "make the customer happy" differently from the manager's intention. The proper way for the manager to have empowered the employee would have been to discuss the company's return policies, role-play various customer scenarios, and then monitor the employee as the employee applied what had been learned. If or when the employee made errors through the training process, the wrong behavior should have been immediately corrected while good performance received positive reinforcement.

When you, as an employee, demonstrate a willingness to learn, you will have accepted responsibility. **Responsibility** means to accept the power that is being given to you. If you are not being responsible, you are not fully utilizing power that has been entrusted to you. Finally, the whole concept of empowerment and responsibility is useless without accountability. **Accountability** means that you accept the responsibility and must report back to whoever gave you the power to carry out that responsibility. Employees at all levels of an organization are accountable to each other, their bosses, their customers, and the company's investors to perform their best. Each employee must take personal responsibility for his or her performance. Each employee must also be accountable for his or her actions and workplace choices.

One of the best ways to gain respect and credibility at work is to begin asking for and assuming new tasks. If you are interested in learning new skills, speak up and ask your boss to teach or provide you opportunities to increase your value to the company. Assume responsibility for these new tasks and report back (become accountable) on your performance. Remember that worthwhile activities support the company's overall mission. Each project for which you assume responsibility must have a measurable goal. If it lacks a goal, it will be difficult to be accountable for your performance.

As you increase your workplace responsibilities, do not ever be afraid to seek assistance. Also, remember that a great amount of learning and success comes from past failure. When you make mistakes, do not blame others. Determine what went wrong and why. Learn from your mistakes, and view them as opportunities to do better in the future.

Cory is rapidly becoming more confident on the job. Cory wanted to be of more value to the company and began studying the concept of personal responsibility and accountability. Cory was excited about the new concepts that were learned and began requesting extra projects at work. Cory gladly kept the boss informed on the status of each project and reported when each project was successfully completed. The boss noticed how Cory took responsibility not only for personal growth but also for the success of the department. As a result, the boss informs Cory that he is impressed with Cory's willingness to improve and is considering Cory for a promotion.

WORKPLACE RELATIONSHIPS

People who are mature and confident behave consistently around others, while those who are not as secure frequently behave differently around the boss or selected colleagues. Some could argue in favor of this behavior, but it is wrong and immature to behave inconsistently around selected audiences. Boss or no boss, you should behave professionally and respectfully at all times, no matter who is around or watching. This section explains the dynamics of workplace relationships and their impact on performance.

Because we spend more time at work than we do with our families, workplace relationships have a profound impact on productivity. The bottom line is that we must treat everyone respectfully and professionally. It is easy to be respectful and professional to those we like; it is much more difficult doing so with those we dislike. Unfortunately, developing strong friendships at work can be equally as damaging as creating workplace enemies if we fail to keep professional relationships separate from our personal lives. Socializing with our coworkers is both expected and acceptable to a degree, but do not make workplace relationships your only circle of friends. Doing so is dangerous because it becomes difficult to separate personal and work issues. It also has the potential to create distrust among employees who are not included in your circle of workplace friends. Finally, it creates the potential for you to unknowingly or subconsciously show favoritism toward your friends. Even if you are not showing favoritism, those who are not within the circle of friends may perceive favoritism and may become distrustful of you.

As you become more comfortable with your job and company, you will be in various situations that provide opportunities to strengthen workplace relationships with coworkers, executives, investors, vendors, and customers. The following section discusses selected situations and how best to behave in these circumstances.

EXECUTIVES/SENIOR OFFICIALS

It is often difficult to know how to behave in a room full of executives or senior officials such as members of the board of directors. At work, there are several occasions when you may be in the presence of executives and senior officials. These may include meetings, corporate events, and social functions. While it is tempting to pull a senior official aside and tell him stories about your boss or how perfect you would be for an advanced position, this behavior is both inappropriate and unacceptable. It is important to not draw attention to yourself and always project a positive, professional image. Highlight the successes of your department and not personal accomplishments.

If you are in a meeting that you do not normally attend, do not speak up unless addressed or introduced by the chairman of the meeting. If it is convenient, before or after the meeting, it is acceptable to introduce yourself to senior officials. Remember to not interrupt. Be confident, extend a hand, and state, "Hello, Mrs. Jones, my name is Tim Brandon. I work in the accounting department. It's nice to meet you." Keep your comments brief and positive. Your objective is to create a favorable and memorable impression with the executive. Introduce yourself and make eye contact so that the executive can connect a face, name, and department. Do not speak poorly of anyone or a situation. It is also inappropriate to discuss specific work-related issues, such as wanting to change positions, unless you are in a meeting specifically to discuss that issue. Always let the executive guide the conversation and make sure to read the executive's body language. If the executive's body language includes a nodding head and his or her body is facing you, continue talking. If the executive is glancing away or his or her body is turning away from you, that body language is clearly communicating the executive's desire to be elsewhere. Therefore, tell the executive it was nice meeting him or her, excuse yourself, and leave. Use encounters with executives as opportunities to create favorable impressions for you and your department.

▶ YOUR BOSS

Typically, there is no middle ground when it comes to workers and their feelings for their bosses. We either love them or hate them. There are three common types of bosses: the bad (incompetent) boss, the abusive boss, and the good boss. Before we discuss how to handle each type, it is important to remember that bosses are human. Like us, they too are learning and developing their skills. Although they are not perfect, we should assume they are doing their best.

Let us begin with the bad or **incompetent boss**. An incompetent boss is one who does not know how to do his or her job. As with every work situation, no matter how bad the boss, you must remain professional and respectful. Make it your mission to make your boss look good. That's right; make your bad boss look good! Doing so demonstrates your maturity and diminishes the tension between you and your boss. Do not worry about your boss receiving credit for your hard work. Incompetence rises to the top. If your boss is a poor performer, others in the company will know your boss is not producing the good work being presented. Therefore, if you are doing good work, it will get noticed by others in the company. If your boss really is not incompetent and you and your boss just have a personality conflict, do not allow your personal feelings to affect your performance. Focus on staying positive and being of value to your boss. Even when your coworkers want to bad-mouth the boss, which is a common occurrence at work, do not give in to temptation. You must remain professional and respectful. Moreover, use your bad boss experience as a time to learn what not to do when you become a boss.

Sometime in your career, you may experience an **abusive boss**. The abusive boss is someone who is constantly belittling or intimidating his or her employees. Abusive bosses generally behave that way because they have low self-esteem. Therefore, they utilize their legitimate and coercive power to make themselves feel better by knocking someone else down. There are several ways to deal with an abusive boss. If the abuse is tolerable, do your best to work with the situation. Although common with employees of abusive bosses, do not speak poorly of your boss in public. If the situation becomes intolerable and is beginning to affect your performance, you have several options. The first is to seek confidential advice from someone in the human resource management department. This expert can begin documenting and observing the situation and take corrective action or provide needed management training to your boss. Remember to be factual in reporting inappropriate incidents. Human resource managers only want facts, not emotions. While tempting, do not go to your boss's boss. Doing so implies secrecy and distrust. If your boss's boss does not support you and/or your immediate boss finds out, your plan will backfire. Finally, if it looks as if nothing and no one can improve your boss's behavior, begin quietly looking for another job either in another department within the company or at a new company. Remember that as an employee, you have rights. If your boss ever acts discriminatory or harassing toward you, document and report the behavior immediately. Your boss cannot make you perform functions that do not reasonably support those identified in your job description. Abusive bosses commonly have employees run personal errands. If you are asked to perform unreasonable functions, you should politely decline.

If you have a **good boss**, be thankful but cautious. A good boss is one who is respectful and fair and is grooming you for a promotion. It frequently becomes tempting to develop a personal friendship with a good boss. You must remember to keep the relationship professional. While it is okay to share important activities occurring in your personal life with your boss (e.g., spouse and child issues, vacation plans), you should never divulge too much information. Take advantage of your good boss and use him or her as a professional mentor. Identify what management qualities make your boss valued and begin imitating these qualities in your own workplace behavior. Regardless of what type of boss you have, always give your personal best.

◀ **EXERCISE 1: About Your Boss:** *What kind of boss have you worked for—incompetent, abusive, or good? Provide at least two specific examples to support your assessment. If you have never held a job before, ask a friend or family member.*

What kind of boss?	
Examples to support assessment	

▶ # COLLEAGUES

Having friends at work is nice. Unfortunately, when workplace friendships go awry, it affects your job. It is for this reason that you should be cautious about friendships developed at work. A friend is someone whom you trust and who knows your strengths and weaknesses. While we should be able to trust all coworkers, they should not know everything about you. It is important to be friendly to everyone at work. There will be some with whom you want to develop a friendship outside of work, but beware. If there is a misunderstanding either at work or away from work, the relationship can go sour and affect both areas. If one of you gets promoted and suddenly becomes the boss of the other, it also creates an awkward situation for both parties. Even if you can both get beyond this issue, others at work may feel like outsiders or feel you are playing favorites with your friend. Finally, if you only socialize with friends developed at work, you risk the danger of getting too absorbed in work issues. The one common thread that binds your friendship is work. Therefore, it is work that you will most likely discuss when you are together. This can be unhealthy and could potentially create a conflict of interest in the decisions you make at work.

▶ # OTHERS WITHIN THE ORGANIZATION

The topic of friendships in the workplace should be extended to those throughout the organization. You are, however, encouraged to increase your professional network by meeting others within your company. As we build our connection power, we are gaining additional knowledge and contacts to assist us in performing our jobs and perhaps earning future promotions. This is called *networking*. When you interact with others in the organization, remember to keep your conversations positive and respectful of others. Even if the other individual steers the conversation in a negative direction, respond with a positive comment. Do not ever be afraid to defend coworkers when another employee is talking ill about them.

For example, one day, Cory and a friend were sitting in the break room when Vicki, the department's unhappy coworker, walked in. "I just can't stand John!" declared Vicki. "That's too bad. John's a friend of mine," responded Cory's friend. Vicki stood there red-faced, turned around, and left the room. Cory told the friend that Cory never knew he and John were close. "Well," responded the friend, "we're not personal friends, but we work together." The friend went on to explain that it is easy to eliminate negative conversation when you immediately communicate that you will not tolerate bad-mouthing others. Cory thought that was pretty good advice.

Each company should have a **corporate culture** (**organizational culture**). Think of corporate culture as the company's personality being reflected through its employees' behavior. The company's culture is its shared values and beliefs. For example, if the company's management team openly communicates and promotes teamwork, the company will most likely have excellent communication and successful teams. In contrast, executives who are always stressed and reacting to crisis situations will create a workplace atmosphere based on stress and crisis management. A company's corporate culture has an enormous impact on **employee morale**. Employee morale is the attitude employees have toward the company. This attitude is a result of the company's corporate culture.

◀ **EXERCISE 2: Improving Morale:** *What can you do to help improve the employee morale in your workplace?*

What workplace behavior contributes to poor employee morale?

▶ **WHEN RELATIONSHIPS TURN NEGATIVE**

Unresolved conflict happens to the best of relationships. Due to a conflict or misunderstanding, a relationship may go bad. Unfortunately, at work, this happens. Sometimes you have no idea what you have done wrong. In other cases, you may be the one that wants to end the relationship. As stated earlier in the text, you do not have to like everyone at work, but no one should know the better. You must show everyone respect and you must behave professionally, even to your adversaries.

If you are the victim of a bad relationship, you need to take the following steps in dealing with the situation:

▶ If you harmed the other person (intentionally or unintentionally), apologize immediately.
▶ Tell the other person that you value his or her friendship.
▶ If the other person accepts your apology, demonstrate your regret by changing your behavior.
▶ If the other person does not accept your apology and your apology was sincere, you must move on. You must still demonstrate your regret by changing your behavior.
▶ If you lose the relationship, do not hold a grudge. Continue being polite, respectful, and professional to your lost friend.
▶ If the lost friend acts rude or inappropriate, do not retaliate by returning the poor behavior. Respond in kindness.
▶ If the rude and inappropriate behavior impacts your performance or is hostile or harassing, document the situation and inform your boss.

Erin had been one of Cory's favorite coworkers since Cory's first day at work. They took breaks together and at least once a week went out for lunch. One day Cory was working on a project with a short deadline. Erin invited Cory out to lunch and Cory politely declined, explaining why. The next day, Cory asked Erin to lunch and Erin just gave Cory a funny look and turned away. "Erin, what's wrong?" Cory asked. Erin just shook her head and left the room. Cory left Erin alone for a few days, hoping whatever the matter was would boil over and things would be better. After a week of Erin ignoring Cory, things only got worse. Cory decided to try one last time to save the relationship. As Cory approached Erin, Cory said, "Erin, I'm sorry for whatever I've done to upset you and I'd like for us to talk about it." Unfortunately, Erin again gave Cory a hollow look and walked away.

The toughest step when addressing a broken relationship is when the other individual does not accept your apology. We have grown up believing that we must like everyone and that everyone must like us. Because of human nature, this simply is not possible. We cannot be friends with everyone at work. Moreover, people get their feelings hurt and some find it hard to forgive. Your focus at work should be, first and foremost, getting the job done. Any behavior that is not respectful and professional interferes with performance. Remember that the company is paying you to perform. Therefore, if a sour relationship begins to impact your performance, you must respond. First ask yourself if your behavior is contributing to the unresolved conflict. If it is, you must change your behavior immediately. If your wronged coworker is upset or hurt, he or she will most likely begin bad-mouthing you. Do not fuel the fire by retaliating by speaking ill of your coworker. This only makes both of you look petty and immature. Document the facts of the incident and remain a mature adult. If the bad behavior continues for a reasonable period of time and it affects your performance, it is time to seek assistance. This is why documentation is important.

At this point, you must contact your immediate supervisor for an intervention. When you meet with your supervisor, explain the situation in a factual and unemotional manner. Provide specific examples of the offensive behavior and document any witnesses. Do not approach your supervisor to get the other individual in trouble. Your objective is to secure your boss's assistance in creating a mutually respectful and professional working relationship with your coworker. The boss may call you and the coworker into the boss's office to discuss the situation. Do not become emotional during this meeting. Your objective is to come to an agreement on behaving respectfully and professionally at work.

▶ DATING AT WORK

A sticky but common workplace relationship issue is that of dating other employees, vendors, or customers of your place of employment. Because we spend so much time at work, it is natural for coworkers to look for companionship in the workplace. While a company cannot prevent you from dating coworkers who are in your immediate work area, many companies discourage the practice. Some companies go as far as having employees who are romantically involved sign statements releasing the company from any liability should the relationship turn sour. It is highly inappropriate for you to date your boss or if you are a supervisor for you to date your employees. Doing so exposes you, your romantic interest, and your company to potential sexual harassment charges. Your actions will impact your entire department and will most likely make everyone uncomfortable.

If you date customers and vendors/suppliers of your company, use caution. In dating either customers or vendors, you must ask yourself how the changed relationship can potentially impact your job. Remember that you are representing your company 24/7. Therefore, you should never share confidential information or speak poorly of your colleagues or employer. You should be careful to not put yourself in a situation in which you could be accused of a conflict of interest. In short, it is always best to keep your romantic life separate from that of the workplace.

▶ SOCIALIZING

Work-related social activities such as company picnics, potlucks, and birthday celebrations are extremely common. While some individuals enjoy attending these social functions, others clearly do not. You do not have to attend any work-related social function outside of your normal work hours. However, it is often considered rude if you do not attend social functions that occur at the workplace during work hours. If you are working on an important deadline and simply cannot attend, briefly stop by the function and apologize to whoever is hosting the event. If you attend a work-related social function, check to see if guests are being requested to bring items to the party. If you plan on attending, you should bring an item if one is requested. It is considered impolite to show up to a potluck empty-handed. It is also considered rude to take home a plate of leftovers unless offered. Alcohol should not be served on work premises.

Attendance at work-related social events occurring outside the work site is considered optional. If the invitation requires an RSVP, be sure to send your reservation or regrets in a timely manner. If you choose not to attend an off-site activity, be sure to thank whoever invited you. This maintains a positive work relationship. If you do attend, do not show up empty-handed and always thank the host for the invitation when arriving and when leaving. If alcohol is being served at a work-related function off of the work site, use caution when consuming alcohol. It is best to not consume at all; but, if you must consume, limit yourself to one drink.

▶ BREAKS AND THE BREAK ROOM

It is a common practice for offices to have a community coffeepot. This means that coffee is available to everyone in the office. Unfortunately, in most cases, the company does not pay for this benefit. The coffee, snacks, and other supplies are typically provided by the boss or someone else in the office. It is common for people to informally contribute to the coffee fund. If you routinely drink coffee or eat the office snacks, you should contribute funds to help pay for this luxury. The same goes for office treats such as doughnuts, cookies, or birthday cakes. If you partake, offer to defer the cost or take your turn bringing treats one day. Many offices have a refrigerator available for employees to store their meals. It is considered stealing to eat someone else's food. Do not help yourself to food being stored in the community refrigerator. If you store your food in this area, remember to throw out any unused or spoiled food at the end of each workweek. Finally, remember to always clean up after yourself. If you use a coffee cup, wash it and put it away when you are finished. Throw away your trash, and leave the break room clean for the next person.

▶ MISCELLANEOUS WORKPLACE ISSUES

While it is tempting to sell fund-raising items at work, the practice is questionable. Some companies have policies prohibiting this practice. If the practice is acceptable, do not pester people nor make them feel guilty if they decline to make a purchase.

It is common and acceptable to give a gift to a friend commemorating special days such as birthdays and holidays. However, you do not have to give gifts to anyone at work. If you are a gift giver, do so discreetly so as to not offend others who do not receive gifts from you. If you advance into a management position, do not give a gift to just one employee. If you choose to give gifts, you must give gifts to all employees and treat everyone equally.

It is also common for employees to pitch in and purchase a group gift for special days such as Boss's Day and Administrative Assistant's Day. While it is not mandatory to contribute to these gifts, it is generally expected that you contribute. If you strongly object or cannot afford to participate, politely decline without attaching a negative comment. If price is the issue, contribute whatever amount you deem reasonable and explain that you are on a budget. If you are the receiver of a gift, verbally thank the gift giver immediately and follow up with a handwritten thank-you note.

◀ SUMMARY OF KEY CONCEPTS

▶ It is important to take responsibility for the job you perform by being accountable for your actions
▶ Keep workplace friendships positive, but be cautious that these relationships not be your only friendships away from the workplace
▶ If a workplace relationship turns negative, remember to remain professional and respectful
▶ It is best to refrain from dating anyone at work
▶ Practice good etiquette at social functions that occur within the office

◀ KEY TERMS

abusive boss
accountability
corporate culture
  (organizational culture)

employee morale
empowerment
good boss

incompetent boss
responsibility

◀ REFERENCE

Deming, W. E. *Quality, Productivity and Competitive Position,* Cambridge, MA: MIT Press, 1982.

◀ IF YOU WERE THE BOSS

1. How can you get employees excited about assuming additional responsibilities?
2. If you noticed employee morale dropping in your department, how would you respond?
3. How would you handle two employees whose friendship had turned negative?
4. You never give your employees gifts, but one of your employees always gives you gifts for holidays, birthdays, and boss's day. Is it wrong for you to accept these gifts?

◀ WEB LINKS

http://www.librarysupportstaff.com/coworkers.html#principles

http://www.iaap-hq.org/careercenter/Workplace_Relationships.htm

http://www.relationships.com.au/relations_in/landing.asp

◀ WORKPLACE DOs AND DON'Ts

Do take responsibility for your performance and success at work.	*Don't* wait for someone to tell you what to do.
Do display consistent, professional behavior.	*Don't* behave appropriately only when the boss is around.
Do always make your boss look good.	*Don't* speak poorly of your boss.
Do create positive relationships with coworkers.	*Don't* make your workplace friendships your primary friendships away from work.
Do practice business etiquette at work-related social functions.	*Don't* ignore the importance of behaving professionally at work-related social functions.

▶ ACTIVITIES

ACTIVITY 1

You are supposed to attend a meeting the next day. Overnight, you have a family emergency. What should you do? Explain your answer.

_____

_____

_____

_____

ACTIVITY 2

Your boss is always bad-mouthing or belittling your coworkers. You do not like it and you wonder what he says about you when you are not around. What should you do?

_____

_____

_____

_____

ACTIVITY 3

The company that services your office equipment has hired a new salesperson. This person does not wear a wedding ring and flirts with you. If you go out on a date with this person, what are at least three potential problems that could occur (work related)?

1. _____

2. _____

3. _____

ACTIVITY 4

Is it appropriate to discuss the following company information with individuals outside of the company? Why or why not?

INFORMATION	YES OR NO	WHY OR WHY NOT?
1. Key clients/customers		
2. Financial information		
3. Boss's work style		
4. Company mission statement		
5. Names of members of the company board of directors		

▶ SAMPLE EXAM QUESTIONS

1. _____ is the attitude employees have toward the company.

2. If you ever harm another, immediately _____.

3. Any behavior that is not _____ or professional interferes with _____.

4. Be cautious in engaging in _____ with coworkers, customers, vendors, or your boss.

5. You _____ have to attend any work-related social function outside of your normal work hours.

6. If _____ is being served at a work-related function off of the work site, use caution when consuming, or better yet, do not _____.

7. If you partake of office treats, it is good manners to _____.

8. Just like at home, you must always _____ in the break room.

9. It is best to not sell _____ items at work.

13

COMMUNICATION

StockByte Royalty Free CD/Getty Images

COMMUNICATION

OBJECTIVES

- Define the impact effective *communication* has in the workplace
- Name the key elements of the communication process
- Name the three types of communication media
- ► Describe the dangers of becoming emotional at work
- ► Demonstrate proper formatting for *business letters* and *memos*
- ► Demonstrate basic telecommunication etiquette

The most important thing in communication is to hear what isn't being said.

Peter Drucker (1909–2005)

► WORKPLACE COMMUNICATION AND ITS CHANNELS

Imagine going to work; sitting at your desk; and, for one day, sending and receiving no communication. If there were no face-to-face contact, no telephone or cell calls, no meetings, and no memos to receive or write, business would come to a complete standstill. No matter how talented you are at your job, if you cannot communicate with others, you will not succeed, much less have a job. This chapter discusses the process and importance of effective communication in the workplace and provides information on how to improve your workplace communication skills.

At work, you have an obligation to share appropriate, timely, and accurate information with your boss, your coworkers, and your customers. As we jump into the topic of workplace communication, you must remember that improving your communication skills is an ongoing process. Information is power. In regard to workplace communication, your goal is to be known as an over-communicator.

While eating lunch with employees from other departments, Cory listened to employees complain about how their bosses did such a poor job communicating with them. The employees complained that they never knew what was going on within the company. Cory had no reason to complain because Cory has a manager that makes every effort to share whatever information the manager knows with Cory's department. After each managers' meeting, Cory receives an e-mail outlining major topics that were discussed at the managers' meeting. During Cory's department meeting, Cory's manager reviews the information a second time and asks his employees if there are any additional questions. Cory appreciates the fact that Cory's manager enjoys and values communicating important information with his employees.

In the workplace, there are two primary communication channels. These include formal and informal communication. Whether it is formal or informal communication, you have a professional obligation to share timely and relevant information with the appropriate people. **Formal communication** occurs through the formal lines of authority. This can include communication within your immediate department, your division, or throughout your company. Formal communication can occur either vertically or horizontally. Formal vertical communication can occur coming down the organization chart (via written correspondence, policies and procedures, and directives and announcements from management), or going up the organization chart (reports, budgets, and requests). Formal horizontal communication occurs among individuals or departments at the same or close organizational levels.

The second type of communication channel is that of the informal organization. **Informal communication** occurs among individuals without regard to the formal lines of authority. For example, while eating lunch with friends, you may learn of a new policy. A major form of the informal communication network is called the *grapevine*. This informal communication network frequently highlights matters of importance to employees. Although the grapevine is an informal source of communication, it usually is not 100 percent accurate. While it is important to know about current events of the workplace, it is important that you not contribute negative information to the grapevine. If inaccurate information is being shared and you are aware of the facts, clarify the information. If someone shares information that is harmful to the company or is particularly disturbing to you, you have a responsibility to approach your boss and ask him or her to clarify the rumor.

When the grapevine is targeting individuals and their personal lives, it is called *gossip*. Gossip is hurtful and inappropriate. Do not be part of personal attacks on individuals. Any time you contribute to negative conversation, you lose credibility with others. By your actions, you communicate both immaturity and unprofessional behavior. Your job is to clarify misinformation when necessary and assist in defending the rights of others. Should someone begin sharing gossip with you, politely interrupt and tell the individual that you really do not want to hear the information and transition the conversation to a more positive subject. You have a right to defend your coworkers from slander (individuals bad-mouthing others), just as you would expect your coworkers to defend you. After a while, your colleagues will learn that you do not tolerate gossip at work and they will reconsider approaching you with gossip.

In that same manner, refrain from speaking poorly of your coworkers and boss. As a result of human nature, you may not enjoy working with all of your colleagues and bosses. You do not have to like everyone at work, but you must treat everyone with respect. Gossip is a form of disrespect. No matter how much someone annoys you at work, do not speak poorly of him or her. It only displays immaturity on your part and communicates distrust to your colleagues. Even if someone speaks poorly of you, do not reciprocate the bad behavior.

▶ THE COMMUNICATION PROCESS

Communication is the process of a sender sending a message to an individual (receiver) with the purpose of creating mutual understanding. As simple as this definition is, a lot of barriers hinder the process of creating mutual understanding and successful communication. Communication is important for maintaining good human relations. Without basic communication skills, processes break down and an organization may collapse. This is why you need to know and understand the communication process (see Figure 1).

Communication starts with a **sender** wanting to convey a message. The sender must identify what message needs to be sent and how best to send this message. The sender has several options for sending the message. The message can be sent verbally, written, or nonverbally. Identifying the message and how it will be sent is called **encoding.**

Once the sender encodes the message, the message is sent to a receiver. **Decoding** is when the receiver interprets the message. The receiver then sends **feedback** on the sender's message based upon the receiver's interpretation of the original message.

Due to barriers, the communication process can break down. First, the sender must clearly identify the real message that needs to be sent. Once the message is identified, the sender needs to figure out how best to send (encode) the message in a manner that will be properly interpreted (decoded) by the receiver. If the sender is not a strong communicator, his or her verbal, written, or body language may be misinterpreted by the receiver and the message may be doomed before it is even sent. The receiver can assist with the communication breakdown if he or she incorrectly interprets the message.

Another barrier to effective communication is **noise**. Noise is anything that interrupts or interferes with the communication process. The noise can be audible (you can actually hear it with your ears), or the noise can occur in your mind (thoughts).

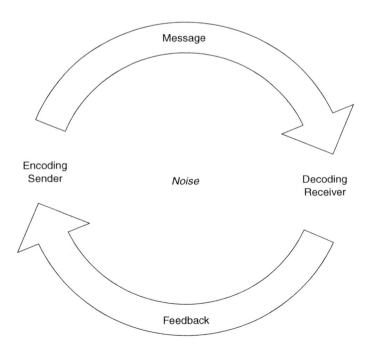

◀ FIGURE 1   Communication Process

◀ **EXERCISE 1: Identify Noises:** *Identify at least four noises you experience during class.*

1. _____

2. _____

3. _____

4. _____

A supervisor in another department really irritates Cory. Cory has never shared this irritation with anyone. One day, Cory was asked to attend a meeting led by the irritating supervisor. As Cory sat in the meeting, Cory had a hard time focusing on the message. Cory's mind was wandering with both audible and mental noise. At the end of the meeting, Cory was embarrassed that there were no notes to share. Cory's dislike for the irritating supervisor affected Cory's ability to listen and be a good receiver. Cory learned a hard lesson that day and made a commitment to be open to every communication, regardless of Cory's like or dislike of the sender.

Communication can only be complete and effective if all of the components of the communication process work together to effectively send the message as it is meant to be sent. In order for this to happen, the sender must choose the right medium and overcome noise. The receiver must then be willing to accept the message and provide feedback to acknowledge that the message has been received correctly.

As previously stated, a key element to effective communication is the communication medium (how the message will be sent). Communication media include verbal, nonverbal, and written communication. Let us further explore these three types of communication media.

▶ VERBAL COMMUNICATION

Verbal communication is the process of using words to send your message. The words you select are extremely important. If you only use basic words in your communications, you may appear uneducated or inexperienced. In contrast, if you use a highly developed vocabulary, you may appear intimidating or arrogant. If others do not know the definitions of the words you are using, they will most likely not ask for clarification for fear of appearing ignorant. Therefore, your intended message will fail. When selecting words for your message, identify whether these words can be misinterpreted in any way. Many times, we assume our receiver is thinking our same thoughts. This is highly unlikely.

Finally, you must learn to stop and listen. Too frequently, a person will have so much to say that he or she does not stop to give the receiver time to respond. The receiver's response is the only way you, as a sender, can verify that your message has been properly received. Therefore, when improving your verbal communication, you must learn when it is appropriate to not speak. Keys to effective listening include making eye contact with the sender and taking notes.

▶ NONVERBAL COMMUNICATION

Nonverbal communication is what you communicate through your body language. You do not have to utter a word and you can still send a very strong message. Body language includes eye contact, facial expressions, tone of voice, and the positioning of your body. Nonverbal communication also includes the use of silence and space.

When people are nervous or excited, they frequently speak fast. When you increase the speed of your speech, you increase the probability that your message will be misinterpreted. Your tone of voice also conveys or creates images. It adds to others' perception of you, which either enforces your message or detracts from the message.

The most obvious form of body language is eye contact. When you look someone in the eye, you are generally communicating honesty and sincerity. At other times, looking someone in the eye and coupling that look with a harsh tone of voice and an unfriendly facial expression may imply intimidation. Those who fail to look someone in the eye risk conveying to their receiver that they are not confident or, worse, are being dishonest. It is important to make eye contact with your audience (individual or group). However, when making eye contact, do not stare. Doing so is considered rude and intimidating. Actively work at making appropriate eye contact with your receiver. If your direct eye contact is making the receiver uncomfortable, he or she will look away. Be aware of his or her response and adapt your behavior appropriately.

Eye contact is part of the larger communication package of your facial expression. A receiver will find it difficult to interpret your eye contact as sincere and friendly when your message is accompanied by a frown. A smile has immense power and value. A nod implies that you are listening or agreeing with a sender's message. Even the positioning of your head can convey disagreement, confusion, or attentiveness.

◄ **EXERCISE 2: Body Language:** *With a partner, take turns communicating the following emotions through body language. Note how the sender signals to communicate the emotion.*

Emotion	Signal
1. Concern	
2. Distrust	
3. Eagerness	
4. Boredom	
5. Self-importance	
6. Interest	

Another important element in body language is the use and positioning of your body. Having your arms crossed in front of your body can be interpreted in several ways: as being cold, angry, or uninterested. When you are not cold, having your arms crossed implies that you are creating a barrier between yourself and the other person. To eliminate any miscommunication, it is best to have your arms at your side. Do not hide your hands in your pockets. In speaking with others, be aware of the positioning of your arms and those of your audience. Also, be aware of the positioning of your entire body. Turn your body toward those to whom you are speaking. It is considered rude to turn your back to or ignore someone when he or she is speaking. In this case, you are using your entire body to create a barrier. Avoid this kind of rude behavior. This only communicates immaturity on your part.

The use of your hands is extremely important in effective communication. Through varied positioning, you can use your hands to nonverbally ask someone to stop a behavior or be quiet or to reprimand another. Your hands will also expose any nervous gestures you may have. Once again, when around others, be aware of the positioning of your hands. If you have any nervous gestures such as popping your knuckles, biting your nails, or continually tapping your fingers, take steps to eliminate these habits.

Apart from a handshake, touching another person at work is not acceptable. People in our society frequently place a hand on another's shoulder as a show of support. However, others could interpret that hand on the shoulder as a threat or sexual advance. Therefore, keep your hands to yourself.

You must also be aware of the space you allow between you and your receiver. Standing too close may be interpreted as intimidation or may imply intimacy. Neither is appropriate for the workplace. Distancing yourself too far from someone may imply your unwillingness to communicate.

Another element that affects nonverbal communication is emotion. You must make every attempt to not become emotional at work. However, reality may cause you to express emotions that oftentimes cannot be controlled. You must make every effort to control your emotions in public. If you feel you are beginning to cry or have an outburst of anger, excuse yourself. Go somewhere private and deal with your emotion. If you are crying or distraught, splash water on your face and regain control of your emotions. If you are getting angry, assess why you are angry, control your anger, and then create a strategy to regain control of how best to handle the situation. Any overt display of anger in the workplace is inappropriate and could potentially jeopardize your job. When you become emotional at work, you lose your ability to logically deal with situations. Practice effective stress management and think before you respond.

Finally, it is important to understand the appropriate use of silence. Silence is perhaps one of the most important communication tools you have. Silence communicates to your audience that you are listening and are allowing the other party consideration. Not immediately responding to a message gives the sender time to clarify or rephrase a message.

◀ **EXERCISE 3: Silence:** *You are trying to negotiate a pay raise with your boss. As you role-play this scenario, practice the effective use of silence. How did the use of silence affect the outcome?*

_____

_____

_____

_____

As you can see, there are a lot of variables involved in effective nonverbal communication. It is important to interpret body language within its entire context. For example, if you are communicating with a colleague with whom you have a positive working relationship and your coworker crosses his or her arms, your coworker is most likely cold. Consider the entire package: environment, relationship, and situation.

▶ WRITTEN COMMUNICATION

Writing is an important element of effective workplace communication. Your written communication conveys your aptitude and attitude. Because the receiver of your message will not have verbal and nonverbal assistance in interpreting your message, it is vital to take great care to ensure that the correct message is being communicated. Because you are not present when the message is received, you must remember that the receiver will be drawing additional conclusions about you based upon the grammar, vocabulary, and presentation/formatting you use in your written communication.

As you advance in responsibility within an organization, you will be required to conduct an increasing amount of written business communications including writing memos, e-mail messages, and business letters. Written business correspondence represents not only your professionalism and intelligence but also that of your organization. It is for this reason that you should consistently present your written correspondence in a professional manner. Make sure all written communication is error free by proofreading the message prior to sending. The key to written communication is to choose words that clearly and concisely communicate your message. You must make sure your message is clear. The three most common forms of written communication in the workplace are letters, memos, and electronic messages. Written communication should be typed (word processed). The only exception to this rule is when you are sending a handwritten thank-you note.

The first step in any professional correspondence is to state an objective. Determine exactly what it is that you want to communicate. Write a draft message and make sure it is free of anger or negative emotions. If the purpose of your correspondence is to address a negative situation (e.g., complaint), make sure your message addresses the situation and not a person. With all written forms of communication, do not send or write any message conveying anger. A good rule of thumb is to always put good news in writing and be cautious when sending negative information in writing. Put bad news in writing only when necessary.

After you have drafted your message and eliminated negative emotions, again review your correspondence and delete unnecessary words. Keep your correspondence short and simple. Do not be too wordy, and try to minimize personalization words (*I, my*) as much as possible. Make sure your correspondence not only communicates your core message but also clearly communicates how you want the reader to respond to your communication. Include contact telephone numbers and a deadline if relevant.

Although it is important to keep your correspondence simple, you want to project a professional image, not that of an elementary student. Get a thesaurus and identify and substitute words to project a more mature image. Make sure you know the definitions of the words you are using and that you are using words appropriately. Utilizing a thesaurus is an excellent way to expand your vocabulary. Remember to not overdo it, and use words in the correct context.

After you have completed writing your message, identify who should receive the message. Share your correspondence only with individuals who need to know the information. However, make sure you have shared the information with individuals whom the correspondence affects. When writing business correspondence, you have several options. These include a business letter, business memo, an e-mail message, and a thank-you note.

▶ THE BUSINESS LETTER

A **letter** is used when your message is being sent to an individual outside of your organization. External audiences may include customers, vendors, suppliers, or members of the community. Letters should be written in proper business format and sent on company letterhead. Every letter sent should be error free. Proofread, sign, and date the letter before mailing. Make sure your message and expected follow-up activity to the letter are clear. Remember, the message needs to be conveyed to the receiver in a professional and concise manner.

Business letters should be written on company letterhead. Company **letterhead** is paper that has the company logo, mailing address, and telephone numbers imprinted on quality paper. Figures 2 and 3 provide an example of the correct letter format.

An important element of a business letter is the mailing envelope. Remember that the envelope helps create a first impression. Make sure you address the envelope with the same information that is in the inside address. The letter should be folded properly. This is done by folding in thirds; start with the bottom and fold it up one-third of the way. Then fold the top over the bottom and put it in the envelope with the opening on the top. Number 10 envelopes are normally used for business letters.

▶ THE BUSINESS MEMO

Business memos (sometimes called *interoffice memorandums*) are used internally, that is, when the written communication is being sent to a receiver within an organization. A memo should include the receiver's name, sender's name, date, and subject. Again, as with a business letter, it is important to include all facts needed to get the message across, but be brief and to the point. In general, memos should be no longer than one page. Figures 4 and 5 illustrate the proper way to format a business memo.

▶ THE BUSINESS E-MAIL

Electronic mail (e-mail) is becoming a more popular form of internal and external communications. With internal e-mail messages, you can directly type a message or attach a formal memo to your e-mail. E-mail creates more efficient communication within an organization and with individuals outside of the organization.

When sending an e-mail, always include a subject in the subject line. The subject line should clearly state the purpose of the e-mail. You should not use *HI* or *HELLO* as the subject line. Because of the spread of common computer viruses, it is also inappropriate to use the words *URGENT* or *IMPORTANT* as a subject line.

As with the use of all workplace equipment, e-mail should only be used for business purposes. Remember that e-mail messages are an important element of professional workplace communication. Therefore, do not use emoticons (happy faces, winks) in your messages. Doing so at work takes away from your professionalism. It is also important to refrain from forwarding messages that are not work related. Maintain an organized and updated electronic address book. Make every attempt to preserve the confidentiality of your address book.

<table>
<tr><td>

(Students do not type QS and DS, these are shown for correct spacing).

Since most business letters will be on letterhead (preprinted business address), you need about a two-inch top margin. Then enter the current *date*.

The *inside address* should have the title, first and last name of receiver.

The *salutation* should have title and last name only.

For the *body*, all lines begin at the left margin. Use a colon after the salutation and a comma after the complementary closing.

Keep the *closing* simple.

The writer's first and last name should be four enters or returns after the closing to give the *writer* room to sign (remember to have the writer sign).

Typist's initials
Enclosure is used only if you add something in the envelope with the letter.

</td><td>

August 1, 2007

QS (4 enters or returns)

Ms. Suzie Student
Word Processing Fun
42 Learn Avenue
Fresno, CA 93225
DS (2 enters or returns)
Dear Ms. Student:
DS
The first paragraph of a letter should state the reason for the letter. If you had any previous contact with the receiver, mention it in this paragraph.
DS
The second (and possibly a third) paragraph should contain details. All information needed to be communicated should be here.
DS
The last paragraph is used to close the letter. Add information that is needed to clarify anything you said in the letter. Also, add any follow-up or contact information.
DS
Sincerely,
QS

Sarah S. Quirrel

Sarah S. Quirrel
Instructor
DS
sbb
Enclosure

</td></tr>
</table>

◀ **FIGURE 2**   Letter Format

▶ THE THANK-YOU NOTE

A thank-you note is a powerful tool for building relationships. When you express thanks, individuals are more likely to continue performing kind acts for you. A thank-you note should be handwritten, in pen, and on a notecard. Thank-you notes do not need to be lengthy; generally, just a few sentences are sufficient. Make it a habit to write a thank-you note when someone does something for you that takes more than five minutes or when someone gives you a gift. Write and deliver the note as soon as possible. Figure 6 shows the correct format and key elements of a thank-you note.

▶ DOCUMENTATION

One final element of effective communication is documentation. Documentation is an important paper trail that assists us in remembering important events that have occurred. Frequently, this is used for personal reasons or as supporting evidence. Documentation may be necessary for an instance in which a policy is not enforced or an abnormal event has occurred that has the potential to evolve into conflict at a later date. These events may support performance issues, business

August 1, 2007

Ms. Suzie Student
Word Processing Fun
42 Learn Avenue
Fresno, CA 93225

Dear Ms. Student:

It was a pleasure speaking with you over the telephone earlier today. I am delighted that you have agreed to serve as a guest speaker in my Communications class. The purpose of this letter is to confirm the details of the upcoming speaking engagement.

As I mentioned in our conversation, the date for your scheduled lecture is Thursday, October 14, 2007. The class meets from 6:00 p.m.–8:30 p.m. You may take as much time as you need, but if possible please allow a student question and answer period. There are approximately sixty students, and the classroom contains state-of-the-art technology. If you have specific technology requests, please do not hesitate to contact me. Enclosed is a parking permit and map of the campus directing you to the appropriate classroom.

Once again, thank you for continued support of our students. I and my students are looking forward to you sharing your communications insight and expertise with us on October 14. If you have any additional information, please do not hesitate to contact me via e-mail at S.Quirrel@teaching.com or call me at 123-456-7890.

Sincerely,

Sarah S. Quirrel

Sarah S. Quirrel
Instructor

sbb
Enclosure

◀ **FIGURE 3**   Letter Example

relationships, and business operations. Every employee should have some method of recording relevant business situations if needed for future reference to protect yourself and/or your employer. Although there are numerous methods of documenting and retaining important information and events, the basic elements to be recorded remain the same.

Effective documentation records the *who, what, when, where,* and *why* of a situation. Basic elements in effective documentation include the date, time, and location the event occurred. It is also important to note the event itself (e.g., who said what or did what). Also, note who was present when the major event occurred and how witnesses to the event behaved or responded to the event. Your documentation is for your personal reference. Therefore, your documentation can be kept electronically, in a journal, or through minimal notations on a calendar. Whatever system you choose, remember to keep your documentation in a secure, private location. It is not necessary to—nor should you—record every event that occurs at work. If there are any supporting memos, be sure to keep copies in a private file, preferably in a secure location. If you are ever called upon to defend your actions, you will have the ability to easily gather pertinent information.

(Students do not type DS, these are shown for correct spacing).	
Start the memo about two inches from the top of the page.	**MEMO TO:** Loretta Howerton, Office Manager *(DS)* **FROM:** Lawrence Schmidt, OA/CIS Trainer *(DS)*
Double-space after each *heading.* Bold and capitalize just the headings, not the information. Use initial caps in the *subject line.*	**DATE:** January 6, 2007 *(DS)* **SUBJECT:** Memo Format for Internal Correspondence *(DS)*
Body—single-space, no tabs, left align. Double-space between paragraphs.	A memorandum is an internal communication that is sent within the organization. It is often the means by which managers correspond with employees, and vice versa. Memos provide written records of announcements, requests for action, and policies and procedures. You should use first and last names and include the job title. *(DS)* Templates, or preformatted forms, often are used for creating memos. Templates provide a uniform look for company correspondence and save the employee the time of having to design a memo. Word processing software has memo templates that can be customized. You should customize the template so it has the company name and your department name atthe top. Make sure you change the date format. It should be as it is seen at the beginning of this memo. *(DS)*
Reference initials (typist's initials) *Attachment notation,* only if needed (if you attach something)	sbb Attachment

◀ **FIGURE 4**   Memo Format

MEMO TO: Loretta Howerton, Office Manager

FROM: Lawrence Schmidt, OA/CIS Trainer

DATE: January 6, 2007

SUBJECT: Accounting Department Computer Training

This memo is to confirm that the computer training for the accounting department will occur on February 1, 2007 in the large conference room. Although the training is scheduled from 9:00 a.m.–11:30 a.m., I have reserved the room for the entire morning, beginning at 7:00 a.m.

As we discussed last week, this may be a good opportunity to offer breakfast to the department prior to the training. If this is something you would like to pursue, please let me know by next Tuesday, and I will make the proper arrangements. Thank you again for the opportunity to provide computer training to your team.

sbb

◀ **FIGURE 5**   Memo Example

▶ TELECOMMUNICATION

With the increased use of technology in the workplace, the proper use of cell phones, voice mail, answering machines, and facsimile machines becomes increasingly important. When using a *cell phone,* keep in mind that there are proper times and places to use it and there are times and places where a cell phone should not be used. Just as it is impolite to interrupt someone who is talking,

Include the date.	*June 3, 2007*
Start your note with a salutation and the receiver's name.	*Dear Mrs. McCombs,*
Be brief but specific about why you are thanking the person. Include how you benefited from the person's kindness. Do not begin every sentence with *I*.	*Thank-you for loaning me your book on business etiquette. I especially liked the chapter on social events and dining. Your constant encouragement and mentoring mean so much to me.* *Sincerely,*
Use a complementary closing, and do not forget to sign your name.	*Mason Yang*

◀ **FIGURE 6**   Thank-You Note

it is also impolite to interrupt a conversation with a cell phone ringing and/or answering a cell phone. There are two basic guidelines for using your cell phone. First, it is OK to have a cell phone ring and/or answer your phone if you are alone at your desk or office. Secondly, when at a luncheon or meeting, turn your cell phone off or on vibrate. If it vibrates, do not answer it. Politely excuse yourself from the table or room and take the call in private. Although these guidelines are for business purposes, they should pertain to personal use as well.

If you are not with another individual, make every attempt to answer the *telephone* after the first ring. Smile when you are talking. Although the caller may not be able to visually see you, your smile will be communicated through your attitude and tone of voice. Speak clearly and slowly. Most voices get higher when the rate of speech increases. Be cautious to not speak too softly or too loudly. If you receive a message, remember to promptly return the call. It is rude to not return a message.

If you are with someone else when the phone rings, ignore the call and let the call go into your voice mail. If you must take the call, explain to the individual in your presence that you are expecting a call (or must take the call) and apologize for the interruption. When taking the call, if possible, be brief, take a message, and return the telephone call after you are finished with your face-to-face meeting.

Do not have a voice-mail message that contains music or humor. Your message should be brief and professional. Provide a friendly greeting, and include your name in the message. Remember to check your message mailbox at least once a day. If you are leaving a message on someone else's voice mail, remember to speak clearly and slowly. Always state your name, when you are calling, the purpose of your call, and a return telephone number.

▶ FOUL LANGUAGE

Your words reflect what is going on in your heart and mind. There is never an appropriate time to use profane and offensive language at work. Even in times of stress or at social functions, you are representing your company and must always do so in a professional manner. Practice self-control. Attempt to eliminate foul or offensive language from your personal and professional vocabulary. Doing so will rid your heart and mind of negativity. If you happen to slip by utilizing inappropriate language at work, immediately apologize. Make a mental note of what situation caused you to behave poorly and learn from the experience. Ask yourself how you could have better handled the situation and mentally rehearse a proper, more acceptable method of verbally handling a challenging situation.

▶ POTENTIAL OFFENSIVE NAMES

Names that could be considered sexist and offensive are inappropriate in a business setting. In fact, using inappropriate names toward coworkers will expose you and your company to a potential sexual harassment lawsuit. These include names such as *honey, sweetie,* and *sexy.* Even if the individual acts as if he or she is not offended by the names, the person may actually be offended or insulted but afraid to tell you. Eliminate potentially offensive names from your workplace vocabulary. In addition, do not use gender-specific titles when referring to certain job titles. For example:

INSTEAD OF:	USE:
Postman	Postal carrier
Policeman	Police officer
Waitress	Server
Stewardess	Flight attendant
Maid	Housekeeper

▶ NOT ALWAYS ABOUT YOU

Closing our discussion on communication, we address one word that often dominates our vocabulary. This word frequently turns listeners off; unfortunately, too often, the sender is unaware of its overuse. The word is *I.* Be cautious with the use of this word. Self-centered people use it to draw attention, while others who may not be confident may use the word to protect themselves. They may not know how to turn the conversation to others, so they choose to stay in a safety zone. When you are using verbal communication, think before you speak. If your initial sentence includes *I,* try to rephrase your message.

◀ **EXERCISE 4: Checking for I:** *Take five minutes and interview a classmate about college and his or her career choice. While you are getting to know each other, keep track of how many times your new friend says the word I.*

◀ SUMMARY OF KEY CONCEPTS

▷ Effective communication is necessary for workplace success
▷ The goal of communication is to create a mutual understanding between the sender and the receiver
▷ There are appropriate times to utilize both the formal and informal communication channels
▷ The communication process involves a sender, a receiver, noise, and feedback
▷ It is important to thoughtfully consider the right words to increase the chance of successful verbal communication
▷ Because the receiver of your message will not have verbal and nonverbal assistance in interpreting your message, it is vital to take great care with all written messages
▷ Listening and silence are effective tools for effective communication

◀ KEY TERMS

business memos	feedback	letterhead
communication	formal communication	noise
decoding	informal communication	sender
encoding	letter	

◀ REFERENCE

Parsons, G. *Basics of Communication*. 1982.
http://www.cedresources.ca/docs/modules/comm.doc

◀ IF YOU WERE THE BOSS

1. One of your employees uses bad grammar that is reflecting poorly on your department's performance. How can you get a handle on this problem?
2. Employees keep saying they never know what is going on at work. What steps would you take to increase workplace communication?

◀ WEB LINKS

http://www.career.fsu.edu/ccis/guides/write_eff.html

http://owl.english.purdue.edu/handouts/pw/p_memo.html

http://members.aol.com/nonverbal2/entries.htm#Entries

http://www.casaa-resources.net/mainpages/resources/sourcebook/listening-skills.html

◀ WORKPLACE DOs AND DON'Ts

Do recognize the importance effective and professional communication has in the workplace.	*Don't* ignore opportunities to improve your communication skills on a daily basis.
Do carefully think through your message and the appropriate medium.	*Don't* be in such a hurry to send your message that an incorrect message is sent.
Do always demonstrate professionalism in the formatting, word choice, and grammar in your written communications.	*Don't* write and send messages when you are angry.
Do express kindness to others with both your words and body language.	*Don't* utilize foul language at work or at home.
Do leave professional voice-mail messages that include your name, a return number, and the purpose of your call.	*Don't* have a cute or annoying message on your voice mail.

► ACTIVITIES

ACTIVITY 1

Without infringing on someone's privacy, discreetly observe a stranger's body language for approximately five minutes. Make sure you are far enough away to not hear him or her speak. Name at least two assumptions you can make by simply watching the person's gestures, movements, and expressions.

GESTURE, MOVEMENT, OR EXPRESSION	ASSUMPTION
1.	
2.	
3.	

ACTIVITY 2

Watch a television news show for a half hour. Document at least two facial expressions of an individual being interviewed. Do the individual's facial expressions match his or her statements?

FACIAL EXPRESSION	MATCH STATEMENTS: YES OR NO
1.	
2.	

ACTIVITY 3

Review the following letter and identify five errors. How should they be corrected?

April 21, 2007

Sandra Wong, Vice President
Human Resource Department
Robinson Enterprises
55123 W. Robinson Lane
Prosperity, CA 99923

Dear Ms. Wong,

It was a pleasure speaking with you this afternoon regarding the average salary you pay your receptionists. This data will be useful as our company begins creating a new receptionist position for our California site.

I am most appreciative of your offer to mail me a copy of your most recent salary guide for all production positions. I look forward to receiving that guide in the mail. As a thank-you for your kindness, I am enclosing coupons for our company product.

If there is any information I can provide to assist you, please let me know. Thank-you again for your cooperation.

Sincerely,

Cory Kringle

WHAT ARE THE ERRORS?	HOW TO CORRECT
1.	
2.	
3.	
4.	
5.	

ACTIVITY 4

Review the following memo and identify five errors. How should they be corrected?

MEMORANDUM

Re: Budget Meeting

To: Mason Jared

From: Cory Kringle

Date: May 1

Hey Mason. I wanted to remind you that we have a meeting next week to talk about next year's budget. Bring some numbers and we'll work through them. Bye.

-Cory

WHAT ARE THE ERRORS?	HOW TO CORRECT
1.	
2.	
3.	
4.	
5.	

ACTIVITY 5

Role-play what to say to someone who is inappropriately talking on his or her cell phone, such as someone interrupting your meeting.

▶ SAMPLE EXAM QUESTIONS

1. The two types of workplace communication include _____ and _____ communication.

2. A major form of the informal communication network is called _____.

3. When the _____ is targeting individuals and their personal lives, it is called _____.

4. When _____ are displayed at work, it becomes difficult to think and behave in a logical manner.

5. Nonverbal communication is what we communicate through our _____.

6. _____ communicates to your audience that you are listening and are allowing the other party consideration.

7. Make sure all _____ is error free by proofreading prior to sending.

StockByte Royalty Free CD/Getty Images

14

NETWORKING AND RESUMÉS

OBJECTIVES

Define *networking* and its importance to a professional future

► Develop a professional *networking list*

► Create and update your *resumé*

► Create a *cover letter* and professional reference list

► Create a *job search portfolio*

*Whenever you
are asked if you can
do a job, tell 'em,
"Certainly I can!" Then
get busy and find out
how to do it.*

**Theodore Roosevelt
(1858–1919)**

▶ PROFESSIONAL NETWORKING

There will be a time in your future that you will be looking for a job or a new position. This is why networking now and throughout your career is important. **Networking** is the act of creating professional relationships. Think of networking as a connection device.

A professional network is important when you begin searching for a new job either within or outside your current company. Developing a professional network is easy. You tell a person who tells others, then those people tell others, and soon you have many people who know that you want a job. Look at figure 1 to see how a network grows.

Almost every person you know can be included in your network. Include the following people in your network list:

- ▶ Coworkers
- ▶ Supervisors
- ▶ Instructors
- ▶ Family
- ▶ Friends

Cory has been working as an account clerk for a year now. Throughout the year, Cory has been learning new skills and has learned several new software packages. In addition, Cory has attended several workshops and conferences. Cory knows that in the next year or two the office manager is planning on retiring. Cory would like this position or a similar one. Now is the time for Cory to begin networking. Cory begins by letting coworkers and supervisors know how much Cory has learned in this job. In addition, Cory mentions the new skills and software packages learned over the last year and shares future goals. Cory then tells family members and friends the same thing. This is the beginning of Cory's professional network. Cory creates a written network list and starts keeping track of the people on the list in order to keep them updated.

In addition to adding people you know, there are many other ways to develop and generate your network. One such way is volunteering for community organizations. This gives you a chance to meet many people in different organizations and in different positions throughout the community. Another way is to join clubs. Again, this is a way to meet different people from different companies and from different industries. When you attend workshops, conferences, and seminars, you get a chance to meet people from different corporations that are in your same career field. Another great method to grow your professional network is for you to conduct

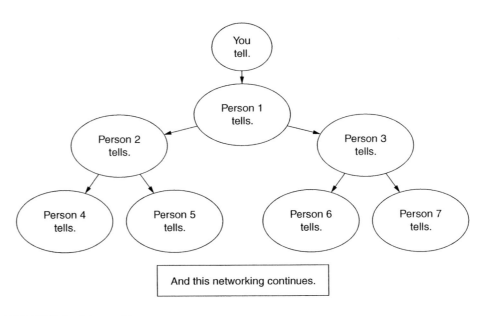

◀ FIGURE 1   Networking

informational interviews. An informational interview is a way to find out about a company or specific career field. You can ask questions about jobs, hiring, and the culture of the company by meeting and talking with others you have added to your professional network.

You are networking when you:

▶ Attend professional or trade association meetings
▶ Talk to other parents when attending a child's sporting or music event
▶ Volunteer for a local park cleanup day
▶ Visit with other members of your social clubs or religious groups
▶ Talk to your neighbors
▶ Strike up a conversation with a stranger waiting at the veterinarian's office
▶ Post messages on mailing lists or in chat rooms
▶ Talk to salespeople who are visiting your office

◀ **EXERCISE 1: Identify Your Current Network:** *Name at least three places where you have met people who could be on your professional network list.*

1. _____

2. _____

3. _____

Once you have established a professional network, it is important to maintain that network. This is done by keeping in touch with the people on your list. Keep them updated with your career growth and plans. You can do this by keeping track of who is included in your network and note the last time you updated your information. A **network list** should include the network contact's name, address, telephone number, and e-mail address so you can easily get in touch with each person. You should provide each contact that is actively assisting with your job search a copy of your most current resumé. Keep the contacts on your network list updated throughout your job search. When keeping in contact with members of your network, be sensitive to their time. Do not annoy or be inconsiderate in your behavior and interactions with individuals in your network.

▶ YOUR RESUMÉ

As you begin your career, you will need to create a resumé. A **resumé** is a formal document that presents a person's knowledge, skill, and abilities to potential employers. Throughout your career, it is important to continue to update your resumé. You may not be planning to find a new job or get promoted now, but a time will come when you need a current resumé. Do not wait until that time to create or update your resumé. It is important that you have all current job-related information on your resumé. You need to continually update and include accomplishments you achieve throughout your career. If you wait until you need a resumé, you may forget the important information. As just discussed in the previous section, you should continually be increasing your skills. Add these new skills and experiences to your resumé.

A career objective is a statement to introduce your skills and interest in the position. If you include a career objective on your resumé, it should be specific to the job for which you are applying. Through research, you will identify company needs; you should then apply this information when writing your objective.

Cyber resumés are designed to be sent through the Internet. Companies often drop these into a database to fill open positions. These resumés are then scanned for key words listed in the job posting. Cyber resumés should be saved in plain text. Do not use tables, text formatting (bold, italics, underline), bullets, or headers.

Once you have completed a resumé, update it at least once a year. After you have reached a significant, new skill level, it will be time to change your resumé format. If you are starting in your career, you should create a resumé using the **functional resumé format.** This format is used to emphasize relevant skills when you lack related work experience. A functional resumé focuses on your skills and education. This is done by listing your career objective, relevant skills, and education before any work experience. Most functional resumés are only one page in length. Refer to Figure 2 for the functional resumé setup. See Figures 3 and 4 for examples.

As you grow in your career, you can change to the **chronological resumé format.** This format emphasizes your related work experience and skills. You should have your employment history, in reverse time order (most recent job first), listed at the beginning of the resumé. Remember to stress major accomplishments and responsibilities of each position. Highlight important activities you have accomplished in your job. Do not assume the reader will know what you have done. Be specific; if necessary, add a second page to your resumé. If your resumé is two pages, be sure you put your name at the top of the second page. Refer to figure 5 for the chronological resumé setup. See Figure 6 for an example.

Make sure your resumé includes both job specific skills and transferable skills. **Job-specific skills** are those that are directly related to a specific job. If you were to leave that job and change careers, those skills would probably not be useful. For example, if you are a medical billing clerk who knows how to use a specific program such as Medical Manager, you will not need to use these skills if you change jobs and become a teacher.

Transferable skills are skills that are transferred from one job to the next. If you change careers, you will still be able to use these skills in any job. For example, if you are a medical billing clerk, you may have consistent contact with patients and must practice patience and be positive when dealing with your customers. If you become a teacher, that skill is transferable to the children in your classroom. You should list both types of skills on your resumé. Employers want you to have the basic skills needed to perform the job, but they also look for transferable skills. They want to know if you are a team player when needed, reliable, a good communicator, get along with others, and so on. The term **soft skills** refers to the people skills needed to get along with others.

Be specific with the skills you list on your resumé, such as computer skills. The term *computer skills* can be too general and typically includes many different areas: networking, programming, applications, data processing, and/or repair. An employer needs to know what specific computer skills you possess. Be specific in your explanation, for example, by informing the employer of your skill level (e.g., basic, intermediate, or advanced) with specific software.

If you are bilingual (speak or write a second language), include this information in your resumé. Let the employer know if you read, write, or just speak that language.

◀ **EXERCISE 2: List Your Skills:** *List as many as possible of your job-specific skills and your transferable skills. If you do not have any job-specific skills, list the job skills you will have after finishing your schooling.*

Job-Specific Skills (Related to Your Career Job)	Transferable Skills (Can Be Used in Any Job)
1.	1.
2.	2.
3.	3.
4.	4.
5.	5.

Organize your skills by listing what is needed for the job first. You need to write with energy. Use action verbs, also referred to as *power words*, and quantify your accomplishments. For example, instead of stating "started a new accounts receivable system," use "developed a new accounts receivable system that reduced turnaround time by 20 percent."

Use power words whenever possible. They describe your accomplishments in a lively and specific way. Use some of the power phrases listed in Table 1 and Table 2.

When creating a resumé, see the resumé setup and sample resumés found later in this chapter and follow these important tips:

✓ Make sure your objective is job specific.
✓ If you are starting out in your career, use a functional resumé; education and skills are listed before work experience. Keep your resumé to one page.
✓ If you have work experience in your career, use a chronological resumé; experience and skills are listed before education. If you need two pages, put your name on the second page.
✓ Include job-specific and transferable skills.
✓ List experience and education with most recent first.
✓ Watch for consistency in tense: if you have words ending in *ing* or *ed* under an area, make sure they all end the same.
✓ Do not use bullets throughout your resumé; use them to emphasize your skills.
✓ Do not use different color fonts or highlights on your resumé.
✓ Make sure your resumé is consistent in both setup and formatting (periods at the end of each line, alignment of dates, date format, bold/italics, etc.).
✓ Do not use a word processing program template.
✓ List your high school in the education section only if you are using a functional format and have not graduated from college.
✓ Use *telephone*, not *phone* (this is slang).
✓ Use the postal abbreviation for your state, for example: the state is *CA*, not *Ca.*, not *Ca*, not *C.A.*
✓ Any reference statement does not belong on your resumé. Do not list references on the resumé. References should be on a separate sheet and provided only when requested.

Create a list of professional references that the potential employer can contact. Instead of listing these on your resumé, create a separate page for references. Do not send this list with your resumé unless it is requested by the employer. However, you should have a copy available because employers usually ask for references after they have interviewed you. Make sure you have asked each person on this list if he or she will be a reference. Also, be sure each person on this list will provide a positive reference. Have at least three names to give as references. Include each reference's name, telephone number, address, relationship, and e-mail if available. References can be past or present employers and supervisors, coworkers, instructors, or someone with whom you have volunteered. Do not use relatives, friends, or religious leaders unless you have worked or volunteered with or for them.

You should have at least three letters of recommendation. A letter of recommendation is a written testimony from another person that states that you are credible. The letters should not be more than two years old. These letters can be from past or present employers, coworkers, instructors, or someone you worked for as a volunteer.

In addition to keeping your resumé updated, you should update your reference list. Make sure your references are relevant to your career. Check to see if they are still willing to serve as references. In addition, make sure you have your letters of recommendation updated.

When you believe your resumé is perfect, have someone you trust review it for punctuation, grammar, and other potential mistakes. Make sure you check it several times before sending it to a potential employer. Look at the Functional and Chronological Resumé Setups for formatting tips.

YOUR NAME

Your Address

City, State ZIP

Telephone Number (Include Area Code)

E-Mail Address (Remove Hyperlink)

OBJECTIVE

Headings can be on the left or centered, 12- or 14-point font, and uppercase or initial cap.
Headings should be formatted the same throughout the resumé.
Make sure the spacing is equal between each section.

QUALIFICATIONS (OR SKILLS)

- Related to the job, they can be job-related skills or transferable skills.
- Most relative to the job are listed first.
- Bullet (small round or small square only) these items to stand out.

EDUCATION

You may list before qualifications.
Do not list high school.
Include the years attended.
List schools in chronological order, most recent attended first.

> Skills and education need to be emphasized. List your skills and education before any work experience.

WORK EXPERIENCE

Include: *Name of Company and City, State*—No Addresses
Job title, if part-time, dates employed (month, year)
List the jobs in chronological order with most recent date first.
List the duties, responsibilities, and achievements.
Be consistent in your setup.
Use the same tense throughout (*ed* or *ing*).
Do not use complete sentences or *I, me,* or *my.*

OTHER CAPABILITIES

Optional—Items in this section may not be directly related to the job but may interest the employer.

Notes to Keep in Mind

- ✓ Watch periods, punctuation.
- ✓ Watch spelling.
- ✓ Keep to one page.
- ✓ Use a regular font, no color, 12-point font (except heading).
- ✓ Use resumé paper, no dark or bright colors.
- ✓ Do not use full sentences or *I, me,* or *my.*
- ✓ References are not necessary; you will have a separate sheet with references.

◀ **FIGURE 2**   Functional Resumé Setup

Cory Kringle

4 Tolearn Avenue

Fresno, CA 93705

559-442-4333

ckringle05@jasper.com

OBJECTIVE

To obtain a position as an Account Clerk with XYZ Company which will allow me to utilize my skills in a dynamic company.

SKILLS

- Knowledgeable and accurate in general ledger and journal posting
- Basic software knowledge of QuickBooks
- Knowledge of account receivables and account payables
- Experience with Microsoft Office, including Word, Excel, Access, PowerPoint, and Outlook
- Ten-key at 150 cspm
- Type 50 wpm accurately
- Excellent English grammar, spelling, and punctuation skills
- Accurately follow oral and written instructions
- Strong attention to detail
- Positive attitude, motivated, and organized

EDUCATION

California State University, Fresno, CA   8/06–present
Accounting

Fresno City College, Fresno, CA   5/06
Associate Degree in Business, Certificate of Completion in Account Clerk Program

WORK EXPERIENCE

S and L Accounting   1/06–5/06
Account Clerk Volunteer (work experience course)
Assisted the accountant by answering telephone, bookkeeping, data entry in Excel and QuickBooks, verifying totals, making copies, faxing, and other clerical duties when needed.

Bret's Hamburger Haven   1/05–12/05
Cashier/Food Service
Worked as a team member to assist customers with food orders, cleaned, handled cash, and trained new employees.

◀ **FIGURE 3** Functional Resumé Example 1

DENISE S. SHORE

1408 North Ferris, Fresno, CA 93702
559-451-5899   dshore02@yahoo.com

OBJECTIVE

To obtain a position as an Office Assistant with XYZ Company that will enable me to utilize my current skills and education.

QUALIFICATIONS

- Type 50 wpm
- Experience with Microsoft Office, including Word, Excel, Access, PowerPoint, and Outlook
- Accurately proofread and edit documents
- Knowledge of records management
- Positive telephone skills
- Excellent oral and written communications skills
- Positive attitude, motivated, and organized
- Excellent customer services skills

EDUCATION

2004–2006	Fresno City College	Fresno, CA

AA Degree Business & Technology
Clerical Administration Certificate

EXPERIENCE

06/2003–present	Target	Fresno, CA

Cashier
Responsibilities include: providing customer service, cashiering, handling of money, placing merchandise on the floor, helping return gobacks, processing of merchandise being put on the floor, stocking of merchandise in back/stockroom, training new hires.

02/1998–05/2003	Burger King	Fresno, CA

Cashiering/Counter Person
Responsibilities included: assisted guests with their orders, ensured a safe and clean work environment, and assisted other team members as needed.

◀ **FIGURE 4**   Functional Resumé Example 2

YOUR NAME
Your Address
City, State ZIP
Telephone Number (Include Area Code)
E-Mail Address (Remove Hyperlink)

OBJECTIVE

> Headings can be on the left or centered, 12- or 14-point font, and uppercase or initial cap.
> Headings should be formatted the same throughout the resumé.
> Make sure the spacing is equal between each section.

WORK EXPERIENCE

Include: *Name of Company and City, State*—No Addresses
Job title, if part-time, dates employed (month, year)
List the jobs in chronological order with most recent dates first.
List the duties, responsibilities, and achievements.
Be consistent in your setup.
Use the same tense throughout (*ed* or *ing*).
Do not use complete sentences or *I, me,* or *my.*

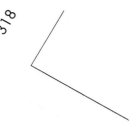

Emphasis is on your work experience in your career. List your work experience first.

QUALIFICATIONS (OR SKILLS)

- Related to the job, they can be job-related skills or transferable skills.
- Most relative to the job are listed first.
- Bullet (small round or small square only) these items to stand out.

EDUCATION

You may list before qualifications.
Do not list high school.
Include the years attended.
List schools in chronological order, most recent attended first.

OTHER CAPABILITIES

Optional—Items in this section may not be directly related to the job but may interest the employer.

Notes to Keep in Mind

✓ Watch periods, punctuation.
✓ Watch spelling.
✓ Use a regular font, no color, 12-point font (except heading).
✓ Use resumé paper, no dark or bright colors.
✓ Do not use full sentences or *I, me,* or *my.*
✓ References are not necessary; you will have a separate sheet with references.

◄ **FIGURE 5** Chronological Resumé Setup

Forrest S. Gunther

2833 Follie Land
Pasadena, CA 93705
214-111-4322
F_gunther@yipae.com

EDUCATION

California State University, Fresno, CA   5/05
Bachelor degree in accounting

Fresno City College, Fresno, CA   5/03
Associate degree in accounting, certificate of completion in account clerk program

PROFESSIONAL WORK EXPERIENCE

Anderson, Bolt, and Company CPA   6/05–present
Accountant
AP, AR, general ledger, general journal, quarterly taxes, and payroll. Supervise account clerks.

Randy and Son Construction   6/03–6/05
Account Clerk
Answer telephone, record journal and ledger for bookkeeping, data entry in Excel and QuickBooks, verify totals, make copies, fax, and other clerical duties when needed.

SKILLS

- Experience and accurate in general ledger and journal posting
- Extensive knowledge of QuickBooks and MAS 90
- Experience with account receivables and account payables
- Experience with Microsoft Office, including Word, Excel, Access, PowerPoint, and Outlook
- Supervisor and leadership skill
- Excellent English grammar, spelling, and punctuation skills
- Accurately follow oral and written instructions
- Strong attention to detail
- Positive attitude, motivated, and organized
- Ten-key at 200 cspm
- Type 60 wpm accurately

◀ **FIGURE 6**   Chronological Resumé Example

◀ **TABLE 1**   Skills Power Phrases

POWER PHRASES FOR SKILLS SECTION

- Ideal oral and written communications skills
- Understanding of office practices and procedures; ability to operate fax machine, copy machine, and ten-key machine; ability to enter data; ability to effectively interpret policies and procedures; work well under the pressure of deadlines; establish and maintain a positive working relationship with others; ability to communicate
- Accurate typing skills at _____ wpm
- Experienced with Microsoft Office, including Word, Excel, Access, PowerPoint, and Outlook
- Excellent English grammar, spelling, and punctuation skills
- Accurately proofread and edit documents
- Strong attention to detail
- Accurately follow oral and written instructions
- Excellent attendance and punctual record
- Maintain confidentiality
- Positive attitude, motivated, and organized

◀ **TABLE 2**   Experience Power Phrases

PHRASES FOR WORK EXPERIENCE

- Prepared reports and other materials requiring independent achievement
- Enjoy working in a flexible team situation
- Established and maintained positive and effective working relationships
- Planned, scheduled, and performed a variety of clerical work
- Maintained office equipment and supplies
- Proofread forms and materials for completeness and accuracy according to regulations and procedures
- Processed and prepared materials for pamphlets, bulletins, brochures, announcements, handbooks, forms, and curriculum materials
- Provided training of temporary or new employees
- Maintained department files and records
- Demonstrated ability to receive incoming calls and route them efficiently
- Processed purchase requisitions, ordered and distributed supplies, and maintained inventory control
- Responsibly planned and conducted meetings

▶ COVER LETTERS

A **cover letter** is most often the first impression a potential employer will have of you. It serves as an introduction to your resumé. Employers use cover letters as screening tools.

When writing your cover letter, use a friendly but professional tone. Include information about the company that shows the employer you have done some research on the company. This may include knowing the key product or service, company growth plans, and/or recent community involvement.

In your letter, point out how you can meet the employer's needs. This is accomplished by reflecting the skills and qualifications the employer is asking for in the advertisement and/or job description. Let the employer know what you can offer the company, not what you want from the company. Do not just duplicate the resumé; instead, expand the areas of interest to the employer.

Be careful not to begin most of your sentences with the word *I*. Instead, focus the attention toward the employer. This puts the company first and makes its needs more important. Do this by beginning the sentence with what the company will receive with your skills. For example:

Instead of writing, "*I* am proficient in Word 2003 and WordPerfect,"
Write, "*Your* company will benefit from my proficiency in Word 2003 and WordPerfect."

When addressing the cover letter, address it to a specific person. This should be the person who is making the hiring decision. Do not address it to a department, the company name, or to whom it may concern. If you have done research and still cannot get a name, use a subject line instead of a salutation. If you have talked to a specific person or with the employer, refer to the previous communication. Make sure you include the specific position you are seeking and how you found out about the job. Request an interview (not the job), include an enclosure notation for your resumé, and close courteously.

Use correct name and title, use spell and grammar check, use left margin justification, and get the employer's permission before sending a letter and resumé. Common mistakes include making typographical or grammar errors, forgetting to including a date, and forgetting to sign the cover letter. Any error communicates a lack of attention to detail. Even minor errors have the potential to eliminate you from any chance of being interviewed.

Be sure you use the proper format for your cover letter. As stated in the resumé section, have someone you trust proofread your letter before sending it to the potential employer. Each paragraph has a purpose. Make sure you have done your research and learned about the position and the company. The cover letter setup in Figure 7 and sample cover letters in Figures 8 and 9 will help you create your cover letter. The cover letter should be printed on the same type of paper used for your resumé. Make sure you sign your cover letter.

Date of Letter

Employer's Name, Title
Company Name
Address
City, State ZIP

Dear Mr./Ms./Dr.:

First Paragraph. Give the reason for the letter, the position for which you are applying, and how you learned of this position. Note any previous contact you may have had with the employer.

Second Paragraph. Tell why you are interested in the position, the organization, and its products or services. Indicate any research you have done on the position and/or the employer.

Third Paragraph. Refer to the attached resumé and highlight relevant aspects of your resumé. Emphasize the skills mentioned in the advertisement or on the job description. Provide specific reasons why the organization should hire you and what you can do for it.

Last Paragraph. Indicate your desire for an interview, and offer flexibility as to the time and place. Thank the employer for his or her consideration and express anticipation in meeting him or her. Include a telephone number for contact.

Sincerely,

(Do not forget to sign your cover letter.)

Your Name
Your Address
City, State ZIP

Enclosure

◀ **FIGURE 7**   Cover Letter Setup

September 25, 2007

XYZ Corporation
Attention Rick Raye
435 East Chesny Street
Santa Rosa, CA 91188

Dear Mr. Raye:

As a recent accounting graduate of Fresno City College I was delighted to learn from your web site of the available account clerk position. The purpose of this letter is to express a strong interest in becoming a XYZ Corporation account clerk at your Santa Rosa Facility. In addition to possessing an A.S. degree in Business and a Certificate of Completion in the Account Clerk Program, I am responsible and consider myself a leader.

XYZ sponsors a variety of community services and employee recognition programs, which I have read a great deal about. Your company has earned my respect, as it has from much of the community for your involvement in after-school programs.

As you will see on the attached resumé, XYZ would benefit from the skills I have learned throughout college. These include: general ledger and journal posting; Microsoft Word, Excel, and Access programs; Quickbooks; and accurate ten-key (150 cspm). In addition, I also offer a superior work ethic, strong communicative abilities, attention to detail, and a keen interest in upgrading my skills.

I am confident that my skills and abilities will make me an ideal candidate for a position in this field. I would appreciate an opportunity to meet with you to discuss how my skills can meet the needs of XYZ. I will contact you by phone within the week to discuss the possibility of an interview.

Sincerely,

(Do not forget to sign here.)

Cory Kringle
4 Tolearn Avenue
Fresno, CA 93705

Enclosure

◀ **FIGURE 8**   Cover Letter Example 1

◀ **EXERCISE 3: List Your References:** *List at least three people you can use as references. Then list at least three people you can ask to write you a letter of recommendation. Include their relationship to you.*

References	Relationship
1.	
2.	
3.	
Letter of Recommendation	Relationship
1.	
2.	
3.	

DENISE S. SHORE

1408 North Ferris, Fresno, CA 93702
559-451-5899   dshore02@yahoo.com

September 21, 2007

Mrs. Lisa Anders
Plenty Office Supplies
1122 Friant Road
Fresno, CA 93725

Dear Mrs. Anders:

I recently spoke with Heidi Johns, an employee at your company; and she recommended that I send you a copy of my resumé. Knowing the requirements for the position and that I am interested in working at this type of establishment, she felt that I would be an ideal candidate for your office assistant position.

My personal goal is to be a part of an organization such as yours that wants to excel in both growth and profit. I would welcome the opportunity to be employed at Plenty Office Supplies since this is the largest and best-known office supply company in the city. Your company has a reputation of excellent products and service.

Plenty Office Supplies would benefit from someone such as I who is accustomed to a fast-paced environment where deadlines are a priority and handling multiple jobs simultaneously is the norm. As you can see on the attached resumé, my previous jobs required me to be well organized, accurate, and friendly. I enjoy a challenge and work hard to attain my goals. Great customer skills are important in a business such as yours.

Nothing would please me more than to be a part of your team. I would like very much to discuss with you how I could contribute to your organization with my office skills and my dependability. I will contact you next week to arrange an interview. In the interim, I can be reached at 559-111-5899.

Sincerely,

(Do not forget to sign here.)

Denise S. Shore

Enclosure

◁ **FIGURE 9**   Cover Letter Example 2

▶ JOB SEARCH PORTFOLIO

As you are conducting your job search, you should begin creating a **job search portfolio.** The job search portfolio is a collection of paperwork you will need for your job search and interviews. The items you collect for your portfolio will be used to keep you organized and prepared while job searching.

It is best to have a binder with tabs to keep this paperwork organized and protected. Because you should not punch holes in your original documents, you should put them into plastic notebook protectors. When you start collecting your paperwork, be sure that you keep your original and at least two copies available at all times while conducting your job search. The copies are for your interviews.

The following is a list of items to keep in your job search portfolio.

ITEM:	IMPORTANCE:
Network list	This is a place to keep it where it is accessible and can be easily updated.
Resumé	Usually asked for by an employer, update once a year.
Cover letter	Usually asked for by an employer, update once a year.
Reference list	Usually asked for by an employer, update once a year.
Letters of recommendation	Usually asked for by an employer, update once a year.
Transcripts	Employers may ask for school transcripts to verify your education. You should have a copy available.
Awards and/or certificates	These are ideal extras you can share with the employer at your interview. Some employers may request certificates for specific skills.
Work samples	These are ideal extras you can share with the employer at your interview. It can prove what you say you can do. Work samples are not necessary in all careers.
Completed application	Although each company will usually have its own application, most of the information requested is the same. By having a completed generic application, you will have most of the information available if you are requested to complete an application while at the job site.
Copy of driver's license	Some employers will ask for this, depending on the job.
Personal commercial	Assists with interview, update at least once a year.
Small calendar, note paper, and pen	Keep track of important dates and use to make notes.
Performance appraisal	Only include if positive.

All items in your portfolio will assist you in your job search and interview process. You will take an **interview portfolio** with you to an interview. The interview portfolio should be a separate folder (such as a paper folder with pockets). Your interview folder should contain copies of the items pertinent to the position for which you are applying. You should bring copies of documents and not your originals. This way you can give them to the employer if necessary. Your resumé, cover letter, and references should be on resumé paper. You will not necessarily take all of the items from your portfolio with you to each job interview. You should have the following for each interview: copies of resumé, cover letter, reference list, application, personal commercial, calendar, note paper, and pen. The other items are included if you want the employer to have a copy because they are relevant to the job. Your folder should remain on your lap while interviewing. If needed, put your personal commercial on the top of the folder in case you get nervous and forget what you have included in this commercial. You can peek at the commercial, but do not read it.

If you are currently working and you start looking for a job, make sure to keep your job search confidential. If you are listing your supervisor as a reference, make sure you let him or her know you are looking and why. Do not quit your current job before being offered a new job. Also, make sure you do not bad-mouth your company or anyone that works for your current or former employer(s).

Even though you now have the experience of being in a career job, you still need to make sure you are prepared when you go on an interview. This means practicing answering interview questions with work-related experiences. Do your homework. Research the company where you will be interviewing, and use that information to let the interviewer know you are interested in working at his or her company.

▶ APPLICATIONS AND PREPARATION

You may be asked to fill out an application to turn in with your resumé packet, or you may be asked to fill out an application after you have been interviewed. If you fill out the application at home, make sure it is typed. If you fill out the application while at the employer's, print neatly and in black ink.

You should have an application filled out in your portfolio so if you are asked to fill one out while at the interviewer's office you have the information needed to complete the application. Make sure you fill out the application completely, but do not list your social security number or birth date. This information should not be given to the prospective employer until you have accepted a job offer.

If you have been convicted of a felony, be honest and check *yes*. Then explain during your interview what you have learned from the mistake. You do not need to reveal any arrests unless you were convicted.

◀ SUMMARY OF KEY CONCEPTS

Professional networking is the act of creating professional relationships. It is an important part of your career process.

- ▶ Almost everyone you know should be a part of your professional network
- ▶ In addition to people you already know, you can develop additional network contacts through various activities
- ▶ You should update your resumé with new skills and accomplishments at least once a year
- ▶ Include both job-specific skills and transferable skills on your resumé
- ▶ Use the correct resumé format for your career time frame
- ▶ A cover letter is most often an employer's first impression of you
- ▶ Make sure your resumé and cover letter are free of typing and grammar errors

◀ KEY TERMS

chronological resumé format	interview portfolio	resumé
cover letter	job search portfolio	soft skills
functional resumé format	job-specific skills	transferable skills
informational interview	network list	
	networking	

◀ IF YOU WERE THE BOSS

1. What would you look for first when reviewing a resumé?
2. What would your reaction be if you were reading a cover letter that had several typing and grammar errors?

◀ **WEB SITES**

http://www.rileyguide.com/network.html#netprep
http://jobsearch.about.com/od/networking
http://www.truecareers.com
http://resume.monster.com
http://jobstar.org/tools/resume/index.htm

◀ **WORKPLACE DOs AND DON'Ts**

Do keep a network list and keep the people on your list updated.	*Don't* be annoying or inconsiderate of your network contacts' time.
Do keep your resumé updated with skills and accomplishments.	*Don't* wait until the last minute to update your resumé.
Do change your resumé format after you have had work experience.	*Don't* use outdated reference names and letters.
Do use the correct format for your resumé.	*Don't* send out a resumé or cover letter that has not been proofread by someone you can trust.
Do check your resumé and cover letter for errors before sending them to employers.	*Don't* forget to sign your cover letter.
Do keep your original job search documents in a portfolio.	*Don't* give employers your original documents and expect them to be returned to you.

▶ ACTIVITIES

ACTIVITY 1

Fill in the following information that will be used to create a resumé.

Skills

JOB-SPECIFIC SKILLS	TRANSFERABLE SKILLS
1.	1.
2.	2.
3.	3.
4.	4.
5.	5.
6.	6.
7.	7.
8.	8.

Education

College Name, City, State
Major information, dates

1. _____

_____

2. _____

_____

Work Experience

Company Name   Dates Worked (month/year)

Job Title

List of duties, not in complete sentence

1. _____

_____

_____

2. _____

_____

_____

ACTIVITY 2

Search for a job you would like to have when you graduate and fill in the following information that will be used to create a cover letter.

Paragraph 1

Position for which you are applying	
How you learned about the job	
Any contact you have had with employer or others about the job	

Paragraph 2

Why are you interested in this job?	
Why are you interested in this company?	
What products or services are provided?	

ACTIVITY 2 (*Continued*)

Paragraph 3

List relevant skills related to the job description.	
List reasons this company should hire you.	

Paragraph 4

Indicate your desire for an interview.	
Indicate your flexibility for an interview (time and place).	

ACTIVITY 3

Create a reference list with at least three names; include the following information.

Reference 1

Name	
Job title	
Place of employment	
Address	
Telephone number	
E-mail address	
Relationship (why is he or she a reference?)	

Reference 2

Name	
Job title	
Place of employment	
Address	
Telephone number	
E-mail address	
Relationship (why is he or she a reference?)	

(*Continued*)

ACTIVITY 3 (*Continued*)

Reference 3

Name	
Job title	
Place of employment	
Address	
Telephone number	
E-mail address	
Relationship (why is he or she a reference?)	

ACTIVITY 4

Using the following Network Table, develop a networking list. At a minimum, include each contact's name, address, and telephone number.

NETWORK TABLE

Network List

NAME	ADDRESS	TELEPHONE NO.	E-MAIL ADDRESS	LAST DATE OF CONTACT

► SAMPLE EXAM QUESTIONS

1. The act of creating professional relationships is referred to as _____.

2. The following people could be included in a professional network: _____, _____, _____, _____, and _____.

3. It is important to update your career resumé at least _____.

4. If you are starting in your career, you should create a resumé using the _____.

5. A/An _____ resumé format emphasizes your related work experience and skills.

6. _____ skills are those that are directly related to a specific job.

7. _____ skills are transferable from one job to the next.

8. Remember to use _____ words whenever possible in your resumé; they describe your accomplishments in a lively and specific way.

15

JOB SEARCH AND INTERVIEW TECHNIQUES

StockByte Royalty Free CD/Getty Images

JOB SEARCH AND INTERVIEW TECHNIQUES

OBJECTIVES

- ► Name key steps in a targeted job search
- ► Identify sources for job leads
- ► Identify how to tailor a resumé and cover letter for a specific position
- ► Identify questions to ask when invited to interview
- ► Identify pre-interview preparation activities
- ► Identify key responses and cues to look for during an interview
- ► Explain key areas of employee rights and how to respond to discriminatory questions
- ► Describe specific statements and behaviors to exhibit at the close of an interview and job offer

All the world's a stage.

William Shakespeare
(1564–1616)

► THE TARGETED JOB SEARCH

After you have created a winning resumé, it is time to begin a targeted job search. A targeted job search leads you through the process of identifying open positions for which you are qualified in addition to identifying companies for which you would like to work. The ultimate goal of a job search is to, of course, secure an interview and a job offer.

The first step in a targeted job search is to identify where you want to work. If your job search is limited to your local area, you will be restricted to employers in your community. If you are willing to commute outside of your area, you must determine how far you are willing to drive (both directions) on a daily basis. Finally, if you wish to move out of the area, you need to identify what locations are most appealing.

A job search is work. It takes time and can sometimes be frustrating. Do not get discouraged if you do not get an interview or job offer on your first try. The purpose of this chapter is to give you the skills and confidence to secure a good job in a reasonable time period.

► SOURCES OF JOB LEADS

There are many sources for job leads. The first and most obvious job lead is directly from your targeted company. Information regarding open positions within your targeted company can be obtained from the company Web site or from visiting the company's human resource department. This is where you will find a list of open positions. If you do not have a targeted company but have an area where you would like to work, conduct an Internet search. Check message boards and job search sites such as monster.com and hotjobs.com. Other job sources include newspaper advertisements, industry journals, industry associations, and current employees who work in your targeted industry and/or company. Most individuals rely on posted job positions. However, many jobs are unsolicited (not made public). This is why it is important to use your professional network. Inform network members of your desire for a job and ask for potential job leads.

If you are unable to find a job lead, we recommend that you send an unsolicited cover letter and resumé to your target company. When sending an unsolicited resumé, you should send two copies: one to the human resource manager and the other to the manager of your target job. Prior to sending your resumé, call the company to secure the names of both managers. Make sure you have identified the correct spelling and gender for both individuals. Sending two resumés to the same company increases the opportunity for you to secure an interview. The targeted department manager will most likely read and file your resumé for future reference. The human resource manager will also review your resumé and may identify other jobs for which you may be qualified.

► TAILORING YOUR RESUMÉ AND COVER LETTER

When you have identified a position for which you are qualified, you should tailor your resumé and cover letter specifically to the job and company for which you are applying. Carefully review the job announcement. If possible, secure a copy of the job description from the company's human resource department if it is not available or attached to the job posting. Identify the key job skills that the position requires and highlight the company needs with your skills. Make sure to include your key qualifications in both your cover letter and resumé. In the cover letter, mention the target company by name, how you learned of the job, and your specific qualifications (reflected from the job posting) that make you an excellent candidate to interview.

Make sure your cover letter and resumé include a daytime telephone number. Because most invitations for job interviews occur over the telephone, your telephone voice mail and/or message machine should be professional. Do not include musical introductions or any other greeting that would not make a positive first impression to a potential employer.

Cory's friend Shelby was a practical joker. Cory enjoyed calling Shelby because her voice-mail message started with a joke or had some strange voice and/or music. However, the last time Cory called Shelby, Cory noticed that Shelby's message was normal. The next time Cory saw Shelby, Cory asked Shelby why her voice message was suddenly so serious. Shelby explained that she had recently applied for a job and had been selected to interview. Unfortunately, every time the interviewer called to arrange an appointment, the interviewer kept getting Shelby's unprofessional message machine and did not leave a message, fearing he had dialed the wrong number.

▶ PRIOR TO THE INTERVIEW

When you are invited to interview, find out with whom you will be interviewing. You may be meeting with one person or a group of individuals. Try to find out how much time the company has scheduled for the interview. If possible, find out how many applicants are being called in for interviews. Although this is a lot of information to secure, if you are friendly, respectful, and professional, most people will share this information.

Arrange your interview at a time that puts you at an advantage to be remembered in comparison to the other candidates. Typically, the first and last interviews are the most memorable. If you are given a choice of times to interview, try to schedule your interview in the morning. People are much more alert at that time, and this puts you at an advantage. Ideally, you want to be the first person interviewed or the last person interviewed prior to the lunch break. If this is not possible, try to be the first person interviewed immediately after the lunch break. Be aware that sometimes you will have no say in when your interview is scheduled. Do not make demands. Politely ask the interview scheduler if it is possible for him or her to tell you who will be conducting the interview and/or if the interview can be at a specific time. The goal is to secure as much information as possible prior to the interview so that you can be prepared.

Prior to your interview, conduct research on the company. Many candidates ignore this step thinking it is unnecessary or takes too much time. Doing so better prepares you for your interview, increases your confidence, and provides you a great advantage over the other candidates who will be interviewing for the same job. Learn as much as you can about the company's leadership, strategy, and any current event that may have affected the company. Review the company Web site. Note the key products/services the company produces. Also, identify the company's key competitors. There are many sources for securing company-specific information. Sources include company-produced brochures/literature, industry journals, the Internet, and interviews with current employees and business leaders. The easiest source for securing information will be from a Web search. In your Web search, identify if and why the company has been in the news. Your Web search may reveal how involved the company is in its community. All of this research will assist you during your job interview.

It is important to have a **personal commercial** that sells your skills and ties these skills to the particular job for which you are interviewing. Once you create your personal commercial, you should modify the personal commercial and adapt it to the requirements for your target job. Your personal commercial should take no more than one minute. The personal commercial should include career goals, education, qualifications, and related job skills. The purpose of the commercial is to sell your skills in a brief statement. Your goal is to sell yourself and match your skills to fit the company needs. Do not include personal information such as marital status, hobbies, or other private areas of your life. Use your personal commercial during your interview when instructed, "Tell me about yourself." If you are not given this instruction during the interview, include your personal commercial at the end of the interview.

◄ **EXERCISE 1: Targeted Personal Commercials:** *Create your personal commercial for a customer service position for a local department store.*

_____

_____

_____

_____

_____

_____

_____

Another very important activity involved in preparing for the interview is to practice interview questions. Table 1 identifies common interview questions, the purpose of each question, and an appropriate answer for each question. Whenever you are answering interview questions, provide examples of your skills and experiences that support your answers.

◄ **TABLE 1**   Interview Questions

QUESTION	ANSWER	DO NOT
Tell me about yourself.	Use your personal commercial modified to the job description.	Do not divulge personal information or background information on where you were born, personal hobbies, and so on.
What are your strengths? mother").	Include how your strengths meet the job requirements and how they will be an asset to the company.	Do not include strengths that are not related to the job. Do not include personal information (e.g., "I'm a good mother").
Tell me about a time you failed.	Be honest. Use an example that is not too damaging. Include the lesson learned from your mistake.	Do not exclude the lesson learned. Do not place blame on why the failure occurred.
Tell me about a time you were successful.	Be honest. Use an example that relates to the job for which you are applying.	Do not take full credit if it was a team effort.
How do you handle conflict?	Be honest. Use an example that is not too damaging. Including how the conflict was positively resolved.	Do not exclude the lesson learned. Do not give specifics on how the conflict occurred and do not use a negative example.
Would you rather work individually or in a team? Why?	State that you prefer one or the other and why, but make sure your answer relates to the job requirements.	Do not state that you will not work one way or the other.
Why do you want this job?	Your answer should convey career goals and how the job supports your current skills. Include company information.	Do not state money or benefits in your response.
How do you deal with stress?	Share positive stress reducers.	Do not state that stress does not affect you. Do not use negative examples.

(Continued)

◀ **TABLE 1**   (*Continued*)

What is your greatest weakness?	Use a weakness that will not damage your chance of getting the job. Explain how you are minimizing your weakness or are turning it into a strength (e.g., "I'm a perfectionist, but I don't allow it to interfere with getting my job done on time").	Do not state, "I don't have any."
Where do you want to be in five years?	Share the goals.	Do not say you want the interviewer's job.
Tell me about a time you displayed leadership.	Use a specific example and try to relate the example to the needed job skills.	Do not appear arrogant.

◀ **EXERCISE 2: Formulating Interview Responses:** *Using the preceding table, identify two questions you would find most difficult to answer. Formulate an answer. Then, with a classmate, role-play an interview asking each other the most difficult questions. Constructively critique each others' answers.*

Question	Answer
1.	
2.	

Conduct a practice day prior to the day of your interview. If possible, drive to the interview location. Ideally, you should do this at the same time as your scheduled interview time to identify potential problems including traffic and parking. Park your car and walk to the location of where the interview will be held. This will enable you to become more comfortable and familiar with your surroundings. Do not go into the specific office, just the general area. Make note of the nearest public restroom. You may need it the day of the interview to freshen up prior to your meeting.

Ensuring your interview attire is clean and professional is another important activity to conduct prior to the day of the interview. Dress at a level above the position for which you are interviewing. For example, if you are interviewing for a clerk position, dress like you are interviewing for a supervisor position. Make sure your clothes are spotless and fit appropriately. Check your shoes. Ladies, it is a good idea to have an extra pair of nylons available. Check your hair and fingernails to ensure they are professional and appropriate for an interview. Do not overdo your perfume/aftershave or jewelry. Remember that cleanliness is important.

Purchase a package of thank-you notes. The thank-you notes should be simple and professional. The evening before your interview, write a draft thank-you note on a piece of paper.

The thank-you note should be brief (three to four sentences). In the note, thank the interviewer for his or her time. State that you enjoyed learning more about the position, you are very interested in the job, and look forward to hearing from the interviewer soon. This draft note will be used as a foundation for notes you will be writing immediately after your interview. Place the draft note, the package of thank-you notes, and a black pen in your car.

◀ **EXERCISE 3: Thank-You Note:** *In preparation for an upcoming interview with a local retailer, write a draft thank-you note.*

Finally, prepare your interview portfolio. Include extra copies of your resumé; a notepad and pen for note taking; your reference list; an extra copy of a most recent performance evaluation, if applicable; and copies of any other documents that pertain to the job. Place your portfolio in your car.

▶ THE DAY OF THE INTERVIEW

Before leaving your home, look in the mirror. Make sure everything fits properly and you project a professional appearance. Practice extending your hand and introducing yourself. The more you practice, the more comfortable you will be. Plan to arrive at your destination fifteen minutes early. This gives you plenty of time to deal with unforeseen traffic and/or parking issues. If there is a public restroom available, go to the restroom and freshen up. Check your hair (and makeup, if applicable). Enter the meeting location five minutes prior to your scheduled interview. This is where your interview unofficially begins. Remember that first impressions matter and that every interaction with every representative of the organization must be professional.

Immediately upon entering the interview location, introduce yourself to the receptionist. Offer a smile and a handshake, then clearly and slowly state your name. For example, "Hi, I'm Cory Kringle, and I am here for a 9:00 a.m. interview with Mr. Wong for the accounting clerk position." If you recognize the receptionist as the same individual who arranged your interview appointment, make an additional statement thanking the individual for his or her assistance. For example, "Mrs. Jones, weren't you the one that I spoke with on the phone? Thank-you for your help in arranging my interview." Be sincere in your conversation, and convey to the receptionist that you appreciate his or her efforts. The receptionist will most likely ask you to have a seat and wait to be called into the interview. Take a seat and relax. While you are waiting, use positive self-talk. Mentally review your personal commercial, qualifications, and the key skills you want to convey to those conducting the interview.

Cory's friend Shelby had finally been asked to interview with one of her target companies. Shelby really wanted the job but was afraid she was not going to do well during her interview. Cory worked with Shelby the evening before the interview by role-playing interview questions and reviewing Shelby's company research. The next day, when Shelby arrived for the interview, she arrived early, thanked the receptionist, and took a seat. As Shelby waited to be called into the interview, she began getting extremely nervous. Remembering Cory's tips, Shelby briefly closed her eyes and used positive self-talk to improve her attitude, increase her confidence, and calm her nerves.

▶ THE INTERVIEW

During the interview, your goal is to communicate confidence. You also need to communicate how your knowledge, skills, and abilities will be an asset to the company. When the appropriate time arrives, you will be invited into a room for your formal interview. When your name is called, stand up and approach the individual who called your name. If it is not the receptionist who called you, extend a smile and a handshake, then clearly and slowly state your name. For example, "Hi, I'm Cory Kringle. It's nice to meet you." Listen carefully to the individual's name. He or she will escort you to an office or conference room where the interview will take place.

The interview may be conducted several ways. It may only involve one person; it may involve several individuals (commonly referred to as a panel interview); or it may include testing. Testing activities may include typing tests, lifting, and demonstrating skills that are included in the job requirements and/or job duties. If you enter a room and there is someone in the room that you have not met, extend a smile and a handshake and introduce yourself. Once again, listen for names. Do not be seated until you are invited to do so. Although you may be offered something to drink, it is best to decline the offer so there is nothing to distract you from the interview. When seated, if possible, write down the names of the individuals you have just met. That way, you can inject the interviewer's name into your conversation.

If the interview is taking place in an office, look around the room to get a sense of the person who is conducting the interview (assuming it is his or her office). This provides useful information for conversation, should it be necessary. Depending on the time available and the skills of the interviewer(s), you may first be asked general questions such as, "Did you have trouble finding our office?" The interviewer is trying to get you to relax. In addition to relaxing, use these questions to connect with your interviewer by including his or her name in your response. For example, if there are family photos or a piece of artwork, ask your interviewer a simple, nonintrusive question such as, "What a nice picture, Mr. Wong. Is this your family?"

During the interview, pay attention to body language—both yours and that of the individual conducting the interview. Sit up straight, sit back in your chair, and try to relax. Be calm but alert. Keep your hands folded on your lap or ready to take notes, depending on the situation. If you are seated near a desk or table, do not lean on the furniture. Do not cross your legs. Remember to make eye contact, but do not stare down the interviewer.

When asked a question, listen carefully. Take a few seconds to think and digest what the interviewer truly wants to know about you. Formulate an answer. All interview answers should relate back to the job qualifications and/or job duties. Your goal is to convey to the interviewer how your skills will assist the company in achieving success. Keep your answers brief but complete. Your job is to sell yourself. Whenever possible, inject information you learned about the company during your research.

Interview questions are either structured or unstructured. Structured questions address specific issues. An example of a structured question is: "How long have you worked in the retail industry?" The purpose of a structured interview question is to secure specific information. An unstructured question is more general. The purpose of an unstructured interview question is to identify if the candidate can appropriately sell his or her skills. An example of an unstructured interview question is: "Tell me about yourself." When you are instructed to "talk about yourself," make sure you state your personal commercial. Whenever possible, pull job samples from your portfolio if you are referring to a specific skill. Relate all answers back to the job for which you are applying.

▶ DISCRIMINATION AND EMPLOYEE RIGHTS

Title VII of the Civil Rights Act was created to protect the rights of employees. It prohibits employment discrimination based on race, color, religion, sex, or national origin. Other laws prohibit pay inequity and discrimination against individuals over forty years of age, individuals with disabilities, and individuals who are pregnant. This does not mean that an employer must hire you if you are a minority, pregnant, over forty, or have a disability. Employers have a legal obligation to provide every qualified candidate equal opportunity to interview. Their job is to hire the most qualified candidate. Unfortunately, some employers often ask interview questions that can be discriminatory. Table 2 was taken from the California Department of Fair Employment and Housing to provide acceptable and unacceptable employment inquiries.

◀ **TABLE 2** Illegal Interview Questions

ACCEPTABLE	SUBJECT	UNACCEPTABLE
Name	**Name**	• Maiden name
Place of residence	**Residence**	• Questions regarding owning or renting
Statements that employment is subject to verification if applicant meets legal age requirement	**Age**	• Age • Birth date • Date of attendance/completion of school • Questions that tend to identify applicants over forty
Statements/inquiries regarding verification of legal right to work in the United States	**Birthplace, citizenship**	• Birthplace of applicant or applicant's parents, spouse, or other relatives • Requirements that applicant produce naturalization or alien card prior to employment
Languages applicant reads, speaks, or writes if use of language other than English is relevant to the job for which applicant is applying	**National origin**	• Questions as to nationality, lineage, ancestry, national origin, descent or parentage of applicant, applicant's spouse, parent, or relative
Statement by employer of regular days, hours, or shifts to be worked	**Religion**	• Questions regarding applicant's religion • Religious days observed
Name and address of parent or guardian if applicant is a minor Statement of company policy regarding work assignment of employees who are related	**Sex, marital status, family**	• Questions to indicate applicant's sex, marital status, number/ages of children or dependents • Questions regarding pregnancy, child birth, or birth control • Name/address of relative, spouse, or children of adult applicant
Job-related questions about convictions, except those convictions that have been sealed, expunged, or statutorily eradicated	**Arrest, criminal record**	• General questions regarding arrest record

If an interviewer asks you a question that is illegal or could be discriminatory, do not directly answer the question; instead, address the issue. For example, if the interviewer states, "You look Hispanic. Are you?" Your response should not just be "yes" or "no." Politely smile and say, "People wonder about my ethnicity. What can I tell you about my qualifications for this job?" Most employers do not realize they are asking illegal questions. However, some employers purposely ask inappropriate questions. In this case, you need to decide if you want to work for an employer that intentionally asks illegal questions. If employers are behaving inappropriately during an interview, one would wonder how they will treat the applicant after he or she is hired.

It is important to protect your rights. Please note that it is inappropriate to disclose personal information. During your interview, avoid making any comment referring to your marital status, children, religion, age, or any other area of protected rights.

◀ **EXERCISE 4: Handing Illegal Interview Questions:** *With a classmate, role-play an interview. During the interview, ask one legal question and one illegal question. Practice answering the illegal question with confidence but in a nonoffensive manner.*

Illegal Question	Answer
1.	
2.	

▶ TOUGH QUESTIONS AND TOUGH ANSWERS

Unfortunately, some job seekers have had negative work-related experiences that they do not want to disclose during an interview. Disclosing such information could be potentially devastating to a job interview if it is not handled properly. Some of these experiences include being fired, having a poor performance evaluation, or knowing that a former manager will not give you a good job reference if called. Perhaps you behaved in a negative manner prior to leaving your old job.

If you did have a difficult situation and are not asked about the situation, you have no need to disclose the unpleasant event. The only exception to this rule is if your current or former boss has the potential to provide a negative reference. If this is the situation, tell the interviewer that you know you will not receive a positive reference from him or her and request that the interviewer contact another manager or coworker who can provide a fair assessment of your performance.

Being honest and factual is the best answer to any difficult question. If you were fired, performed poorly, or left in a negative manner, state the facts. Tell the interviewer that you have matured and realize that you did not handle the situation appropriately. Do not speak poorly of your current or previous employer, boss, or coworker. It is also important to not place blame on who was right or wrong in your negative workplace situation. Remember that every experience, be it positive or negative, is a learning experience.

► CLOSING THE INTERVIEW

After the interviewer has completed his or her questioning, you will be asked if you have any questions. Having a question prepared for the close of your interview demonstrates to your prospective employer that you have conducted research on the company. A good question refers to a current event that has occurred within the company. For example, "Mr. Wong, I read about how your company employees donated time to clean up the ABC schoolyard. Is this an annual event?" A statement such as this provides you one last opportunity to personalize your interview and demonstrate that you researched the company. This is also a good time to share any relevant information you have in your portfolio.

Do not ask questions that imply you did not research the company or that you only care about your needs. Inappropriate questions include questions regarding salary, benefits, or vacations. These questions imply that you care more about what the company can do for you than what you can do for the company. However, it is appropriate to ask what the next steps will be in the interview process, including when the hiring decision will be made.

After the interviewer answers your general question, restate your personal commercial and ask for the job. An example of a good closing statement would be: "Once again, thank-you for your time. As I stated at the beginning of our meeting, I feel I am qualified for this job based upon my experience, knowledge, and demonstrated leadership. I would like this job and believe I will be an asset to the XYZ company." The purpose of the job interview is to sell yourself. A sale is useless if you do not close the sale.

After you make your closing statement, the interviewer will signal that the interview is over. He or she will do this either through conversation or through body language (he or she may stand up and walk toward the door). Prior to the close of the interview, ask the interviewer for a business card. As you are handed the card, shake the interviewer's hand and, once again, thank him or her for his or her time and state that you look forward to hearing from him or her. Remember to continue communicating confidence, friendliness, and professionalism to every company employee you encounter on your way out of the building.

When you return to your car, retrieve your draft thank-you note. If necessary, modify your draft thank-you note to include information that was shared during your interview. Then hand-write a personalized thank-you note to each individual who interviewed you. Use your finest handwriting and double-check your spelling and grammar. Refer to the business cards for correct name spelling. After you have written your note, hand deliver it to the reception area and ask the receptionist to deliver the notes. Your goal is to make a positive last impression and stand out from the other candidates.

QUESTIONS YOU MAY ASK THE INTERVIEWER

1. Does your company have any plans for expansion?
2. What type of formal training does your company offer?
3. What is the greatest challenge your industry is currently facing?
4. What is the next step in the interview process?
5. What are the hours of the position?
6. When will you be making a hiring decision?

QUESTIONS YOU *SHOULD NOT* ASK DURING AN INTERVIEW!

1. How much does this job pay?
2. How many sick days do I get?
3. What benefits will I get?
4. What does your company do?
5. How long does it take for someone to get fired for poor performance?

▶ AFTER THE INTERVIEW

After delivering your thank-you notes, return to your car and congratulate yourself! If you did your best, you should have no regrets. Prior to leaving the company, jot down notes regarding specific information you learned about your prospective job and questions you were asked during the interview. Through the excitement of an interview, you may forget parts of your meeting if you do not immediately write notes. Finally, make a mental note of what you did right and areas in which you would like to improve upon next time you need to interview. This information will be helpful in the future. Remember that it may take several interviews to land a job, so do not be disappointed if you do not get a job offer on your first attempt.

▶ NEGOTIATION

Within a few weeks, you should hear back from the company. At that point, you may be called in for a second interview or may receive a job offer. You may be told that your job offer will be contingent upon your reference checks. This will be a good time to call the individuals on your reference list to give them an update on your job search. This way they will be prepared to respond to the individual conducting your reference check.

If you are a final candidate for the job, the interviewer may ask you about your salary requirements. Prior to stating your salary requirement, you should sell your skills. For example, "Mr. Wong, as I mentioned in my initial interview, I have over five years' experience working in a professional accounting office; therefore, I feel I should earn between $XXX and $XXX." In order to negotiate an acceptable salary, you must first conduct research and compare your research to the salary range that was included in the job posting. Check job postings and conduct online research to determine local and regional salaries. In your search, attempt to match the job description as closely as possible to that of the job for which you are applying. Depending on your experience, start a few thousand dollars higher than your desired starting salary and do not forget to consider your experience and/or lack of experience. Some companies do not offer many benefits but offer higher salaries. Other companies offer higher salaries and fewer benefits. You need to weigh these factors when determining your desired salary. If you are offered a salary that is not acceptable, use silence and wait for the interviewer to respond. This minute of silence may encourage the employer to offer a higher salary.

Cory's friend Shelby was invited to a second interview. Prior to the interview, Cory and Shelby once again prepared for potential questions and situations Shelby might encounter during the interview. In their practice, Cory asked Shelby about her starting salary. Shelby said she did not care; she would just be happy to get a job. Cory reminded Shelby that she needed to sell her skills and go into the interview with a desired target salary. Cory and Shelby then conducted an Internet search of both local and statewide jobs that were similar to the one Shelby wants. Fortunately, the next day, when the interviewer asked Shelby about her desired starting salary, Shelby was prepared to answer.

▶ WHEN YOU ARE NOT OFFERED THE JOB

As stated at the beginning of the chapter, a job search is like a full-time job. It takes time and can sometimes be discouraging. If you are not called in for an interview or do not get a job offer, do not be discouraged.

If you are not called in for an interview, evaluate your resumé and cover letter. Check for typographical or grammatical errors. Make sure you have listed important skills that reflect the needs of the job for which you are applying. Have someone who knows you and your skills—and whom you trust—review your cover letter and resumé. Many times, a fresh perspective will catch obvious errors or opportunities for improvement.

If you are invited to interviews but do not receive a job offer, do not be discouraged. Remember to make every experience a learning experience. Sit down and carefully review each step in the interview process and grade yourself. Consider your pre-interview preparation, interview day appearance, your interview answers, your ability to interject your company research into each interview answer, and your overall attitude. Any area that did not receive an *A* grade is an area poised for improvement.

There are several steps you can take to increase the probability for success in your next interview. Consider your overall appearance. Make sure you convey professionalism. Ensure that your clothes are clean and that they fit properly. Have a hairstyle that is flattering and well kept. Make sure your fingernails and jewelry are appropriate and do not deter from your personality and job skills.

Mentally review job interview questions that were asked and the responses you provided. Remember that every answer should communicate how your skills will assist the target company in achieving success. Review the amount of company research you conducted. Did you feel amply prepared or did you just conduct the bare minimum? If you felt you did conduct the appropriate amount of research, assess whether you fully communicated your research to the interviewer.

Assess your body language and attitude. Stand in front of a mirror and practice your answers to difficult and/or illegal questions. If possible, have a friend videotape you and provide a critical evaluation of your appearance, attitude, and body language. Check for nervous gestures, and keep practicing until you are able to control these nervous habits.

Finally, be honest with your overall performance. Did you ask for the job? Did you immediately send a thank-you note to your interviewer(s)? You must sell your skills through your mannerisms, answers, and attitude. Your goal is to stand head and shoulders above the other candidates.

◀ SUMMARY OF KEY CONCEPTS

- A targeted job search leads you through the process of identifying open positions for which you are qualified in addition to identifying companies for which you would like to work
- There are many sources of job leads, including directly from the company, an advertisement, and a professional network
- You should review common interview questions and formulate answers as part of your interview preparation
- You should modify your personal commercial and adapt it to the requirements of your target job.
- Conduct a dry run prior to the day of your interview
- During your interview, communicate how your knowledge, skills, and abilities will be assets to the company
- There are laws that protect employees from discrimination
- At the close of the interview, you should ask for the job. The purpose of the job interview is to sell yourself

◀ KEY TERM

personal commercial

◀ REFERENCE

State of California Department of Fair Employment and Housing. *Pre-Employment Inquiry Guidelines.* CA, DFEH-161, Sacramento, CA, 2001.

◀ IF YOU WERE THE BOSS

1. What kind of information should you share with your current staff members as they prepare to interview a new employee?
2. How would you handle a prospective employee who disclosed inappropriate information during the job interview?

◀ WEB SITES

http://jobstar.org/electra/question/sal-req.cfm
http://www.collegegrad.com/intv
http://www.careercc.com/interv3.shtml
http://interview.monster.com
http://www.rileyguide.com/interview.html

◀ WORKPLACE DOs AND DON'Ts

Do realize that a targeted job search takes time.	*Don't* get discouraged if you do not get an interview or job offer on your first try.
Do explore various sources of job leads including your personal network, the Internet, and industry journals.	*Don't* limit your job leads to newspaper advertisements.
Do tailor your resumé and personal commercial to the needs of your targeted employer.	*Don't* have unprofessional introductions on your voice-mail message.
Do try to schedule your interview at a time that puts you at an advantage over the other candidates and secure information that better prepares you for the interview.	*Don't* make demands with the individual scheduling the interview.
Do learn as much as you can about the company, its strategy, and its competition.	*Don't* forget to include your research information in your interview answers.
Do practice interview questions and formulate answers that highlight your skills and experience.	*Don't* show up to an interview unprepared.
Do remember that your interview begins the minute you step onto company property.	*Don't* let your nerves get the better of you on a job interview.
Do know how to handle inappropriate questions that may be discriminatory.	*Don't* answer an illegal question. Instead, address the issue.

► ACTIVITIES

ACTIVITY 1

Identify a local company for which you would like to interview. Using the following table, conduct a thorough targeted job search on this company. Answer as many of the questions as possible.

1. Company name	
2. Company address	
3. Job title	
4. To whom should the cover letter be addressed?	
5. What are the job requirements?	
6. What is the duration of the job?	
7. What are the hours/days of work?	
8. What are the working conditions?	
9. Is there room for advancement?	
10. What kind of training is offered?	
11. What other positions at this company match my qualifications?	
12. What are the average starting salaries (benefits)?	
13. Is traveling or relocation required?	
14. Where is the business located (home office, other offices)?	
15. What are the products or services that the employer provides or manufactures?	
16. What is the mission statement?	
17. What kind of reputation does this organization have?	
18. What is the size of the employer's organization relative to the industry?	
19. What is the growth history of the organization for the past five, ten, or fifteen years?	
20. How long has the employer been in business?	
21. Who is the employer's competition?	

ACTIVITY 2

Using an Internet job site or other medium, identify four job leads that match your career goals and current qualifications.

JOB LEAD	INTERNET SITE ADDRESS OR MEDIUM NAME AND DATE
1.	
2.	
3.	
4.	

ACTIVITY 3

Write out at least two different statements you can use during a telephone conversation when you are invited to interview at a specific time. Make one statement for when you accept the interview time and make the other statement for when you must change the time. Make sure your statements attempt to secure all relevant interview information.

INITIAL STATEMENT	RELEVANT INTERVIEW INFORMATION NEEDED

ACTIVITY 4

Using information obtained in your target company research (Activity 1), write out three common interview questions and answers. Integrate relevant company information in your answers.

QUESTION	ANSWER
1.	
2.	
3.	

ACTIVITY 5

Using information gathered in Activity 2, conduct a salary search. Develop a grid illustrating the highest salaries and lowest salaries for these positions. Using your research data, write out a statement you could use to negotiate a higher salary.

LOWEST SALARY	HIGHEST SALARY

Your Statement of Negotiation

► **SAMPLE EXAM QUESTIONS**

1. The purpose of a/an _____ is to identify _____ and identify companies for which you would like to work.

2. One of the most obvious job sources is utilizing your _____.

3. Your telephone message should be _____.

4. In addition to finding out with whom you will be interviewing, find out how much _____ the company has scheduled and _____ are being called in to _____.

5. Prior to your interview, _____.

6. If possible, prior to the interview day, _____.

7. When asked a difficult question, it is important to be _____ and _____.

Index

OWENS COMMUNITY COLLEGE
P.O. Box 10,000
Toledo, OH 43699-1947